JESUS CHRIST OUR COMPLETE OFFERING

HOW THE LEVITICAL OFFERINGS FORESHADOWED CHRIST

DAVID D. BERGEY

JESUS CHRIST OUR COMPLETE OFFERING
Copyright © 2017   by David D. Bergey   All rights reserved
First Edition

No part of this book may be reproduced, stored in a retrieval system, or transmitted, in any form or by any means: electronic, mechanical, photocopy, recording, or any other, except for brief quotes in printed reviews, without permission of the author.

Printed in the United States of America

ISBN: 978-0-578-19441-7

All Scriptures quoted are from the Authorized King James Version unless otherwise noted.

New Revised Standard Version Copyright © 1989 by the Division of Christian Education of the National Council of Churches of Christ. All rights reserved.

THE HOLY BIBLE, NEW INTERNATIONAL VERSION® NIV® Copyright © 1973, 1978, 1984 by International Bible Society. Used by permission. All rights reserved.

Tanakh Copyright © 1985 by the Jewish Publication Society. All rights reserved.

Revised New Testament of the New American Bible © 1986. All rights reserved by the Confraternity of Christian Doctrine.

The Amplified New Testament, © 1954, 1958, 1987, Lockman Foundation, La Habra, Calif. All rights reserved.

Walter J. Cummins, *A Journey through the Acts and Epistles*, Franklin, Ohio: Scripture Consulting, 2006. All rights reserved.

For Mary McSherry Bergey

Contents

Preface   9

Part One   The Substitute Offering

Chapter 1   His Finished Work   18
     Fully Accomplishing what God Gave Him to Do

Chapter 2   Our Complete, Once-and-for-All Savior   33
     The Once-and-for-All Sacrifice
     Complete in Him

Chapter 3   Isaiah 53:   47
The Messiah Bears our Sins, Sorrows and Sickness
     The Transfer of the Ages

Chapter 4   The Law: A Shadow of Christ   62
     Substitution Foreshadowed

Chapter 5   Patterns of the True Things to Come   73
     The Day of Atonement: A Pattern of True Things to Come
     The Passover Sacrifice: A Pattern of the True Things to Come
     Old Testament Sacrifices: Tutorials of Christ

Part Two   The Levitical Offerings

Chapter 6 The Categories of the Offerings   90
    Sin or Sin Offering?
    Public and Private Offerings
    Sweet Savor and Sin Offerings

Chapter 7 Trespass Offering or Restitution Offering   103
    The Trespass Offering Addressed Property Violations against Neighbor
    The Trespass Offering Addressed Treachery toward God
    The Trespass Offering: Full Restoration and Restitution
    He Paid it All and Much More
    No Verdict of Condemnation
    The Trespass Offering: a Portrayal of Christ's Accomplishments

Chapter 8 Sin Offering or Purification Offering   137
    Purifying by the Blood
    The *Chattath,* Sin Offering, can be called Purification Offering
    First Usage of Sin Offering the Bible
    The Red Heifer Sin Offering
    Jesus Christ, Our *Chattath* Offering

Chapter 9 The Sweet Savor Offerings   171
    Incense=Prayer
    Qatar, to Burn as Incense
    Sweet Savor: Soothing Fragrance of Rest
    Christ, Our Sweet Savour Offering
    Our Three-fold Intercession

Chapter 10 Peace Offering   189
    Only the Best for God: Censing the Fat on the Altar
    Sharing Fully in the Peace Offering

JESUS CHRIST OUR COMPLETE OFFERING

    Three Varieties of the Peace Offering
    Joy and Thanksgiving Accompanying the Peace
        Offering
    Sacrifices of Thanksgiving in the New Testament
    The Significance of the Eating Sacrifices
    Peace Offering: Double Demonstration of
        Identification
    Our Identification with Christ
    He is our Peace Offering

Chapter 11 Meal Offering or Gift Offering   **226**
    Minchah: Meal Offering or Gift Offering
    A Scene of Reconciliation: The *Minchah* Offering
        Defined
    Christ, Our Gift Offering

Chapter 12   **246**
Meal and Drink Offerings: Precursors of Communion
    I Corinthians 10: Eating and Drinking Symbolizing
        our Identification with Christ's Sacrifice
    I Corinthians 11:
        Proclaiming the Lord's Death till He Come
    Discerning the Lord's Body
    Asking for God's Remembrance

Chapter 13 Burnt Offering or Ascending Offering   **280**
    The Burnt Offering: Completely Offered unto God
    Olah: The Ascending Offering
    Jesus Christ, The Sacrifice that Ascended
    Jesus Christ, our Continual Burnt Offering

Chapter 14
The Burnt Offering: Utterly Devoted to God   **295**
    Genesis 22: Abraham's Burnt Offering
    Abraham's Accounting
    Jephthah's Burnt Offering

Jesus Christ: He Gave His All
Living Sacrifices Alive from the Dead

Chapter 15 Wave Offering or Elevation Offering   **319**
The First Fruits Offerings: Belonged to the Lord
Waving the Sheaf of the First Fruits
The Resurrection: Christ, the First Fruits Offering
Wave Offering of the Leaven Loaves on Feast of
    Pentecost
Elevated into His Kingdom

Chapter 16   **343**
The Day of Atonement: The Grand Portrayal of Christ
Scapegoat
Ascending Sacrifices on the Day of Atonement
Models in Motion

Part Three   The Complete Offering

Chapter 17 Christ's Complete Sacrifice on Display: **367**
   Viewing the Old Testament Offerings as a Whole

Chapter 18 His Complete Offering   **375**

Chapter 19 Complete in Him: **383**
Our Identification with Christ
Sacrificial Identification in the Old Testament
Walking in Newness of Life: Living our Identification
    with Christ

Chapter 20 Complete Deliverance in the Lamb of God 399
The Word of the Cross is the Power of God
The Lamb of God: Sacrifice for the Ages

Appendix One
The Probable Location of the Crucifixion   **414**

JESUS CHRIST OUR COMPLETE OFFERING

Golgotha: A Place of Polling
"The Place of the City"
Arrest and Punishment at the Scene of the Crime
Significance of the Mount of Olives
We have an Altar

Appendix Two   Defining *telos* and related Greek   427
words used in *Jesus Christ Our Complete Offering*

Appendix Three   The Hebrew word *Choli*   430

Appendix Four   The First Sin Offering in the Bible   434

Scripture Index   438

Subject Index   445

Preface

Christ's complete sacrifice makes you complete. He paid it all so you could have it all. "You are complete in him" is God's point of view according to Colossians 2:10. I wrote this book to help you see the great salvation Christ fully accomplished for us on the cross.

As a young teen, I was riding through a dark city in the back of my parents' car. I saw a lit sign that stated, "JESUS SAVES." I was frustrated. I thought how does that sign explain anything or help anyone?

I had already accepted Christ as my Lord and believed that God had raised him from the dead. Yet, in that moment, that bright sign seemed trite and pointless.

For me this book may well be the end of a life-long search to define the salvation that Jesus Christ accomplished. As I wrote this book some fifty years later, I saw how our salvation by Christ must be the greatest gift ever bestowed on humanity.

Christians generally understand that Christ died for them on the cross at Golgotha. They may also recognize that the savior took their place as a substitute on the tree. Others have grown in their understanding to see that the Son of God bore their sin and sickness. In this book, we will try to expand our appreciation of the full completeness of his offering and our redemption.

Remarkably, we can gain vivid insight into Christ's sacrifice by looking at the sacrifices of the Old Testament. These Levitical sacrifices were not merely obscure rites and

JESUS CHRIST OUR COMPLETE OFFERING

practices of some ancient tribes. The offerings of the Law were designed by God to depict and teach about the coming Christ. In fact, these could be called "tutorials of redemption." They foreshadowed the greatest subject of all time—the redemption of humanity by the sacrifice of the Lamb of God.

Today, computers provide step by step, interactive learning programs called tutorials. These tutorials often teach by having the student rehearse each move until the task is completed. One may repeat the tutorial program as often as needed. The sacrifices instituted by Moses by revelation from God were a vast and detailed system of interactive learning designed to demonstrate how God would redeem humankind.

Understanding these offerings and their exact function can bring joy and light to the believer because they show forth Christ and his redemptive work. Each offering of the Old Testament is—in its own way—a small portrait of Christ. These specific offerings of the Old Testament portray Christ in different ways.

Each Mosaic offering displays at least one distinctive function of the person of Christ or the work of Christ. Each glistens with at least one aspect of the multifaceted diamond of Christ's work on the cross. These sacrifices, taken as a whole, reveal facets of our redemption and salvation with a brilliant radiance.

Our Lord's sacrifice was so massive in its scope and magnitude that no one single sacrifice could give a full pattern of him who was to come. Rather, the distinct characteristics of each sacrifice illustrated one or more of the aspects of Christ's accomplishments. The scope of his ultimate sacrifice can be appreciated when the offerings are

Preface

looked at as a whole. The distinguishing aspects of these Old Testament offerings give a vivid portrayal of him who was to come.

We could just vaguely agree that Jesus was our sacrifice and leave it at that. Or we can dig deeper into God's Word and make an effort to see exactly how each sacrifice paralleled aspects of our redemption.

While this sounds rather straightforward, it will take some diligence to first become familiar with these sacrifices. We are exhorted to be diligent workmen of the Word of Truth in II Timothy 2:15. We will need to read sections of Leviticus to become familiar with these sacrifices. We will also look at various Hebrew words in the Old Testament or Greek in the New Testament to get more a precise definition of an individual word or phrase.

For example, when Isaiah 53:10, prophesies of the coming Christ, said he is an "offering for sin." The words "offering for sin" are translated from one word in the Hebrew, *asham*, meaning "trespass offering." This is not a general statement about Jesus dying for our sins, but is rather an explicit comparison of Christ to a specific offering in Leviticus.

This book is divided into three sections. The first part of the book, "The Substitute Offering," lays the groundwork to examine the offerings of the Law. This first section is illustrated by the cover of the book, a painting by my daughter, Tara Bergey. When my 10-year-old granddaughter, Amélee, first saw the painting, she declared that the title should be, "The Lord is my shepherd." I think that is what most Christians would think when seeing this picture. However, the cover depicts the scapegoat as described in Leviticus:

JESUS CHRIST OUR COMPLETE OFFERING

> Leviticus 16:21 and 22:
> And Aaron shall lay both his hands upon the head of the live goat, and confess over him all the iniquities of the children of Israel, and all their transgressions in all their sins, putting them upon the head of the goat, and shall send *him* away by the hand of a fit man into the wilderness:
> And the goat shall bear upon him all their iniquities unto a land not inhabited: and he shall let go the goat in the wilderness.

The cover of this book is of a man leading the young goat out into the wilderness. This scapegoat foreshadows the coming redeemer as a substitute who would carry all our sins to the cross.

The second section of the book, "The Levitical Offerings," covers six distinctive offerings of the Old Testament: trespass, sin, peace, meal, burnt, and wave offering. We will ask of each sacrifice: What is its function? What are its characteristics? What is its most prominent point of distinction from the other offerings? Once this is understood, we can ask how this offering corresponds to Christ. Only then can we see the simple and straightforward correlations that particular offering has to the great focus of the ages: the sacrifice of Christ.

Only after we get a clear concept of the particular offering we are studying, can we grasp how it relates to Christ in the New Testament without any guesswork or speculation. Rather than quoting scholars and building on their assumptions, we will allow the Bible to define its own terms.

These studies of the individual offerings are not presented as an end in themselves, but rather to see how they portray Christ and his redemptive work. The object of this book is

Preface

not to become wrapped up in a study of the Old Testament sacrifices, but rather to become immersed in Christ and what he has accomplished for us.

The third section of this book is entitled: "The Complete Offering." We will view the Old Testament offerings as a whole, seeing a full spectrum of Christ's sacrifice. We look at our deliverance and the utter completeness of our identification with the savior. The centrality of his death on the cross will resound for all eternity.

I started to write about this subject about 20 years ago. The launching pad for this book was a short book I wrote in the year 2000: "Our Identification with Christ's Sacrifice." This topic is reinforced and expanded on with new information from the Scriptures. In 2004, I released a book entitled, *Jesus Christ Our Approach Offering*. It related how many of the Levitical offerings were, in essence, approach offerings. These foreshadowed Christ, the great approach offering, who opened the way into God's presence.

I would have preferred to write this book sooner, but it took time to grow in my understanding of the offerings and how they fit with Christ. What has kept me immersed and interested in this topic for all these years is the dynamic and practical application this study has on my own Christian life. I saw how our identification, our full sharing with Christ, is illustrated in the Old Testament sacrifices. I learned how Christ, as our complete savior, bore our sins on the cross as well as our physical sickness and mental pain.

In looking at the sacrifices of the Law of Moses, there were many variations and details. At times, the complexity was daunting. However, the more I looked at the sacrifices of the Law, the more I saw how with one clarion voice they spoke of my identification with the great sacrifice to come. I also

JESUS CHRIST OUR COMPLETE OFFERING

saw more vividly how he bore my sin and sickness. The layers of detail in the Old Testament sacrificial system were challenging. But a simple message rang out: what he bore **for** me and what I shared **with** him.

While this book is about the complete and perfect work of Jesus Christ, it is neither a complete or perfect work on the subject. My aim is that by reading about Christ's sacrifice in light of the Levitical sacrifices you will see Christ and his accomplishments with a finer lens. This book should also reinforce what you already know.

> I Corinthians 1:18:
> For the preaching [*logos*=word] of the cross is to them that perish foolishness; but unto us which are saved it is the power of God.

This verse says that the "word of the cross" is foolishness to those who do not believe. To many, the word of the cross is silliness. Some look at the crucifixion with the eyes of the senses. All they see in the death of Christ is a tortured but gallant martyr who inspired his followers to start a major religion. But we see so much more. We see a suffering savior who carried our sins and our sicknesses. We behold a resurrected lord giving us the power of God to live what he has accomplished.

Our endeavor in this study is to come to a greater understanding of the "*logos* of the cross." To many this pursuit may appear foolish, "but unto us which are saved it is the power of God." My prayer is that, as we perceive the word of the cross with more clarity and certainty, God's triumphant power will be more at work in our lives.

Preface

How to use this book

By using the Subject or Scripture Indexes, this book can serve as a reference guide. By using the Table of Contents you can choose topics of interest and skip to the subjects that interest you. Or you can read the book in order. The introductory chapters (especially 6 and 9) can be essential.

Please note that [words in brackets] within Scripture quotes are additional information that I have added. For example: Hebrew words from the Old Testament and Greek words from the New Testament are often bracketed in Scripture quotes.

The Hebrew and Greek words are *italicized* and transliterated into English according to the Young's Concordance. As you probably know, our English Bibles were mostly translated from the Hebrew language in the Old Testament and the Greek in the New Testament.

Occasionally I use **bold type** in Scripture quotations for my emphasis. Bold type is for teaching purposes **only** and should in no way be attributed to the Bible itself.

JESUS CHRIST OUR COMPLETE OFFERING

Acknowledgments

This book is dedicated to my wife, Mary, without whose love and patient support this project would not have been possible. I trust that her rewards await in heaven for putting up with me.

The members of my home fellowship have my thanks, especially my four children, who endured occasional teachings about the book of Leviticus and Old Testament offerings without too much eye-rolling or sighing.

I owe a debt of gratitude to the following, who read through the entire book and offered their suggestions and assistance. My long-time editor, Karen Heckler, read the first rough draft and then the final one. I call her the first and the last. I will always treasure the input Walter Cummins offered me. His patient explanations, valuable insights, and corrections made this a better book.

Mary Wall, Dan Bader, and my wonderful daughter-in-law, Lalee Bergey, also read the manuscript in its entirety, giving me helpful feedback. I am thankful to God for bringing them into my life. These all have made me a better writer and, on occasion, a better workman of God's Word. They must have believed in me and my book, having put so much time and effort into helping me. Of course, any errors or oversights are mine alone.

In the course of editing, I developed a lymphoma which required medical attention. With the help of some very good medical professionals and God's hand of victory, I was healed. I am so thankful to God and His deliverance becoming reality: "**He** sent from above, **He** took me, **He** drew me out of many waters. **He** delivered me from my strong enemy…"(Psalm 18:16 and 17). May He always be the Prime Mover in my life.

Part One

The Substitute Offering

Chapter 1

His Finished Work

It was about three in the afternoon when Jesus of Nazareth died on a hill outside Jerusalem. He had been crucified on a wood post earlier that day. He was so much more than another heroic martyr who died for a just cause. He was the fulfillment of what God had promised in the Old Testament Scriptures regarding the Messiah—the Christ. On that day, Jesus Christ bore the sins of all humanity.

Most observers to the grisly scene would have viewed the crosses lined up with Jesus in the midst. As those men hung there in agony, those who looked on would have seen the sun darken for three hours and would have felt an earthquake. They may have noticed the Roman soldiers casting lots over Jesus' cloak. They could have heard them mock him or seen them pierce the lord's side. Whatever their observations, very few saw the spiritual reality of what was accomplished that day. Although they were witnesses to the atrocious scene, the eyes of the senses could not have understood how the horribly beaten man on the middle cross was shouldering the sins of all humanity.

To those who had previously followed Jesus Christ, the awful death of this wonderful man of God must have seemed like a devastating setback. It would have been the

His Finished Work

demolition of their hopes. The next three days and three nights would be the darkest in human history.

Jesus had healed multitudes. He had fed thousands. He had even raised some from the dead. Only days before his crucifixion, he had approached Jerusalem from "the descent of the Mount of Olives" with the multitudes cheering, "Hosanna, blessed is the king of Israel that cometh in the name of the LORD."[1] He was the king of Israel entering the gates of the holy city. What excitement and expectation must have filled the hearts of the believers in Christ who witnessed those events! However, what they observed that afternoon was a horribly beaten man dying on a stake.

For thousands of years prior to this event, God had been preparing people for the day when the Messiah would lay down his life as a sacrifice. Moses and the other prophets who spoke for God foretold of the Christ and what he was to accomplish.

The Bible is about the massive quandary facing God — the reconciliation of humanity to Himself. In the first two chapters of Genesis, the opening passages of Scripture, no problem exists. Man and woman had been created in a state of union with God in Paradise.

In the last two chapters of the Bible, Revelation 21 and 22, again no problem exists. Paradise has been restored with the new heaven and new earth. Sandwiched in between the two chapters opening the Scriptures and the two chapters closing the Scriptures, we have the daunting problem of God and His fractured relationship with humanity. In between these chapters, the solution is presented: Christ. When Christ came and fully accomplished the redemption of humanity on the

---

[1] Luke 19:37 and 38, John 12:13.

JESUS CHRIST OUR COMPLETE OFFERING

cross, God resolved the issue of His severed relationship with Adam's descendents.

The whole of the Scripture is united in one aim—to explain Christ. To overcome its severed relationship with God, humanity needs to accept and understand what God did in Christ. The entire Bible relays information about the Christ. In the Old Testament, the Christ is spoken of prophetically and by pattern in anticipation of the coming savior. The New Testament looks back on what Christ accomplished and proclaims the redemptive realities of his finished work.

Looking at the opening chapters of Genesis we can consider the idyllic state of man and the environment God had placed him in. In surveying the fully restored earth and created man, Genesis 1:31 records God's observation: "And God saw every thing that he had made, and, behold, it was very good..."

There is no inkling of any problem existing between God and newly created man. When God originally created Adam and Eve, he made them with body, soul and spirit. Also, God gave them dominion over all the earth in an environment that is described as "very good."[2]

Then in Genesis 3, all was lost by the original fracture of the relationship between God and man. This breach in the relationship continues for the rest of the Bible until the last two chapters of Revelation when all is reconciled.

---

[2] Genesis 1:28: "And God blessed them, and God said unto them, Be fruitful, and multiply, and replenish the earth, and subdue it: and have dominion over the fish of the sea, and over the fowl of the air, and over every living thing that moveth upon the earth." For a more complete study of man's original conditions and the conditions that resulted from Adam's sin, see Walter J. Cummins, *The Acceptable Year of the Lord* (Franklin, Ohio: Scripture Consulting, 2005). Chapter 1 "The World's Need for a Savior."

His Finished Work

In Genesis 2:17 God instructs Adam and Eve of "the tree of the knowledge of good and evil, thou shalt not eat of it: for in the day that thou eatest thereof thou shalt surely die." God emphatically declares that on the very day they would eat of that tree, they would certainly die.[3]

Chapter 3 records the tragic event. They did eat of the tree and were expelled from paradise. On that day, they died in that they lost the spirit of God that the Creator had originally given to them. Additionally, they lost the dominion and authority God had given and were driven from the garden in which everything in their environment was "very good."

> Romans 5:12:
> Wherefore, as by one man [Adam] sin entered into the world, and death by sin; and so death passed upon all men, for that all have sinned.

Sin, death, and sickness entered into the world by Adam's violation of Genesis 2:17. The death that passed upon all humanity is the death brought about by Adam's loss of spirit. Death (the loss of spirit life) had passed upon all men and women. Therefore, humankind is separated from God, without easy and free access to Him, which Adam and Eve had once enjoyed. All born after Adam and Eve have breathing bodies and living souls, yet the spirit of God, the likeness and image of God, is absent.

With the fall of man, in a very real sense, man had lost a part of himself. Man and woman were now incomplete, having only body and soul, lacking the spirit of God. Jesus Christ's mission was to completely redeem humanity so they could be once again whole: body, soul and spirit.

---

[3] For more on Genesis 2:17, see David Bergey, *Jesus Christ Our Approach Offering* (Redlands, CA, 2004) 31.

JESUS CHRIST OUR COMPLETE OFFERING

Ephesians gives us a look at the fallen condition of humanity and what Christ accomplished by his sacrifice.

> Ephesians 2:12 and 13:
> That at that time ye were without Christ, being aliens from the commonwealth of Israel and strangers from the covenants of promise, having no hope, and without God in the world:
> But now in Christ Jesus ye who sometimes were far off are made nigh [near] by the blood of Christ.

As a consequence of Adam and Eve's sin, the status of the nations of the world was reduced to, "...having no hope, and without God in the world."

Many years after the fall of man, God established a covenant with the nation of Israel. Yet, as Ephesians 2:12 suggests, those outside that framework remained excluded and estranged. Aliens, strangers, having no hope, without God—this is quite a list and a sad condition. Also the neighborhood was rather grim: "in the world."

When all the false gods and false hopes are stripped away, all that was left of fallen humanity was this ruined condition: having no hope, without God, in the world. Humanity without God lives in desperation, in anxiety and in the darkness of this world.

After this succinct description of fallen man's dire position, verse 13 contrasts this with glowing light and positive simplicity: "But now in Christ Jesus ye who sometimes were far off are made nigh [near] by the blood of Christ."

The expression "the blood of Christ" refers to his sacrifice on the cross. Those of us who are far off are brought near to God; the alienation and estrangement from God have been

His Finished Work

resolved by Christ's sacrifice. This amazing reversal in our status from "far off" from God to "nigh" was accomplished by Christ's finished work on the cross—by "the blood of Christ." Our standing before God was drastically altered by Christ's perfect work on the tree at Golgotha. Christ's finished work has brought us from outsiders to insiders.

> Romans 8:31 and 32:
> What shall we then say to these things? If God be for us, who can be against us?
> He that spared not his own Son, but delivered him up for us all, how shall he not with him also freely give us all things?

God gave up His Son as the ultimate sacrifice to redeem and save humanity after the fall of Adam. God demonstrated a love that defied description in offering His only begotten Son for us.

Verse 32 speaks of freely giving us "all things," not just one thing. We can accept that Jesus died for our sins and we are saved and leave it at that. Or we can dig deeper into the Scriptures and make an effort to see in more detail what occurred that day when he gave his life on the cross.

In this study of "*Jesus Christ the Complete Offering*," we shall examine what the Scriptures say regarding his sacrifice for mankind. Many of us are familiar with the records that speak of Christ's death for our sins. Yet there is much more to consider regarding God's promises, commandments, and declarations pertaining to what the Christ was to do. The scope and magnitude of Christ's achievements on the cross will begin to emerge as we delve into these records in the Scriptures.

JESUS CHRIST OUR COMPLETE OFFERING

In viewing the crucifixion, we will go beyond the eyes of the senses that only see another wretched martyr breathing his last breath. We will see from God's Word what happened that day on Golgotha.

Fully Accomplishing what God Gave Him to Do

There is a record in the gospel of John that shows how Jesus was vitally concerned about completing his God-given mission.

> John 4:31-34:
> In the mean while his disciples prayed him, saying, Master, eat.
> But he said unto them, I have meat to eat that ye know not of.
> Therefore said the disciples one to another, Hath any man brought him ought to eat?
> Jesus saith unto them, My meat is to do the will of him that sent me, and to finish[4] his work.

A crucial starting point of this study involves understanding that Jesus Christ chose to do the will of God and he was devoted to finishing the work that God had sent him to do. Jesus Christ chose to accomplish all God wanted him to do.

> John 5:36:
> But I have greater witness than that of John: for the works which the Father hath given me to **finish**, the same works that I do, bear witness of me, that the Father hath sent me.

Here Jesus Christ spoke of works which the Father gave him to accomplish in full. It was not only to do certain works, but

---

[4] The word, "finish," in John 4:34 and 5:36 is translated from the Greek word, *teleioō*. Please see Appendix Two for an explanation of this Greek word.

His Finished Work

to carry out those works in full. These works would then bear witness that the Father had truly sent him. As we continue to read the passage in this chapter, many other truths on this subject emerge.

> John 5:37-39:
> And the Father himself, which hath sent me, hath borne witness of me. Ye have neither heard his voice at any time, nor seen his shape.
> And ye have not his word abiding in you: for whom he hath sent, him ye believe not.
> Search the scriptures; for in them ye think ye have eternal life: and they are they which testify [bare witness] of me...

Jesus had cited a number of things that had testified of him. The completion of the works God had given him to do would bare witness (verse 36). The Father Himself bore witness (verse 37). The Scriptures also bore witness (verse 39).

Christ said the Scriptures should be carefully searched because they testified of him. When he said "search the scriptures" he was referring to the Old Testament writings. Of course, at this time, what is called the New Testament had not yet been written.

> Verse 46:
> ...For had ye believed Moses, ye would have believed me: for he wrote of me.

In verse 46, Jesus said, "He [Moses] wrote of me." The books of Moses are the first five books of the Bible: Genesis, Exodus, Leviticus, Numbers and Deuteronomy. In looking at these books, we will see that Moses wrote of Christ not only in a single prophecy, but in multiple prophecies, promises, types, shadows and illustrations. Our study will focus in detail on these Scriptures to see how Moses foretold of Christ by way of the Old Testament sacrifices.

Immediately prior to his death, Jesus told his twelve apostles about the upcoming crucifixion.

> Luke 18:31-34:
> Then he took unto him the twelve, and said unto them, Behold, we go up to Jerusalem, and all things that are written by the prophets concerning the Son of man shall be accomplished.[5]
> For he shall be delivered unto the Gentiles, and shall be mocked, and spitefully entreated, and spitted on:
> And they shall scourge him, and put him to death: and the third day he shall rise again.
> And they understood none of these things: and this saying was hid from them, neither knew they the things which were spoken.

Here Jesus Christ defines precisely what finishing the works his Father had given him to do would entail. He took the twelve apostles aside and let them know what would occur. He told them about his coming death and its great significance in verse 31: "...all things that are written by the prophets concerning the Son of man shall be accomplished." The prophecies of the Old Testament about the Messiah's suffering and death were to be fully accomplished and brought to a complete end. The events he described would be the total fulfillment of those prophecies concerning the Messiah's suffering and death.

The twelve apostles, however, did not understand. They had seen the lame walk, the blind see and the dead rise—but

---

[5] The word, "accomplished," is translated from the Greek word, *teleō*. See Appendix Two for more explanation.

His Finished Work

they simply could not absorb this statement concerning his death. They did not grasp what Jesus was talking about. These disciples, who had witnessed such wonders, simply could not receive that this great man of God would die.

After the crucifixion and resurrection, Christ helped two disciples on the road to Emmaus overcome their lack of understanding.

> Luke 24:25-27:
> Then he said unto them, O fools, and slow of heart to believe all that the prophets have spoken:
> Ought not Christ to have suffered these things, and to enter into his glory?
> And beginning at Moses and all the prophets, he expounded unto them in all the scriptures the things concerning himself.

There were only two—no large crowds, only two. Can one imagine any prominent teacher or leader in any field spending so much time with only two students? Add to this, two students whom that teacher would address as "fools, and slow of heart." Apparently Christ had a different perception of what was important than most do today.

How blessed these two disciples must have been! Later, as recorded in verse 32, they said one to another "Did not our heart burn within us, while he talked with us by the way, and while he opened to us the scriptures?" Their hearts became alive as Christ unfolded the Old Testament Scriptures concerning himself.

Let's look at a record regarding the last supper shortly before Jesus' arrest and crucifixion.

JESUS CHRIST OUR COMPLETE OFFERING

> Luke 22:37:
> For I say unto you, that this that is written must yet be accomplished[6] in me, **And he was reckoned among the transgressors:** for the things concerning me have an end [*telos*].

The phrase in bold print is a quote from Isaiah 53. Jesus declared of this prophecy in Isaiah, that it "must yet be accomplished in me." In chapter three, we will examine Isaiah 53 in detail and see how Jesus Christ completely carried out these words that were written hundreds of years before he was born.

According to this record in Luke, Jesus said clearly that the specific revelation in Isaiah 53 was to be accomplished in him. His crucifixion was the fulfillment of this prophecy. Jesus added, "for the things concerning me have an end." Looking at the Greek text of the New Testament, we see that the word translated "end" is *telos*. The Greek word *telos* means "a full and complete end," not merely a cessation but a total fulfillment and completion. (See Appendix Two). The prophecies in the Old Testament were brought to total fulfillment and completion in Jesus Christ.

If a contractor has fully completed the job as described in a contract, everything is totally finished. When the final payment is given after all the work is fully accomplished, that is the end. It is not merely a matter of the work stoppage, but the job having been completed, carried out to fulfillment and the full and final payment received.

John 17 is a record of Jesus praying to God right before the crucifixion.

---

[6] "Accomplished" is translated from the Greek word, *teleō*. See Appendix Two.

His Finished Work

> John 17:1-4:
> These words spake Jesus, and lifted up his eyes to heaven, and said, Father, the hour is come; glorify thy Son, that thy Son also may glorify thee:
> As thou hast given him power over all flesh, that he should give eternal life to as many as thou hast given him.
> And this is life eternal, that they might know thee the only true God, and Jesus Christ, whom thou hast sent. I have glorified thee on the earth: I have **finished**[7] the work which thou gavest me to do.

In prayer to his heavenly Father, Jesus looked beyond the cross to future realities such as God glorifying Christ and giving eternal life to the believers. Christ also said, "I have finished the work which thou gavest me to do." The phrase "I have finished" is used as a figure of speech to refer to what he was going to do in the very near future—carry out to full consummation and completion the work God gave him to do.

> John 19:16-30:
> Then delivered he him therefore unto them to be crucified. And they took Jesus, and led *him* away.
> And he bearing his cross went forth into a place called *the place* of a skull, which is called in the Hebrew Golgotha:
> Where they crucified him, and two other with him, on either side one, and Jesus in the midst.
> And Pilate wrote a title, and put *it* on the cross. And the writing was, JESUS OF NAZARETH THE KING OF THE JEWS.

---

[7] The word, "finished" is translated from the Greek word, *teleioō*. See Appendix Two.

JESUS CHRIST OUR COMPLETE OFFERING

This title then read many of the Jews: for the place where Jesus was crucified was nigh to the city: and it was written in Hebrew, *and* Greek, *and* Latin.

Then said the chief priests of the Jews to Pilate, Write not, The King of the Jews; but that he said, I am King of the Jews.

Pilate answered, What I have written I have written.

Then the soldiers, when they had crucified Jesus, took his garments, and made four parts, to every soldier a part; and also *his* coat: now the coat was without seam, woven from the top throughout.

They said therefore among themselves, Let us not rend it, but cast lots for it, whose it shall be: that the scripture might be fulfilled which saith, They parted my raiment among them, and for my vesture they did cast lots. These things therefore the soldiers did.

Now there stood by the cross of Jesus his mother, and his mother's sister, Mary the *wife* of Cleophas, and Mary Magdalene.

When Jesus therefore saw his mother, and the disciple standing by, whom he loved, he saith unto his mother, Woman, behold thy son!

Then saith he to the disciple, Behold thy mother! And from that hour that disciple took her unto his own *home*.

After this, Jesus knowing that all things were now **accomplished**,[8] that the scripture might be **fulfilled**,[9] saith, I thirst.

Now there was set a vessel full of vinegar: and they filled a spunge with vinegar, and put *it* upon hyssop, and put *it* to his mouth.

---

[8] The words, "accomplished" in verse 28 and "finished" in verse 30 are translated from the Greek word *teleō*. See Appendix Two.
[9] "Fulfilled" is translated from the Greek word, *teleioō*. See Appendix Two.

His Finished Work

> When Jesus therefore had received the vinegar, he said, It is **finished**: and he bowed his head, and gave up the ghost.

One of the Lord's last utterances before his death was, "It is finished." Jesus did not say, "I am finished." When Christ said "It is finished," to what did he refer? The work his Father had given him to bring to a final consummation was now at an end. The multiple prophecies and types of Christ's sacrifice written about in the Old Testament were fully accomplished. By his crucifixion, Jesus Christ brought to a complete and full end all that the Old Testament Scriptures spoke of his great sacrifice.

Christ stated in Luke 18:31: "all things that are written by the prophets concerning the Son of man shall be accomplished." He finished the work God had given him to do, accomplishing all that was required for the salvation of humanity. He had a job to do and he completed it in every detail. All things written by the Old Testament prophets were being fulfilled; not one prophecy or type was disregarded.

This monumental finished work of Christ's sacrifice is also mentioned in I Peter.

> I Peter 1:18 and 19:
> Forasmuch as ye know that ye were not redeemed with corruptible things, as silver and gold, from your vain conversation received by tradition from your fathers;
> But with the precious blood of Christ, as of a lamb without blemish and without spot.

To redeem means to buy back. Our redemption was not purchased by the wealth of this world but with the precious

JESUS CHRIST OUR COMPLETE OFFERING

blood of Christ, as of a lamb without blemish or without spot. Our redemption was fully paid for on the cross. Then three days and three nights later, God raised Christ from the dead.

As our substitute offering, without blemish or spot, Jesus Christ brought to a full end his sacrificial work. In the upcoming chapters, we will consider how our savior stood as a substitute on our behalf. We will see a perfect savior that performed a perfect work. He left nothing undone, imperfect or incomplete. As a direct result, our salvation is not partial. Our redemption is not deficient in any respect. Our quest is to behold Christ and his work of redemption with greater clarity so we can securely rest in his finished work and not in ours.

Chapter 2

Our Complete, Once-and-for-All Savior

We have seen that Jesus Christ was far, far more than a courageous martyr who died for a just cause. According to the Gospels, he brought to full completion the mission his Father sent him to do. He completely fulfilled the Old Testament prophecies about his suffering and death. With his last breath, he proclaimed, "It is finished," knowing that all the Scriptures were fulfilled and his mission was accomplished. The sacrificial work God had given him to do was carried out to completion, accomplishing all that was required for the redemption of fallen humanity.

In this chapter, we'll consider some of the benefits that we enjoy as a result of Christ's finished work. We will read about our eternal status as sons of God, completed by his perfect sacrifice.

Let's look at a passage in the book of Hebrews, which also speaks of Christ's finished work.

> Hebrews 2:9:
> But we see Jesus, who was made a little lower than the angels for the suffering of death, crowned with

JESUS CHRIST OUR COMPLETE OFFERING

glory and honour; that he by the grace of God should taste death for every man.

This verse opens with the phrase, "...we see Jesus..." We behold our Lord Jesus Christ not only as one enduring the crucifixion, but we see him as having accomplished his work, "crowned with glory and honor." We are to look beyond the cross unto the finished, completed work of Christ. The results of the sacrifice of our lord on the cross should not be an unseen reality for us—we should **see** what he has achieved.

A notable truth concerning his sacrifice is "...that he by the grace of God should taste death **for** every man." The crux of this truth hinges on the profound yet small word, "for" which means "in place of," or as a substitute. By the grace of God, Jesus Christ stood as a substitute so that by his sacrifice, Christ tasted death for every human being. As we shall see, the animal sacrifices of the Old Testament foreshadowed Christ's perfect sacrifice, also serving as substitutes.

> Verse 10:
> For it became him, for whom are all things, and by whom are all things, in bringing many sons unto glory, to make the captain of their salvation perfect[1] through sufferings.

Here our position is significantly elevated: "...bringing many sons unto glory..." We are sons of God brought unto glory! Certainly as we see Jesus and his fully accomplished sacrifice, we can truly open our eyes to who we are as well: sons of God brought to glory.

---

[1] In the book of Hebrews, we should recognize that the word, "perfect" is translated from the Greek word, *teleioō*. See Appendix Two.

Our Complete, Once and for All Savior

> Verses 11 and 12:
> For both he [Jesus] that sanctifieth and they who are sanctified are all of one: for which cause he is not ashamed to call them brethren,
> Saying, I will declare thy name unto my brethren, in the midst of the church will I sing praise unto thee.

Who sanctified us? Jesus did, by his accomplished work on the cross. Hebrews 10:10 declares that "...we are sanctified through the offering of the body of Jesus Christ once *for all.*" Hebrews 13:12 states that Jesus sanctified "...the people with his own blood." One of the monumental accomplishments of his "once for all" sacrifice is our sanctification. Biblically, to sanctify means to separate, to mark off, to set apart from the common lot dedicated or devoted to some special purpose.[2]

By Christ's accomplishments we have been separated out from the mass of humanity. His work has marked us as distinctive in God's sight, set apart for God's purposes. As sons of God we have been removed from the realm of the profane and the common, into the kingdom of God.

Since we are sanctified, because we are one with him, he is not ashamed to call us brethren. Then again in verse 12, he speaks of us as "his brethren."

> Verses 13-15:
> And again, I will put my trust in him. And again, Behold I and the children which God hath given me.

---

[2] For more on our sanctification, please see Walter J. Cummins, *Scripture Consulting Select Studies* (Franklin, Ohio: Scripture Consulting, 2010) 315 and David Bergey, *Jesus Christ Our Approach Offering*, 144-152.

JESUS CHRIST OUR COMPLETE OFFERING

> Forasmuch then as the children are partakers of flesh and blood, he also himself likewise took part of the same; that through death he might destroy him that had the power of death, that is, the devil;
> And deliver them who through fear of death were all their lifetime subject to bondage.

Here it speaks of "…the children which God hath given me." Since Christ is not ashamed to call us brethren, this is a radical transformation in our standing! We have gone from dead in trespasses and sin to become children of God. We've changed from without God and without hope in this dark world into God's kingdom. We're no longer abandoned orphans in this world. We are now brothers of Jesus Christ — sons of God brought unto glory.

In the world, people can be sensitive or quick to grasp their status or standing in a community or group. This is true no matter what rung of society. Whether that community is an institute of academics researching some arcane subject or a gang involved in criminal activities. One's standing in a community or group often gives people a sense of themselves. While social standing can be fleeting, we should be quick to grasp a sense of our eternal status as sons of God.

As Hebrews states here, we are high on the ladder as sons of God and brothers of our Lord Jesus Christ. This status of sonship is indeed an elevated standing Christ has acquired for us as sons of God. We certainly should have an altered sense of ourselves because we have moved from without God and without hope into the realm of sons of God.

In verse 14, it states that by this death, Jesus Christ "might destroy him that had the power of death, that is, the devil."

Our Complete, Once and for All Savior

In the coming age of glory, the devil and death will be destroyed (I Corinthians 15:26; Revelation 20:10). But right now we can be delivered from the bondage of fear of death because we have eternal life. The reality of living for eternity ought to transform even our short-term outlook.

> Verses 16 and 17:
> For verily he took not on him the nature of angels; but he took on him the seed of Abraham
> Wherefore in all things it behoved him to be made like unto his brethren, that he might be a merciful and faithful high priest in things pertaining to God, to make reconciliation for the sins of the people.

Christ was in all things made as his brethren; he was human. Since sin came by a human, Adam, it is logical and just that it was to be discharged by a human. Jesus Christ, as a man without sin, was an equivalent sacrifice to be substituted for all mankind. A man of the seed of Abraham, made like unto his brethren, paid the price for humanity's redemption and salvation. What a perfect savior! By his sacrifice he has set us apart as sons of God, bound for glory.

The Once-and-for-All Sacrifice

Let's consider another passage about Jesus Christ, our complete savior.

> Hebrews 5:8 and 9:
> Though he were a Son, yet learned he obedience by the things which he suffered;
> And being made perfect he became the author of eternal salvation unto all them that obey him;

JESUS CHRIST OUR COMPLETE OFFERING

By his death on the cross our savior achieved our salvation. Hence Jesus Christ has become the author of eternal salvation to all them that obey him.

Hebrews 7 goes on to explain further the completeness of our savior, calling Jesus Christ the high priest seated at the right hand of God.

> Hebrews 7:22-28:
> By so much was Jesus made a surety of a better testament.
> And they truly were many priests, because they were not suffered to continue by reason of death:
> But this man, because he continueth ever, hath an unchangeable priesthood.
> Wherefore he is able also to save them to the uttermost that come unto God by him, seeing he ever liveth to make intercession for them.
> For such an high priest became us, who is holy, harmless, undefiled, separate from sinners, and made higher than the heavens;
> Who needeth not daily, as those high priests, to offer up sacrifice, first for his own sins, and then for the people's: for this he did **once** [*ephapax*], when he offered up himself.
> For the law maketh men high priests which have infirmity; but the word of the oath, which was since the law, maketh the Son, who is consecrated[3] for evermore.

In verse 27, the Greek word rendered "once" in the Authorized King James Version is *ephapax*, which many of the other English translations render "once for all." Jesus Christ's sacrifice was once and for all time, a singular and

---

[3] "Consecrated" is translated from the Greek word, *teleioō*. See Appendix Two.

Our Complete, Once and for All Savior

unique event. The sacrifice of Christ was absolutely definitive: once-and-for-all. When he offered himself, it was the full and final offering for God's people for all time.

The Greek word *ephapax* also occurs in the following verse.

> Romans 6:10:
> For in that he died, he died unto sin once [*ephapax*]: but in that he liveth, he liveth unto God.

Christ laid down his life as the consummate sacrifice once and for all, with absolute finality. Yet he lives—God raised him from the dead.

> Hebrews 4:14-16:
> Seeing then that we have a great high priest, that is passed into [through] the heavens, Jesus the Son of God, let us hold fast our profession.
> For we have not an high priest which cannot be touched with the feeling of our infirmities; but was in all points tempted like as we are, yet without sin.
> Let us therefore come boldly unto the throne of grace, that we may obtain mercy, and find grace to help in time of need.

After Christ gave his life as the final sacrifice, God raised him from the dead and then he ascended, passing through the heavens. Now we have a preeminent high priest who has ascended through the heavens, interceding for us in the very presence of God.

Our lord is able to help, to intercede on our behalf. He has suffered, he has been tempted. In all points he has been tempted as we are, yet he remained without sin.

JESUS CHRIST OUR COMPLETE OFFERING

Jesus has a heartfelt bond with God's people, empathically feeling with them. He is not unaware or insensitive in our times of need. The Gospels speak of Christ's deep compassion for his people on many occasions.[4] Indeed, his very motivation in giving himself to die was the love he had for God's people:

> Ephesians 5:2:
> And walk in love, as Christ also hath loved us, and hath given himself for us an offering and a sacrifice to God for a sweetsmelling savour.

Christ gave himself up as a substitutionary sacrifice on our behalf because he loved us. Evidently this yearning compassion our lord had toward God's people has not come to an end since his resurrection and ascension into the heavenlies. He still can be "touched with the feelings of our infirmities." This very real empathic connection Christ has with us could be considered another dimension of the completeness of our savior.

Our lord is truly an everlasting savior! He was born just like any other human being. He lived among us. He died in great anguish and disgrace. Despite these temptations, he never sinned. He carried out the mission God gave him to its utter conclusion. His sacrificial work was full and consummate. God raised him from the dead and he then ascended. Now, at God's right hand, he lives to make intercession for us. He is the complete savior — able to save us to the uttermost as we approach God by him.

---

[4] Matthew 9:36; 20:34; Mark 1:41; 6:34; 8:2.

Our Complete, Once and for All Savior

Complete in Him

The following verse is key to understanding how the sacrifices of the Law looked forward to Christ.

> Hebrews 10:1:
> For the law having a shadow of good things to come, and not the very image of the things, can never with those sacrifices which they offered year by year continually make the comers thereunto perfect [complete].[5]

The word "comers" may be translated "those who approach."[6] The sacrifices of the Old Covenant were offered "year by year continually," yet those sacrifices could never make the offerers complete. While the offerings of the Old Testament gave the supplicants some limited measure of approach to God, these were only shadows of the good things to come. These offerings could never bring those who approached into a finished state in their relationship with God.

Previously in Hebrews the inadequacy of the Old Covenant is stated:

> Hebrews 7:19: For the law made nothing perfect ...
> Hebrews 9:9: ...could not make him [priests of Old Covenant] that did the service perfect, as pertaining to the conscience.

---

[5] The word, "perfect" is translated from the Greek word, *teleioō*, in Hebrews 2:10, 5:9; 7:19; 9:9; 10:1,14. See Appendix Two.
[6] The Amplified Bible says: "...those who approach;" Revised Version and Working Translation: "...those who approach..."

JESUS CHRIST OUR COMPLETE OFFERING

The Law and Levitical priests were never able to make them perfect or complete. Animal sacrifices could never result in a finished work.

> Hebrews 10:10-14:
> By the which will we are sanctified through the offering of the body of Jesus Christ once for all [*ephapax*].
> And every priest standeth daily ministering and offering oftentimes the same sacrifices, which can never take away sins:
> But this man, after he had offered one sacrifice for sins for ever, sat down on the right hand of God;
> From henceforth expecting till his enemies be made his footstool.
> For by one offering he hath perfected for ever them that are sanctified.

As verse ten declares, we are sanctified through the offering of the body of Jesus Christ once and for all. Reading the verse carefully, we see it says we are sanctified once and for all by the offering of the body of Jesus Christ.

Here the finality and completeness of Christ's sacrifice is linked directly to **our** sanctification. Our salvation is locked irreversibly to the absolute reality of Christ's sacrifice. Just as Christ's offering of himself was a once-and-for-all final definitive event, so also is our salvation. Our sanctification has the same definitive force as his sacrifice!

According to verse 10, we are sanctified once and for all by the offering of the body of Jesus Christ. His sacrifice has set us apart, sanctified us, definitively and completely. Our salvation has a sense of absolute finality.

Our Complete, Once and for All Savior

Christ's offering on our behalf was a unique and individual event with irreversible finality. In like manner, our sanctification, our salvation and our redemption was also an unparalleled event with irreversible finality.

> Hebrews 10:14:
> For by one offering he hath perfected[7] for ever them that are sanctified.

As far our salvation is concerned, we are a completed work; we are finished, brought to a full end. Now we are His workmanship created in Christ Jesus. By Christ's finished work on the tree at Golgotha, our salvation is forever a finished work.

A comparison of Hebrews 10:1 and 14, offers a glaring contrast between those who approached God under the Old Covenant and those who now approach God through the sacrifice of Christ. What a counterpoint—<u>never complete</u> in contrast to <u>complete forever</u>.

Those who approached by Old Testament Sacrifices:
NEVER COMPLETE

Those who approach by Christ's Sacrifice:
COMPLETE FOREVER

Now we can contemplate the full impact a completed sacrifice and a complete savior has directly on us: a perfect

---

[7] "Perfected" is translated from the Greek word, *teleioō*. See Appendix Two.

JESUS CHRIST OUR COMPLETE OFFERING

offering yields a perfect salvation. Or put another way, a fully completed offering produces a fully completed salvation. Now this profound gem in Colossians 2:10 can be grasped more clearly: "And ye are complete in him, which is the head of all principality and power."

> Hebrews 7:25
> Wherefore he is able also to save them to the uttermost[8] that come unto God by him, seeing he ever liveth to make intercession for them.

We have complete salvation and deliverance available today because Christ lives to make intercession for us. Again, look at the utter totality of our salvation!

Jesus Christ achieved a consummate work on the cross. As such, our savior is complete, always living to intercede for us. So then as a result, we have a salvation accomplished in full, lacking nothing, to the uttermost. By his complete offering we have been made complete.

Those who gaped in horror at the crucifixion did not see the reality of a complete sacrifice for all humanity, a complete savior for all time and a complete salvation for all God's people. But we perceive what they did not: "But we see Jesus, who was made a little lower than the angels for the suffering of death, crowned with glory and honour; that he by the grace of God should taste death for every man." The salvation he accomplished for us was absolutely perfect and all encompassing.

These marvelous realities bring to mind that classic response of those who heard the gospel after the Day of Pentecost in Acts 2:37: "men and brethren, what shall we do?" Hebrews

---

[8] "Uttermost" is translated from the Greek word, *panteles*, from *pan* meaning "all" and *telos*. See Appendix Two.

Our Complete, Once and for All Savior

tells us. In light of these glorious truths, the book of Hebrews instructs us on how to exercise our completeness.

> Hebrews 4:16:
> Let us therefore come boldly unto the throne of grace, that we may obtain mercy, and find grace to help in time of need.
>
> Hebrews 10:19:
> Having therefore, brethren, boldness to enter into the holiest by the blood of Jesus,

Our response to our absolute, definitive, accomplished salvation is to approach God with boldness.[9] Our boldness before God has been accomplished for us in Christ. It does not say to enter into God's presence groveling with the head lowered. We can be open with God and pour out our hearts to Him. By Christ's final sacrifice we can walk face to face with our Heavenly Father without fear and self-loathing. We have an unquestioned right to approach God with boldness.

> Ephesians 2:8-10:
> For by grace are ye saved through faith; and that not of yourselves: it is the gift of God:
> Not of works, lest any man should boast.
> For we are his workmanship, created in Christ Jesus unto good works, which God hath before ordained that we should walk in them.

Our salvation is totally by grace, not of ourselves or by our own works. It is by the offering of God. There are no grounds for blowing one's own horn because our

---

[9] Also see: "Chapter Six: Our Right of Boldness in Approaching God" and "Appendix A: Boldness: Our Privilege as Citizens of Heaven," David Bergey, *Jesus Christ Our Approach Offering*.

JESUS CHRIST OUR COMPLETE OFFERING

redemption and sanctification was accomplished by the sacrifice of our Lord Jesus Christ.

We can add nothing to this glorious completeness. Nothing can be added to it or be taken from it. We cannot increase or improve upon what Christ has done. However, we are to grow in our appreciation and realization. We can increase our acknowledgment and our enjoyment of the accomplished realities of Christ's sacrifice.

The sacrifice of Christ and our resultant standing before God applies equally to the poorest or youngest child of God as well as to the highest and most learned. God makes no distinction—man does that. On occasion, our walk may be marked by failures, difficulties, weakness, setbacks, and sins. Our walk is quite a different matter from our complete salvation. Our fellowship with God is distinct from our position in Christ as sons of God. Our walk cannot effect what Christ has accomplished in the slightest degree.

He was the equivalent sacrifice that fully paid the price for humanity's redemption. The completeness and finality of his work is mirrored in the completeness and finality of what we have received. We should occupy ourselves with Christ and his accomplishments. Let the word about Christ dwell in us richly. What a comfort to the soul it brings—that our salvation rests not on our work but on HIS. Indeed, what a quiet certainty it brings to our lives when we recognize our salvation is by his accomplishments, not ours.

Chapter 3

Isaiah 53:
The Messiah Bears our Sins, Sorrows and Sickness

We have seen that Jesus Christ finished the work of redemption that God had sent him to do. He did all that God had spoken of him in the Scriptures. We have also noted that the sacrifices of the Mosaic Law were not able to fully accomplish those things that the Christ was to achieve by his sacrifice. He wrought a complete salvation which is available today. God had spoken in previous times of what the Christ was to do, and Jesus Christ was fully aware of those promises, commandments, and declarations regarding his mission.

We previously considered something Jesus said at his last supper. Let's look at that record again.

> Luke 22:37:
> For I say unto you, that this that is written must yet be accomplished in me, **"And he was reckoned among the transgressors:"** for the things concerning me have an end.

JESUS CHRIST OUR COMPLETE OFFERING

"And he was reckoned among the transgressors," with bold print and quotation marks added, is a direct quote from Isaiah 53:12. In this verse, of which Jesus spoke, he said that this prophecy "must yet be accomplished in me." Christ said explicitly that he would completely fulfill this prophecy of Isaiah. Jesus also said, "for the things concerning me have an end." The *New American Bible* renders this phrase, "and indeed what is written about me is coming to fulfillment."

In Luke 22, Jesus plainly identified himself with the prophecy in Isaiah 53. A reference to the same record in Isaiah 53 is also given in the Gospel of Mark.

> Mark 15:22-28:
> And they bring him unto the place Golgotha, which is, being interpreted, The place of a skull.
> And they gave him to drink wine mingled with myrrh: but he received it not.
> And when they had crucified him, they parted his garments, casting lots upon them, what every man should take.
> And it was the third hour, and they crucified him.
> And the superscription of his accusation was written over, THE KING OF THE JEWS.
> And with him they crucify two thieves; the one on his right hand, and the other on his left.
> And the scripture was fulfilled, which saith, **And he was numbered with the transgressors.**

Jesus was crucified at Golgotha, where others were also crucified beside him. According to Mark 15:28, those things were done in fulfillment of the record in Isaiah 53:12 which spoke of his being "numbered with the transgressors."

Let's look at this passage beginning in Isaiah 52:13.

Isaiah 53

Isaiah 52:13 and 14:
Behold, my servant shall deal prudently, he shall be exalted and extolled, and be very high.
As many were astonied [astounded] at thee; his visage was so marred more than any man, and his form more than the sons of men:

In verse 13, God speaks of His servant being exalted to the utmost degree, and then in the next verse it attests that his form and visage was "so marred more than any man."

Verses 13 and 14 are set in shocking contrast to each other. This forms a figure of speech called *Antithesis*. In these two verses, two utter extremes are juxtaposed, set side by side, forming a violent contrast to shock the mind.[1] In verse 13 the Messiah's glorification is the loftiest conceivable. In verse 14 his degradation is the deepest possible. The height of his eminence is held in brutal contrast to the depth of his wretchedness. The figure of speech *Antithesis* is used repeatedly in this passage. The aim of this figure is not smooth reading, but to seize our attention. Similar to many other figures of speech, it has one end, to get the reader to take notice. Many Old Testament prophecies feature shocking contrasts that accentuate the impossibility of fulfillment except by divine means.[2]

When the true Messiah would come, his exaltation would be of the highest and his degradation would be of the deepest. The Gospels tell us how this declaration came to pass. With

---

[1] E.W. Bullinger, *Figures of Speech Used in the Bible* (Grand Rapids, Michigan: Baker Book House, 1968) 715.
[2] The first prophecy of Christ in Scripture, Genesis 3:15, also forms a startling contrast that accentuates the impossibility of fulfillment except by divine means. In combat, how does one go on to crush the head of an opponent once his heel is crushed? Also see II Kings 6:25; 7:1.

the benefit of hindsight in verse 14, we can see a prophecy of Christ's crucifixion, while the previous verse refers to God exalting Christ by the resurrection and ascension. Even though seemingly impossible, God brought this prophecy to pass.

> Isaiah 52:15-53:1:
> So shall he sprinkle many nations; the kings shall shut their mouths at him: for that which had not been told them shall they see; and that which they had not heard shall they consider.
> Who hath believed our report? and to whom is the arm of the LORD revealed?

"Arm of the Lord revealed" is an oriental expression which indicates the arm being raised to do battle (Jeremiah 21:5). Here it speaks of God fighting for his people.[3]

Only five verses earlier Isaiah 52:10 states: "The LORD hath made bare his holy arm in the eyes of all the nations; and all the ends of the earth shall see the salvation of our God." The expression "bare his holy arm" refers to raising the arm to do battle. Here God does battle to bring about the salvation and redemption of his people. He fights for His people as never before. He presents the final sacrifice for all time, for all people, which will save them from their sins.

> Isaiah 53:2 and 3:
> For he shall grow up before him as a tender plant, and as a root out of a dry ground: he hath no form nor

---

[3] Christopher C Geer, *Appreciating Oriental Insights in the Bible*, Student's Study Guide to Set 2 (Glasgow, Scotland: Word Promotions, 1998) 6. Also see: Leland Ryken and others, eds., *Dictionary of Biblical Imagery* (Downers Grove, IL: Inter-Varsity Press, 1998) 43.

Isaiah 53

comeliness; and when we shall see him, there is no beauty [majesty] that we should desire him.
He is despised and rejected of men; a man of sorrows, and acquainted with grief: and we hid as it were our faces from him; he was despised, and we esteemed him not.

This servant of the Lord was to be rejected of men and despised. He was to suffer to the extreme. The last clause of verse 2, "…when we shall see him, there is no beauty that we should desire him," and all of verse 3 is referring to his crucifixion. When they looked upon the crucified savior, they saw no kingly majesty that they had seen only days previous when the multitudes heralded him as the king as he entered Jerusalem (John 12:13). The senses observer only saw a severely beaten man hanging on a tree, despised, and accursed.

But in the following verses, we have a new concept introduced, a reality that was not seen by the eyes of those beholding the crucifixion. The outward appearance alone gave no hint of what God was carrying out.

> Isaiah 53:3 and 4:
> He is despised and rejected of men; a man of sorrows [*makob*], and acquainted with grief [*choli*]: and we hid as it were our faces from him; he was despised, and we esteemed him not.
> Surely he hath borne our griefs [*choli*], and carried our sorrows [*makob*]: yet we did esteem him stricken, smitten of God, and afflicted.

The words "grief" or "griefs" in verses 3 and 4 are a translation of the Hebrew word, *choli*. The Hebrew word, *choli*, is used 22 times in the Hebrew Old Testament. All 22 verses have a direct reference to disease or sickness.[4] Yet the Authorized King James Version in Isaiah 53 mistranslates *choli* as "grief" and "griefs."

Verse 3 should read that he was "...acquainted with sickness:" Verse 4 should declare: "Surely he hath borne our sickness."

The *New International Version* also mistranslates *choli* as "suffering" in verse 3 and as "infirmities" in verse 4. Those who read Isaiah 53:4 in these popular versions would not notice that Christ carried their sicknesses.

However, in the next verse God clarifies and repeats the truth, which has been translated correctly.

> Isaiah 53:5:
> ...and with his stripes we are healed.

In the New Testament, I Peter 2:24 reiterates the prophecy: "...by whose stripes ye were healed." God speaks with vivid clarity that the sacrificial work of Christ bore not only sin, but sickness as well. Here in Isaiah 53, the coming savior is revealed as a righteous servant who would pay the price for our physical wholeness.

In Isaiah 53:4, we see more than a servant of the Lord enduring intense suffering. We now have new, additional information. This suffering servant would bear the sickness and carry the sorrows of God's people.

He not only bore our sin, he bore the consequences of sin as well. In a previous chapter we noted that the transgression of Adam and Eve and their subsequent death from loss of

---

[4] See Appendix Three. As the appendix list demonstrates, the only precise translation of *choli* must be sickness or disease.

Isaiah 53

spirit life brought tremendous repercussions on humanity. Sickness and sorrows were some of the calamitous aftereffects.

The Authorized King James Version of Isaiah 53 also states that the Messiah will carry our sorrows. The Hebrew word translated "sorrows" in Isaiah 53:4 is *makob* meaning "pain" or "sorrow," often including mental anguish.[5] The first occurrence of this word, *makob*, in the Hebrew Old Testament is in Exodus.

> Exodus 3:7 and 8:
> And the LORD said, I have surely seen the affliction of my people which are in Egypt, and have heard their cry by reason of their taskmasters; for I know their sorrows [*makob*].
> And I am come down to deliver them out of the hand of the Egyptians, and to bring them up out of that land unto a good land and a large, unto a land flowing with milk and honey...

The children of Israel languished in slavery, oppressed under their Egyptian taskmasters. God saw their affliction and heard their cry. In verse 8, He says: "And I am come down to deliver them out of the hand of the Egyptians..." God's will was the deliverance of His people. He wanted the Israelites to be delivered from their captivity. We can read the record of Israel's deliverance from slavery in Exodus. God rescued them with mighty signs and wonders.

Later God facilitated the deliverance of all His people from oppression and bondage with the coming of the Messiah. Jesus Christ bore our pains and our mental anguish. Jesus Christ lifted up and carried away our mental bondage and

---

[5] *Gesenius' Hebrew and Chaldee Lexicon* (Grand Rapids, MI: Baker, 1979) 470.

JESUS CHRIST OUR COMPLETE OFFERING

oppression to the cross. In addition to our physical ailments, our mental prisons and our emotional bondage were heaped on the shoulders of our savior. What inner joy and rejoicing this should bring to our lives!

Matthew, chapter 8 quotes Isaiah 53:4:

> Matthew 8:16 and 17:
> When the even was come, they brought unto him many that were possessed with devils: and he cast out the spirits with his word, and healed all that were sick:
> That it might be fulfilled which was spoken by Esaias [Isaiah] the prophet, saying, Himself took our infirmities, and bare our sicknesses.

With the personal presence of His righteous servant on earth, God began to fulfill His Word as revealed hundreds of years before by the prophet Isaiah. Jesus "...cast out the spirits with his word, and healed all that were sick." The words of the scrolls of Isaiah were being accomplished—unfolding in manifestation. The healing and deliverance ministry of the Lord Jesus Christ must have been a thrill to behold.

But the greater thrill would have been the realization that the savior of the world was on earth, walking among men. These were exhilarating times, on the cusp of a new age of deliverance for God's people. But what was more exciting—the redemption of humanity by the offering of the life of God's Messiah—was to soon occur.

Matthew 8:16 states that "he healed all that were sick" which parallels verse 17: he "bare our sicknesses." Likewise, "took our infirmities" corresponds to Jesus curing those possessed; casting "out the spirits with his word." The casting out of

Isaiah 53

devil spirits was a direct fulfillment of the prophecy in Isaiah 53:4 of the Messiah bearing pain and mental anguish. Devil possession would be the extreme of pain and mental anguish.

Sometimes those described as "possessed with devils," in biblical times may today be referred to as "mentally ill." Regardless of the vocabulary used or the cause—Jesus Christ bore it all! He paid the price for our healing.

The Transfer of the Ages

Returning to Isaiah 53, we see more that was accomplished by his sacrifice.

> Isaiah 53:5 and 6:
> But he was wounded **for** our transgressions, he was bruised **for** our iniquities: the chastisement of our peace was upon him; and with his stripes we are healed.
> All we like sheep have gone astray; we have turned every one to his own way; and the LORD hath **laid on him** the iniquity of us all.

In addition to being despised and rejected, this man was wounded for our transgressions; he was bruised for our iniquities. Jehovah laid on this man of God the iniquity of all of God's people.

According to Isaiah 53, God was to legally transfer the sins and sicknesses of His people to this man. The Lord God "laid on him the iniquity of us all." This righteous man, laid low with so much suffering, also had all the sins and sicknesses of God's people weighing down on him as well.

JESUS CHRIST OUR COMPLETE OFFERING

What a dire soul in such a miserable circumstance! His face and body are so marred that he hardly resembled a man. On top of that, the Lord God lays on him the iniquity of us all. This wretched man has the sin, the sickness and the sorrows of His people transferred onto his shoulders. He not only bears the sins; he carries the sicknesses and pains as well. Look at all that was heaped upon him!

Here God reveals the actual realities of the crucifixion that the senses could not behold. It declares in verse 5 that he was wounded **for** our transgressions. This small but significant word "for" has been put in bold print to highlight the concept of substitution. This man stood as a substitute. He suffered the penalty of sin in place of God's people. He carried their sin, sickness and mental anguish so they don't have to.

> Isaiah 53:7-9:
> He was oppressed, and he was afflicted, yet he opened not his mouth: he is brought as a lamb to the slaughter, and as a sheep before her shearers is dumb, so he openeth not his mouth.
> He was taken from prison and from judgment: and who shall declare his generation? for he was cut off out of the land of the living: **for** the transgression of my people was he stricken.
> And he made his grave with the wicked, and with the rich in his death; because he had done no violence, neither was any deceit in his mouth.

As if there was any doubt, these verses remove any possibility that this righteous servant may have survived his horrible treatment. This wonderful man was "cut off out of the land of the living," meaning he died. Then, verse 9 makes an astounding statement: his grave was with the rich. This is a startling enigma: his death was dishonorable and

Isaiah 53

held up for public disgrace, but in contrast, his burial was prestigious among the rich. The first part of verse 9 could be translated more accurately as follows. "His grave was assigned with criminals, yet he was with a rich man in his death."

Joseph of Arimathea made a daring entrance into the presence of Pilate after the crucifixion to obtain the body of Jesus for burial (Matthew 27:57-60). Remarkably, this prophecy was fulfilled by the actions of only one man — Joseph of Arimathea. Instead of being thrown into a common grave for criminals, the body of Jesus Christ was placed in a tomb, which only the affluent would have.

> Isaiah 53:10:
> Yet it pleased the LORD to bruise him; he hath put him to grief: when thou shalt make his soul an offering for sin [*asham*=trespass offering], he shall see his seed, he shall prolong his days, and the pleasure of the LORD shall prosper in his hand.

Here again is the figure of shocking contrasts. How can God prolong his days while also making his life an offering for sin? Again, the answer is found in the Gospels. On Golgotha, his life was given as an offering; three days and three nights later, God raised him from the dead.

The words "offering for sin" are one word in the Hebrew text of the Old Testament — *asham*. Usually in the Authorized King James Version, *asham* is translated as a "trespass offering." The trespass offering is one of the main offerings of the Old Covenant and is explained in detail in Leviticus.

As we shall see later, there are two offerings for sin under the Old Testament. One is the "sin offering" — its main

JESUS CHRIST OUR COMPLETE OFFERING

purpose is purification and the other is the trespass offering its main purpose is restitution.

Here in Isaiah 53:10, God specifically calls Christ an *asham* or trespass offering. This plain statement, calling Christ a trespass offering, is a cornerstone verse from which we can draw a straight line to the Levitical sacrifices. In chapter seven, we will embark on a study of this offering and see its exact significance as well as how it applies to the sacrifice of Christ.

> Isaiah 53:11 and 12:
> He shall see of the travail of his soul, and shall be satisfied: by his knowledge shall my righteous servant justify many; for he shall **bear their iniquities**.
> Therefore will I divide him a portion with the great, and he shall divide the spoil with the strong; because he hath poured out his soul unto death: and he was numbered with the transgressors; and he **bare the sin** of many, and made intercession for the transgressors.

These closing verses mention again how the Messiah will bare the sins and iniquities of many. The sins and iniquities have been transferred to this righteous servant of God. For this reason, God shall see the travail of his soul, and God will be "satisfied." God's satisfaction is in the legal sense: this righteous servant has satisfied the requirements of justice. He paid in full everything that was lacking or owed. The sins of God's people have been carried away, restitution has been paid; the demands of justice have been met—all by the suffering and death of this righteous man.

The following chart is from Isaiah 53, which describes what God's righteous servant was to do as a substitute; on whom

Isaiah 53

God would transfer the sin, sickness and pains of God's people.

What was Transferred to the Messiah in Isaiah 53:

Verse 4	**borne** our griefs [sicknesses]
	carried our sorrows [pains]
Verse 5	wounded **for** our transgressions,
	bruised **for** our iniquities:
	the chastisement of [for] our peace
	was **upon** him;
	and with his stripes we are healed
Verse 6	**laid on him** the iniquity of us all
Verse 8	**for** the transgression of my people was he stricken
Verse 11	he shall **bear their iniquities**
Verse 12	he **bare the sin** of many

In most modern legal systems, there is no parallel of satisfying justice by transferring guilt by one party to an innocent party. The crimes of one cannot be transferred to another; the innocent cannot take the punishment for the guilty. In fact, a primary aim of most legal systems is to prevent this from happening. The guilty must be punished and the innocent protected. However, even in our legal systems, a parent could pay a fine for a child or hire an accomplished and expensive defense attorney to plead the case.

As we saw in Isaiah 53, under God's justice, it is permissible to transfer sins of a guilty one to an innocent. This truth is fundamental to both the Old and New Testaments. If sin

JESUS CHRIST OUR COMPLETE OFFERING

cannot be transferred, then Christ could not have borne our sins. And if he did not bear our sins, we are yet without hope. Christianity is built on the proposition that Christ is the sacrifice that bore the sin of the world.

Starting in Genesis, when animal sacrifices were offered, the concept was conveyed that the innocent offering bore the guilt for the offerer. Here in Isaiah 53, what is depicted in the Law is made explicit. This prophecy states plainly that a righteous servant of God will lay down his life and bear the sins of God's people, by becoming a trespass offering. The prophecy of Isaiah 53 is completely fulfilled in Matthew, Mark, Luke and John. All the iniquities were transferred to Jesus of Nazareth as he suffered and died on Golgotha.

HOW did God accomplish our redemption and salvation? Here in Isaiah 53, it declares the means God used to achieve our salvation. The method God utilized to facilitate our salvation was straightforward: take all of our sins and lay them on someone else! In the next chapter, we will consider how the sacrificial system that God gave to Moses by revelation constantly reiterates the concept of this transfer of sin. Every time an animal died as a sacrifice, the implied message was that the innocent was dying as a substitute for the guilty. On Golgotha all was brought into full consummation with the crucifixion of Christ. All the types and the prophecies of the Old Covenant of the coming complete sacrifice of the Messiah were fulfilled.

In this Old Testament revelation of Isaiah we see what actually happened that afternoon when Christ died. Luke 22:37 is a clear signpost, pointing us to Isaiah 52:13 – 53:12. The unseen realities behind the death of our Lord Jesus Christ are explained in this prophecy of Isaiah. It gives details of what his death on the cross accomplished. Isaiah prophesied how a righteous servant of Jehovah would bear

Isaiah 53

the sins of God's people. Also, how the sins would be transferred onto an innocent sacrifice and the legal means God would use to cleanse His people from their sins. Here in Isaiah 53, we see why all of history pivoted on this event of the crucifixion.

Chapter 4

The Law: A Shadow of Christ

Jesus Christ brought to full consummation the Old Testament prophecies concerning himself. He made this clear to the two disciples on the road to Emmaus: "And beginning at Moses and all the prophets, he expounded unto them in **all** the scriptures the things concerning himself." (Luke 24:27). Afterward, he spoke of these matters to other disciples.

> Luke 24:44 and 45:
> And he said unto them [the disciples], These are the words which I spake unto you, while I was yet with you, that **all** things must be fulfilled, which were written in the law of Moses, and in the prophets, and in the psalms, concerning me.
> Then opened he their understanding, that they might understand the scriptures,

Jesus opened their eyes to the totality of his fulfillment of all the Old Testament writings. Christ fulfilled all that was stated in the Old Testament in regard to himself.

The Law: A Shadow of Christ

> Hebrews 9:28-10:3:
> So Christ was once offered to bear the sins of many; and unto them that look for him shall he appear the second time without sin unto salvation.
> For the law having a **shadow of good things to come** [Christ and his accomplishments], and not the very image of the things, can never with those sacrifices which they offered year by year continually make the comers thereunto perfect.
> For then would they not have ceased to be offered? because that the worshippers once purged should have had no more conscience of sins.
> But in those sacrifices there is a remembrance again made of sins every year.

Because the Law was a shadow of the good things to come, these sacrifices looked forward to the perfect sacrifice to come, but they could never make the Old Testament offerer complete. These offerings under the Law of Moses were a shadow, a silhouette, an outline of the promised Messiah who would offer himself. The "good things to come," which the sacrifices foreshadowed, was the coming savior and the results of his accomplishments in our lives. While these offerings were not the very image or reality of "good things to come," they gave a shadow outline of the "once for all" sacrifice of Jesus Christ. These sacrifices were initiated by God in anticipation of the true and perfect sacrifice of Jesus Christ.

As we shall see, the grand purpose of the offerings was for God to direct Israel to where true salvation would come. The sacrifices of the Law depicted an innocent victim enduring in their stead the righteous penalty for sin. Understanding the Old Testament offerings can enable us to grasp Jesus Christ and his perfect work of redemption more clearly.

JESUS CHRIST OUR COMPLETE OFFERING

Hebrews 10:3 states another purpose of these Old Testament sacrifices: "But in those sacrifices there is a remembrance again made of sins every year." In offering a sacrifice, the separation, alienation and enmity from God and the sin of the Israelites was recalled to mind. These sacrifices reminded people of the need for a redeemer.

Hebrews 10:2 says, referring to the offerings, "…the worshippers once purged…" This statement suggests that these offerings granted some limited and temporary cleansing or forgiveness of sins. As we shall see in future chapters, with the sin and trespass offerings this was the case. However, being provisional, these offerings could never secure a complete and perfect salvation.

Colossians gives us another example of how the Mosaic Law was a shadow of the good things to come.

> Colossians 2:16 and 17:
> Let no man therefore judge you in meat, or in drink, or in respect of an holyday [feast], or of the new moon, or of the sabbath days:
> Which are a shadow of things to come; but the body is of Christ.

No one is to pass judgment on the believer in matters of food or drink or regarding the feast days, new moon, or Sabbath days. These various days of the Old Testament calendar are a shadow of things to come. The feast days were set on the yearly calendar; the new moon on the monthly; the Sabbath day, weekly.

The Law: A Shadow of Christ

The three terms—feast, new moon, and Sabbath—are often used together in the Old Testament.[1]

> I Chronicles 23:31:
> And to offer all burnt sacrifices unto the LORD **in the sabbaths, in the new moons, and on the set feasts**, by number, according to the order commanded unto them, continually before the LORD:

> II Chronicles 2:4:
> Behold, I build an house to the name of the LORD my God, to dedicate it to him, and to burn before him sweet incense, and for the continual shewbread, and for the burnt offerings morning and evening, **on the sabbaths, and on the new moons, and on the solemn feasts** of the LORD our God. This is an ordinance for ever to Israel.

Notice how the feast, new moon and Sabbath are marked by sacrificial offerings. There are other ordinances concerning these days, but most often, the primary event was the offering of various sacrifices.[2]

The sacred calendar of the Old Covenant—feasts, new moons, and Sabbaths—were "a shadow of things to come; but the body is of Christ."

> Acts 5:15:
> Insomuch that they brought forth the sick into the streets, and laid them on beds and couches, that at the

---

[1] Other examples of "feast, new moon and Sabbath" used together: II Chronicles 8:13; 31:3; Nehemiah 10:33; Ezekiel 45:17; Hosea 2:11. In Isaiah 1:11-14, in verse 14, God says of those observing these special days: "Your new moons and your appointed feasts my soul hateth: they are a trouble unto me; I am weary to bear them." How much more would this be true under the New Covenant!
[2] Numbers 28 and Leviticus 23.

JESUS CHRIST OUR COMPLETE OFFERING

least the shadow of Peter passing by might overshadow some of them.

The shadow of Peter was only an outline, a silhouette of his actual body. In Colossians 2:17, the real thing is Christ, while the Law was a shadow outline of him who was to come. The reality depicted by the various holidays, rituals and sacrifices of the Law was Christ. These sacred days of the Old Testament, as well as the sacrifices that accompanied them, foreshadowed Christ and his accomplishments.

Substitution Foreshadowed

We have seen that the Law of Moses was a shadow of the good things to come. Therefore, let's look at a specific example of how the sacrifices of the Law foreshadowed Christ. Hebrews 9:28 states, "Christ was once offered to bear the sins of many." Then in Isaiah 53, we read that the coming savior was to bear the sins and iniquities of God's people.

As previously noted, God transferred the guilt of humanity onto Jesus Christ—He "laid on him the iniquity of us all." Christ stood as a substitute, suffering the penalty of sin—death.

How exactly is this concept of substitution foreshadowed in the Old Testament sacrifices?

> Genesis 22:13:
> And Abraham lifted up his eyes, and looked, and behold behind him a ram caught in a thicket by his horns: and Abraham went and took the ram, and offered him up for a burnt offering **in the stead** of his son.

The Law: A Shadow of Christ

We will look at Genesis 22 in more detail when we examine the burnt offering. Yet from this verse alone we can see that Abraham sacrificed a ram "in the stead of his son." This offering served as a substitute in place of Isaac. As we will see in chapter 14, this is one of the great records in the Old Testament looking forward in anticipation of Christ and his sacrificial work.

Another preeminent chapter that portrays the work of our savior is Leviticus 16. This superb chapter describes the activities of the Day of Atonement and unfolds a treasure trove of messianic shadows and types. Of all the holy days under the Law that foreshadowed the reality of what Christ would accomplish, none present it in more graphic detail than the Day of Atonement. We will examine this very holy day of the Law at length in later chapters. However, as with Genesis 22, at this time we will only focus on the point of substitution.

> Leviticus 16:7-10:
> And he shall take the two goats, and present them before the LORD at the door of the tabernacle of the congregation.
> And Aaron shall cast lots upon the two goats; one lot for the LORD, and the other lot for the scapegoat.
> And Aaron shall bring the goat upon which the LORD'S lot fell, and offer him for a sin offering.
> But the goat, on which the lot fell to be the scapegoat, shall be presented alive before the LORD, to make an atonement with him, and to let him go for a scapegoat into the wilderness.

On the Day of Atonement two goats were selected; one was offered on the altar, and the other was to be the scapegoat set free in the wilderness. The second goat called the scapegoat was presented alive before the Lord.

Aaron laid his hands on the goat and then it was taken out into the wilderness and abandoned. This domesticated animal would then in all likelihood perish in the wilderness.

> Leviticus 16:21 and 22:
> And Aaron shall lay both his hands upon the head of the live goat, and confess over him all the iniquities of the children of Israel, and all their transgressions in all their sins, **putting them upon the** head of the goat, and shall send *him* away by the hand of a fit man into the wilderness:
> And **the goat shall bear upon him all their iniquities** unto a land not inhabited: and he shall let go the goat in the wilderness.

Before releasing the scapegoat, Aaron carried out a procedure that is central to our study. He laid his hands on the head of the goat and confessed the sins of the people. Verse 22 then declares, "and the goat shall bear upon him all their iniquities." Aaron transferred the sins upon the goat, causing this sacrifice to bear all the iniquities.

Putting his hands on the goat identified the offerer with the offering. The sin of the nation of Israel was laid upon the scapegoat by the high priest, and then, in turn, all the innocence of the offering was transferred to the Israelites.

From God's point of view, there was a full sharing between the offerer and the animal sacrificed. The offering shared fully in sin and the consequences of sin — death. And, in turn, the one presenting the sacrifice shared fully in the innocence of the offering. This laying of the hands on the animal to be sacrificed was, in essence, a double transfer.

The Law: A Shadow of Christ

The scapegoat is quite an extraordinary illustration of the coming Christ. This Old Testament sacrifice was a visual lesson in how God would save His people from their sins. The sins of the guilty would be transferred to the innocent. Just as the sins of Israel were borne by the scapegoat, so the sins of humanity would be borne by the Messiah. The scapegoat was a clear silhouette of the "good things to come" of Hebrews 10:1. It was a good thing that sins could be transferred to an innocent sacrifice. It was certainly a very good thing that Christ would bear all of the sins of humanity to satisfy God's justice so that we could be saved.

In addition to the Day of Atonement, this gesture of laying the hand on the head of a sacrificial animal was also practiced with other sacrifices.

> Leviticus 1:4:
> And he shall put his hand upon the head of the burnt offering; and it shall be accepted **for** him to make atonement **for** him.

Placement of his hand on the head was an integral part of this offering that symbolized identification or a full sharing with that offering. Just as Leviticus 16:21 explained, placing the hand on the head of the sacrifice signified a transfer. The burnt offering bore the sins of the Old Covenant believer.

The English words, "for" occur twice in the verse with the meaning, "on behalf of." The Israelite put his hand on the head of the offering that it may be acceptable on the offerers' behalf and to make atonement on his behalf as a substitute. The sacrifice stood as the representative before God, and died in his place.

JESUS CHRIST OUR COMPLETE OFFERING

The Hebrew word, *nasa*, is critical to our study of this transference of sin from one party to another. *Nasa* means to bear, to take away, in the sense of lifting up and carrying.

Nasa: to bear

The Scapegoat bore sin by laying on of hands
Leviticus 16:22: "…the goat shall bear (*nasa*) upon him all their iniquities"

The Messiah bore our sin and sickness
Isaiah 53:4: "Surely he hath borne (*nasa*) our sicknesses…"
Isaiah 53:12:   "…he bare (*nasa*) the sin of many…"

As this chart shows, **nasa** is used referring to bearing sin in both Leviticus 16:22 and Isaiah 53:4, 12—all focal verses in our study. The wording in Leviticus 16 and in Isaiah 53 is similar. Remember Isaiah 53? "Surely he hath borne our sickness…carried our sorrows…he shall bear their iniquities…he bare the sin." Just as the scapegoat, our sins were transferred to the Messiah.

The Hebrew word, *nasa*, is used in Isaiah 53:4 and 12, where it speaks of the Messiah bearing the sins and sickness of God's people. This is HOW God accomplished our redemption and salvation: an innocent one carried the sins of the guilty.

The transference of sin from the guilty to the innocent is fundamental in both the Old and the New Testaments. While the animal sacrifices of the Old Covenant were only

The Law: A Shadow of Christ

shadows of the ultimate sacrifice who was to come, these illustrations are remarkably precise in depicting HOW God would facilitate the redemption of humanity. The principles of sacrifice are set forth by God's revelation in the five books of Moses. The Levitical sacrifices, while only a foreshadowing, are accurate, depicting the means, the method, and the mode by which God would redeem mankind: the transfer of sin from the guilty to the innocent.

All of the sacrifices of the Old Testament illustrated Christ because every time an animal was presented as an offering to God, it died in place of the person offering the sacrifice. That animal was presented to God as a substitute for the offerer, and then died on his behalf. The concept of substitution is intrinsically built in to every animal sacrifice. While there are myriads of details in the Old Covenant sacrifices, there is one big simple message: substitution. The big picture—the one straightforward lesson—of every sacrifice, was that the lifeblood of that animal was shed on behalf of the life of the Israelite presenting the offering.

The sacrifices of the Old Testament form a critical part of the unfolding revelation of God's plan of redemption. The book of Leviticus did not come by "the will of man" but was the words of God written down by Moses.[3] These Levitical practices were instructions from God on how to offer sacrifices to approach God and find some measure of forgiveness. But they were much more—these sacrifices taught important concepts about God's eternal plan to redeem humanity.

When the Son of God arrived to fulfill this plan, God's people had a treasure trove of images and ideas ready at hand. They knew exactly how an innocent animal would die

---

[3] II Peter 1:21: "For the prophecy came not in old time by the will of man: but holy men of God spake as they were moved by the Holy Ghost."

JESUS CHRIST OUR COMPLETE OFFERING

in their place as a substitute, by the transference of their sins onto it. And, as we shall later see in more detail, the Mosaic sacrificial system served as a pattern and type of the complete sacrifice who was to come—Christ. These Old Covenant sacrifices pointed to and found their true meaning in THE Lamb of God, Jesus of Nazareth.

Chapter 5

Patterns of the True Things to Come

We examined how Hebrews 10:1 speaks of the Law being "a shadow of the good things to come." Hebrews 8 and 9 provide valuable background information and specifics of how the Old Covenant was a shadow of Christ. It would be worth our time and effort to delve into these chapters to explore how the Levitical system was the pattern of the true things to come.

> Hebrews 8:1 and 2:
> Now of the things which we have spoken this is the sum: We have such an high priest, who is set on the right hand of the throne of the Majesty in the heavens; A minister of the sanctuary, and of the true tabernacle, which the Lord pitched, and not man.

The opening verses of chapter 8 bring us to a main point of Hebrews: Jesus Christ as the high priest is seated at God's right hand. He serves in the true tabernacle in the heavens, before the face of God, where he intercedes for us. This is what Jesus Christ is doing right **now**. He not only died for us, now he lives for us!

JESUS CHRIST OUR COMPLETE OFFERING

> Verse 3:
> For every high priest is ordained to offer gifts and sacrifices: wherefore it is of necessity that this man have somewhat also to offer.

The Old Testament priests were commanded to offer a multitude of sacrifices under the Law. What did Christ offer up in sacrifice as the high priest of the heavenly sanctuary? Only a few verses earlier in Hebrews 7:27 it tells us: "Who [Christ] needeth not daily, as those high priests, to offer up sacrifice, first for his own sins, and then for the people's: for this he [Christ] did once when he offered up himself." Our savior did not offer the blood of bulls and goats in an earthly sanctuary, but he presented his own blood as a once-and-for-all sacrifice.

> Hebrews 8:4 and 5:
> For if he were on earth, he should not be a priest, seeing that there are priests that offer gifts according to the Law:
> Who serve unto the **example** [illustration[1]] and **shadow** of heavenly things, as Moses was admonished of God when he was about to make the tabernacle: for, See, saith he, that thou make all things according to the **pattern** [type, model[2]] shewed to thee in the mount.

Christ's singular offering and heavenly service in the heavenly tabernacle was foreshadowed and illustrated by

---

[1] "Example" is translated from the Greek word, *hupodeigma*, meaning illustration, sample, example or copy. Ceslas Spicq, *Theological Lexicon of the New Testament*, translated and edited by James Ernest (1978, Peabody, Mass: Hendrickson, 1994) Volume III, 404.

[2] "Pattern" is translated from the Greek word, *tupos*, transliterated over into our English word, "type," and it means "copy, model, pattern or example."

this Levitical system. These priests presented offerings were not only a "shadow" as Hebrews 10:1 states, but also served as illustrations of Christ's work to come in the true tabernacle.

> **Priests offered gifts and sacrifices according to the Law:**
> **Illustration, Model and Shadow**
> of heavenly things

As Hebrews 8:5 says, the tabernacle was built by Moses according to the design God revealed to him on Mount Sinai. In Hebrews 9:23 it calls the earthly tabernacle that Moses built was designed as "the patterns of things in the heavens." This would indicate that this earthly sanctuary was a copy of the tabernacle in heaven.[3] When Christ ascended into this true heavenly tabernacle, he fulfilled the position of high priest and sacrifice.

> **The earthly, Mosaic Tabernacle was modeled after the Heavenly Tabernacle**

We have seen how Hebrews explains that the Old Testament tabernacle, high priest and sacrifices were examples, shadows, patterns, and models of the true things to come. Our focus in the following sections will be on how the sacrifices of the Law illustrate Christ and his work for us.

---

[3] Also see: Walter J. Cummins, *Riches of God's Grace in the New Covenant* (Franklin, Ohio: Scripture Consulting, 2010). 44.

JESUS CHRIST OUR COMPLETE OFFERING

The Day of Atonement: A Pattern of True Things to Come

Hebrews chapter 9 opens with a description of the Mosaic tabernacle:

> Hebrews 9:1-6:
> Then verily the first covenant had also ordinances of divine service, and a worldly sanctuary.
> For there was a tabernacle made; the first [section], wherein was the candlestick, and the table, and the shewbread; which is called the sanctuary.
> And after the second veil, the tabernacle which is called the Holiest of all;
> Which had the golden censer, and the ark of the covenant overlaid round about with gold, wherein was the golden pot that had manna, and Aaron's rod that budded, and the tables of the covenant;
> And over it the cherubims of glory shadowing the mercyseat; of which we cannot now speak particularly.
> Now when these things were thus ordained, the priests went always into the first [section of the] tabernacle, accomplishing the service of God.

The tabernacle Moses built according to God's exact instructions had two sections.

> Verse 7:
> But into the second [section, the holy of holies] went the high priest alone once every year, not without blood, which he offered for himself, and for the errors of the people:

Verse 7 refers to the Day of Atonement when the high priest entered the holy of holies once every year. Although the

Patterns of the True Things to Come

book of Hebrews never mentions the Day of Atonement by name, it references what occurred on this holy day many times.[4]

Previously we noted from Leviticus 16 that on the Day of Atonement the high priest selected two goats. After casting lots, one goat was designated to be sacrificed on the altar as a sin offering and the other became the scapegoat. The key to this section of Hebrews is understanding what happened to the goat that was sacrificed on the altar.

> Leviticus 16:15:
> Then shall he kill the goat of the sin offering, that is for the people, and bring his blood within the vail [in the holy of holies], and do with that blood as he did with the blood of the bullock, and sprinkle it upon the mercy seat, and before the mercy seat:

After sacrificing this other goat for a sin offering, the high priest entered into the inner chamber of the tabernacle and sprinkled the blood to purify the tabernacle.[5]

> Hebrews 9:8:
> The Holy Ghost this signifying, that the way into the holiest of all was not yet made manifest, while as the first tabernacle was yet standing:

The high priest was the only one permitted into the holy of holies and the Day of Atonement was the only time when the high priest was allowed to enter into the holy of holies. In this chamber is where the presence of God abode. All

---

[4] Hebrews 5:3; 9:7, 25; 10:1-3; 13:11.
[5] As we shall see in Chapter 15, Leviticus 16:16-20 goes on to explain that this sprinkling of the blood of the sin offering makes atonement for the tabernacle because of the uncleanness of the children of Israel, cleansing and hallowing the holy place, reconciling the tabernacle.

approach was barred to that inner sanctuary of the tabernacle, except by this one man, on this one day of the year. By this restricted access to the holy of holies, God signified that The Way was not yet open. Jesus Christ's ascension into the most holy sanctum of heaven paved the way for access into God's presence.[6]

> Verse 9:
> Which was a **figure** [parable] for the time then present, in which were offered both gifts and sacrifices, that could not make him that did the service perfect, as pertaining to the conscience;

The word "figure" is a translation of the Greek word, *parabolē*, meaning an illustration, comparison, or parable. The offerings of the priests in the tabernacle were an illustration or parable of Christ's sacrifice and service in the heavenly tabernacle. According to E. W. Bullinger in *Figures of Speech Used in the Bible*, a parable is an extended simile containing likenesses, comparing resemblances to teach a spiritual truth.[7] As the sacrifices of the Old Testament are compared to Christ's sacrifice, likenesses and resemblances can be seen in them.

Similarly, we saw in Hebrews 8:5, the offerings presented by the priests were a pattern of heavenly things. The Old Testament tabernacle, priesthood, and sacrifices depicted Christ and his service in the true tabernacle of heaven.

---

[6] For more information see: David Bergey, *Jesus Christ Our Approach Offering*, Chapter 5.
[7] E.W. Bullinger, *Figures of Speech Used in the Bible*, 751.

Patterns of the True Things to Come

Verses 10-12:
Which stood only in meats and drinks, and divers washings, and carnal ordinances, imposed on them until the time of reformation.
But Christ being come an high priest of good things to come, by a greater and more perfect[8] tabernacle, not made with hands, that is to say, not of this building [creation];
Neither by the blood of goats and calves, but by his own blood he entered in once into the holy place, having obtained eternal redemption for us.

The high priest's entry into the Mosaic tabernacle on the Day of Atonement with the blood of the sin offering corresponded directly to Christ's ascension into the heavenly sanctuary with his own blood. When our savior entered into the greater and more perfect tabernacle in heaven, the "good things to come" had arrived! Our eternal redemption had been accomplished.

Verses 21-25:
Moreover he [Moses] sprinkled with blood both the tabernacle, and all the vessels of the ministry.
And almost all things are by the law purged with blood; and without shedding of blood is no remission. It was therefore necessary that **patterns**[9] of things in the heavens should be purified with these; but the heavenly things themselves with better sacrifices than these.
For Christ is not entered into the holy places made with hands, which are the **figures**[10] [copies] of the

---

[8] *Teleios*, see Appendix Two.
[9] "Patterns:" Greek: *hupodeigma* meaning illustration, sample, example or copy.
[10] "Figures:" Greek: *antitupos*, transliterated into English word, antitype, meaning a copy or representation of an earlier type. The earthly tabernacle was an antitype or copy of the original and true heavenly one.

JESUS CHRIST OUR COMPLETE OFFERING

true; but into heaven itself, now to appear in the presence of God for us:
Nor yet that he should offer himself often, as the high priest entereth into the holy place every year with blood of others.

In verses 23 and 24, the earthly tabernacle that Moses built is called "the patterns of things in the heavens," and "figures of the true." Every year on the Day of Atonement, the high priest entered the holy place, which copies the true tabernacle in heaven, with blood from the sin offerings. In contrast, Christ entered into heaven itself by his own blood once. He accomplished purification for all mankind, as well as for the true holy place in heaven.

> Hebrews 9:26-10:1:
> For then must he often have suffered since the foundation of the world: but now once in the end of the world hath he appeared to put away sin by the sacrifice of himself.
> And as it is appointed unto men once to die, but after this the judgment:
> So Christ was once offered to bear the sins of many; and unto them that look for him shall he appear the second time without sin unto salvation.
> For the law having a **shadow** of good things to come...

When it declares, "he shall appear the second time," plainly the "good things to come" have not yet all arrived! While Christ's sacrificial work is finished and we have received so many good things, there is yet more in store for us: "...in the ages to come he might shew the exceeding riches of his grace in his kindness toward us through Christ Jesus." (Ephesians 2:7).

Patterns of the True Things to Come

On the great Day of Atonement, the tabernacle, high priest, and offerings formed a pattern to illustrate and to teach the Messiah's work.

> **Day of Atonement**
>
> **High Priest:** Enters into earthly tabernacle
>
> **Tabernacle:** Cleansed by blood
>
> **Sacrifice:** Sin Offerings

> **Christ at the Ascension**
>
> **High Priest:** Enters into heavenly tabernacle
>
> **Tabernacle:** Cleansed by Christ's blood
>
> **Sacrifice:** Christ, the final offering for sin

On the Day of Atonement there was the greatest interaction between the three prime elements of the Mosaic revelation that foreshadowed Christ: priest, sacrifice, and tabernacle. These intersected in remarkable synergy. As we have seen, Hebrews explains how this interaction parallels Christ.

On the Day of Atonement, the sacrificial law reaches its supreme expression. Here, the high priest attains his highest mission. Here, the tabernacle receives its fullest use. Here, we behold a most majestic foreshadowing in the Old Testament revelation of Christ and his accomplishments.

JESUS CHRIST OUR COMPLETE OFFERING

Our focus in the following chapters will be on Leviticus and on how the sacrifices of the Law illustrate Christ and his work for us.

The Passover Sacrifice:
A Pattern of the True Things to Come

When I Corinthians 5:7 states, "...For even Christ our Passover is sacrificed for us," it suggests that the Passover and accompanying sacrifice was a pattern of Christ. As we will consider, aspects of the sacrifice of the Passover correspond directly to Christ. Specific characteristics and functions of this sacrifice serve as a model of Christ. This Old Testament sacrifice of the Passover is a type or illustration of Christ.

A distinctively unique aspect of the Passover sacrifice compared with other offerings and sacrifices is the absolute focus on the time **when** it was to be sacrificed. Exodus 12 says of the Passover:

> Exodus 12:2, 3 and 6
> ...it shall be the first month of the year to you.
> Speak ye unto all the congregation of Israel, saying, In the tenth day of this month they shall take to them every man a lamb, according to the house of their fathers, a lamb for an house...
> And ye shall keep it up until the fourteenth day of the same month: and the whole assembly of the congregation of Israel shall kill it in the evening [in Hebrew: between the two evenings].[11]

The Passover offering was to be sacrificed in the late afternoon on the 14th day of the first month.

---

[11] Flavius Josephus. *The Complete Works of Josephus*, trans. William Whiston (Grand Rapids, MI: Kregel, 1960). 588.

Patterns of the True Things to Come

One characteristic of the Passover that distinguishes it from all other sacrifices is the stipulation of the exact month, the exact date, and the exact time of day when the Passover sacrifice was to be slain. This is in sharp contrast to the five offerings of Leviticus 1-7: the burnt offering, meal offering, peace offering, sin offering, and trespass offering did not exclusively belong to only one day of the year.

A careful study of the Gospels reveals that Christ laid down his life as a perfect sacrifice on the exact date as well as the specific time of day that the Passover sacrifice was offered.[12] In this way, the distinguishing characteristic of the Passover sacrifice speaks prophetically about the coming Christ in a way no other sacrifice does. With this distinctive characteristic of timing, an exact correspondence to Christ's offering comes into focus. Jesus Christ, our Passover, laid down his life precisely when the Passover sacrifice was slain. With the simultaneous timing of both, we see a most vivid portrayal and fulfillment of Christ's sacrifice.

However, this remarkable correlation between the timing of Christ's crucifixion in the Gospels and the Passover sacrifice in Exodus 12 is not superficially obvious and does not leap out at the reader. To realize how the timing of the crucifixion corresponded with the Passover sacrifice of Exodus 12, one would need to study the Gospel records carefully.

Once this parallel is understood, it becomes strikingly apparent **how** the killing of the Passover sacrifice illustrated Christ's sacrifice. This is not speculative typology—the Gospels say Christ *was* slain on the exact month and on

---

[12] Many Bible scholars have documented this: The Companion Bible (London: Bagster, 1972) appendix 156. Victor Paul Wierwille, *Jesus Christ, Our Passover* (New Knoxville, OH: American Christian Press, 1980), 1-30.

precisely the day and at the exact time of day that the Passover was sacrificed in Exodus 12. This fits together the Scriptures of the Old and New Testaments.

II Timothy 2:15 exhorts us to be workman of the Word of Truth. As we spend time working the Scriptures, without any guesswork or speculation, we will see magnificent parallels between Christ and these sacrifices.

Old Testament Sacrifices: Tutorials of Christ

In this section, we have focused on the big picture of Christ's work for us: substitution. It is helpful to look at the scope of substitution before looking at the other examples of the Old Testament sacrifices.

For most of us initially, these sacrifices can blur into an indistinct and vast system of the Mosaic sacrificial rituals. But the burnt offering, meal offering, peace offering, sin offering, trespass offering, and Passover offering all had precise functions with exact meanings. While these offerings may be indistinct to us, none of these offerings were ambiguous or unclear in their Old Testament usage or function.

In the Old Testament many terms are used to refer to the various sacrifices. The words describing sacrifices are not vague or general but are specific and precise in their meaning and usage. As we read Leviticus, we could make the mistake of seeing the terms used for offerings or sacrifices as generic words used for offerings. However, the Hebrew text of the Old Testament uses the various Hebrew words for offerings and sacrifices with distinct clarity and accuracy.

Patterns of the True Things to Come

Passover Offering:	*pesach*
Trespass Offering:	*asham*
Sin Offering:	*chattath*
Peace Offering:	*shelem*
Meal Offering:[13]	*minchah*
Burnt Offering:	*olah*
Wave Offering	*tenuphah*

Each offering had its own particular name, unique rituals and distinctive functions. However, the offerings had many similarities as well as differences.

We have seen that an innocent animal's shed blood for a guilty human was a very common similarity, which made substitution an integral part of the sacrifices. God drove this point home by repetition. However, simple repetition was not the only way God revealed Christ in the offerings. As we progress through our study, we shall see each of the offerings had one or more major points of exceptional uniqueness. Each sacrifice had at least one major distinctive characteristic that set it apart from the other sacrifices.

As with the Passover sacrifice of Exodus 12, the sacrificing of an animal as a substitute was common to many other sacrifices that were instituted under the Law. Also, the Passover offering was to be eaten by the offerer, just as the peace offering was. Both have in common the eating of the sacrifice. However, one characteristic of the Passover

---

[13] Rendered "meat offering" in the King James Version. In a bizarre twist of archaic English word usage, the only offering in Leviticus 1-7 with **no meat** is the "meat offering." Since, in our current usage, "meat" means the flesh of an animal, this offering will be rendered "meal offering." Many versions call this sacrifice the "grain offering," but since the Law stipulated "flour" (Leviticus 2:2, 4) "meal offering" is more fitting.

sacrifice that distinguishes it from all others was timing: the exact month, the exact day of the month, and the time of day were stipulated. In contrast to the Passover offering, the burnt offering, meal offering, peace offering, sin offering, and trespass offering were not limited to being offered only on one day of the year.

Galatians 3:23-25 explains that the Law was a "tutor" to lead us to Christ.[14] In the words of the Authorized King James Version, the Law was a "schoolmaster to bring us unto Christ." Today we have computer programs that provide step-by-step, interactive learning programs called tutorials. These tutorials often teach by having the learner rehearse each move until the task is completed. One may repeat the tutorial program as often as needed. The sacrifices instituted by Moses by revelation from God were a vast and detailed system of interactive learning designed to demonstrate how God would redeem humankind. Modern computer programmers were not the first to use interactive, step-by-step learning programs.

The sacrificial experience for the Old Covenant believer could, and often did, involve all of the five senses. The Israelite offering an animal heard with his ears and saw with his eyes the priest killing the animal. With the gesture of placing his hand on the animal's head, he felt. He smelled the pleasant aroma as the animal burned on the altar.[15]

---

[14] In the *Working Translation*, "tutor" is translated from the Greek word, *paidagōgos*, from which we get the English word "pedagogue," meaning teacher or "pedagogy," meaning the profession of teaching.

[15] Animals given in sacrifice were skinned before being placed on the altar. The smell of the sacrifice was not an acrid of burning of the hair but rather the smell of grilling meat. Leviticus 7:8.

Patterns of the True Things to Come

With a meal offering, the offerer would get a whiff of the fragrance of the incense as it was mixed with the meal and burned on the altar.[16]

With the Passover and peace offering, the sense of taste would be involved, as a portion was allowed to be eaten by the offerer. In this way, the sacrifices of Leviticus could involve all five senses. It is well-documented that a learning experience is improved when more of the five senses are used.

God initiated a teaching system that involved all five senses, combined with interactive learning. Remarkably, the sacrifices used all five senses to teach substitution and identification. The comprehensive scope of these sacrifices as teaching tools is outstanding! For those of us involved with education at any level, employing all five senses with interactive learning is a revolutionary concept. Moreover, these sacrifices taught the greatest subject of all time—the redemption of humanity by sacrifice of the Lamb of God.

Our study of sacrifices is to see what Christ has accomplished and exactly how he did it. As we examine the unique specifics of each sacrifice, we can see how it is a pattern of the good things to come.

We will never approach the Mosaic tabernacle and present a sacrifice to the sons of Aaron. We have something far superior: a high priest that resides in the true tabernacle in the heavenlies. The Messiah has offered himself for our sins once and for all time, having opened the way for us to approach God with boldness. We can study these Old Covenant sacrifices and see how they illustrated and foreshadowed the good things to come. As the distinctive

---

[16] Leviticus 2:1-9.

JESUS CHRIST OUR COMPLETE OFFERING

functions and characteristics of the individual sacrifices come into view, we may strengthen our grasp of the completeness of the salvation we have in Christ.

Part Two

The Levitical Offerings

Chapter 6

The Categories of the Offerings

The first verse of Leviticus is where our study of Levitical offerings must begin.

> Leviticus 1:1 and 2:
> And the LORD called unto Moses, and spake unto him out of the tabernacle of the congregation, saying, Speak unto the children of Israel, and say unto them, If any man of you bring an offering unto the Lord…

The opening phrase tells us these offerings were God's revelation to Moses. As II Peter 1:21 says of the Scriptures, they, "…came not in old time by the will of man; but holy men of God spake as they were moved by the Holy Ghost."

God spoke to Moses. God summoned Moses out of the tabernacle and gave him detailed revelation regarding each sacrifice. Nothing was left to man's imagination. The book of Leviticus did not come by the will of man.

Leviticus chapter seven closes with the following summary verses:

The Categories of the Offerings

> Leviticus 7:37-38:
> This is the law of the burnt offering, of the meat offering, and of the sin offering, and of the trespass offering, and of the consecrations,[1] and of the sacrifice of the peace offerings;
> Which the LORD commanded Moses in mount Sinai, in the day that he commanded the children of Israel to offer their oblations [offerings[2]] unto the LORD, in the wilderness of Sinai.

The last verse of this section concludes with the same truth set forth in Leviticus 1:1: "…the Lord commanded Moses…" This book came about not by the will of any man, but by the express commandment of God. This foundational truth bookends this unit of Scripture from Leviticus 1:1 through 7:38.

Moses did not draw up the outline of offerings and present it to the people for their approval. Neither was a committee of tribal elders appointed to come up with plans for sacrifices. The book of Leviticus was not a compilation of the views of the priests over a period of time or God's suggestions augmented by the ingenuity of the Levites.

Leviticus states explicitly, about fifty times, that the Lord spoke or said something to Moses. God gave exact revelation on each offering to Moses. The Lord revealed the name of each offering, the distinctive rituals, functions, and purposes of each offering.

---

[1] The "consecrations" or ordination/instillation offerings for the priests are covered in a later chapter.
[2] "Oblations" or "offerings" can be inclusive of both meal offerings and sacrificed animals. The word "sacrifice" only refers a slaughtered animal. In Leviticus the words "oblation" or "offering," are usually translated from the Hebrew word *qorban*. For more on the *qorban*, see David Bergey, *Jesus Christ Our Approach Offering*, 24.

JESUS CHRIST OUR COMPLETE OFFERING

While much of the book of Leviticus deals with various offerings, a "sacrifice" would involve the death of an animal.[3] The term "offering" is more inclusive, referring to sacrifices as well as meal or drink offerings.

Verse 37 lists five different offerings in Leviticus 1-7 that God commanded Moses to institute:

1. Burnt offering
2. Meal offering[4]
3. Peace offering
4. Sin offering
5. Trespass offering

In addition to these five primary offerings, in chapter 14 we will also consider another distinctive offering that is mentioned in this section of Leviticus: the wave offering.

Sin or Sin Offering?

The following verse seems to contradict the statement that each offering is distinctive in and of itself.

> Leviticus 5:6:
> And he shall bring his trespass offering [*asham*] unto the LORD for his sin which he hath sinned, a female from the flock, a lamb or a kid of the goats, for a sin offering [*chattath*]; and the priest shall make an atonement for him concerning his sin.

---

[3] The Hebrew word, *zebach*, meaning a slaughter or a slaughtered animal is usually translated as "sacrifice." (Young's, 829). Of course, the word "sacrifice," has a much broader meaning in current usage.

[4] Rendered "meat offering" in the King James Version. In a odd twist of archaic English word usage, the only offering in Leviticus 1-7 with **no meat** is called the "meat offering." Since, in our current usage, "meat" means the flesh of an animal, this offering will be called "meal offering."

The Categories of the Offerings

As this verse reads in the Authorized King James Version, the trespass offering and the sin offering seem to be interchangeable. He "shall bring his trespass offering" for his sin, a female from the flock, "for a sin offering." This verse, as translated, gives the impression that the sin offering and trespass offering are perhaps one and the same.

The term "trespass offering" is translated from one Hebrew word, *asham*. Also, "sin offering" is translated from one Hebrew word, *chattath*.

In a study of the Levitical offerings, it is essential to recognize that both "trespass" and "trespass offering" are translated from the same Hebrew word: *asham*. Likewise, "sin" and "sin offering" are translated from one Hebrew word: *chattath*. Whether the word "offering" should be supplied depends on the context. The usage in the context is all-important in determining how the word should be translated.

Leviticus 5:6 is in the section on instructions about the sin offering. Four verses later in verse 14, the section on the trespass offering starts. So the word "offering" should not be supplied after "trespass" in Leviticus 5:6 because of the context. A trespass offering mentioned in verse 6 is out of place and confusing.

New Revised Standard Version gives a more accurate translation.

> Leviticus 5:6:
> And you shall bring to the LORD, as your penalty for the sin that you have committed, a female from the flock, a sheep or a goat, as a sin offering.

JESUS CHRIST OUR COMPLETE OFFERING

The Hebrew word, *asham*, should be translated as "penalty" as does the *New International Version, New English Bible* and *Tanakh*.[5] There is no trespass offering spoken of here, but rather a trespass and therefore a penalty for a trespass. The trespass offering and the sin offering have some things in common, yet were two distinct and separate Levitical offerings.

This may seem a fine point, but as our study progresses, we will on occasion notice that the Authorized King James Version may leave out the word "offering" when it should be supplied, while in Leviticus 5:6 it inserts the word "offering" when it should be left out.[6]

That being said, generally the translators got it accurately; as in Isaiah 53:10 where it says, "…thou shalt make his soul an offering for sin." In the Hebrew text, there is not a word for "offering." In the Hebrew it simply reads that he was made an *asham*, a trespass. Yet translators unanimously supply the word "offering" or "sacrifice," understanding from the context that Christ was not made an actual trespass, but rather made a trespass offering.

> *Asham* **may be translated as:**
> -trespass
> -trespass offering

---

[5] Milgrom translates verse 6 most clearly: "And he shall bring as his reparation [*asham*] to the Lord, for the wrong that he has committed, a female from the flock, sheep or goat, as a purification offering." Jacob Milgrom, *The Anchor Bible Leviticus 1-16* (Doubleday, New York, 1991) 293.

[6] Appendix Four, "The First Sin Offering in the Bible" gives an example in Genesis 4:7 where the Authorized King James Version leaves out the word "offering" when it should be supplied.

The Categories of the Offerings

As we will consider later, Isaiah 53:10 refers to a trespass offering not a sin offering. In the next chapters, we will launch into a detailed study of the trespass offering and the sin offering and contrast the various attributes of each.

Here is another example of how a word may be translated in two different ways. In the following verse, the Hebrew word, *chattath,* is used twice with two different meanings:

> Leviticus 4:3:
> ...let him bring for his **sin** [*chattath*] which he hath sinned, a young bullock without blemish unto the LORD for a **sin offering** [*chattath*].

It is obvious from its context in the verse that the first *chattath* refers to an actual sin and the second to an offering for sin. While there is no word in the Hebrew text for "offering" in this verse, all the translations and versions supply the word "offering." E.W. Bullinger in his book, *Figures of Speech Used in the Bible*, classifies the second use of *chattath* in Leviticus 4:3 as the figure, metonymy, where one noun is exchanged for another associated noun.[7]

> ***Chattath*** **may be translated as:**
> -sin
> -sin offering

In the New Testament there are other examples where the word "offering" should be supplied after the word "sin."

> Hebrews 10:6: In burnt offerings and ***sacrifices* for sin** thou hast had no pleasure.

---

[7] E.W. Bullinger, *Figures of Speech Used in the Bible*, 584. Also see: Julia B. Hans, *Go Figure! An Introduction to Figures of Speech in the Bible* (Cambridge, Massachusetts: Merrimack, 2016) 152.

JESUS CHRIST OUR COMPLETE OFFERING

> Hebrews 10:8: Above when he said, Sacrifice and offering and burnt offerings and *offering* **for sin** thou wouldest not...

The italicized words *"sacrifices"* and *"offering"* indicate they were added by the translators, while not in the Greek text. In these verses, these words are properly supplied in the Authorized King James Version because the context clearly warrants it.

> Hebrews 13:11:
> For the bodies of those beasts, whose blood is brought into the sanctuary by the high priest **for sin** [offering], are burned without the camp.

Here is an example where the word "offering" should have been supplied but was not. As we shall see in chapter 8 of this book, a key part of the sin offering is what is done with the blood. Therefore in this verse, the word "offering" should be supplied after sin: "...whose blood the high priest brings into the sanctuary as a sin offering..."[8]

As we consider the offerings in the Scriptures, it is necessary for us to understand that the word "offering" may need to be supplied as warranted by the context.

---

[8] Quoted from *New American Bible*. The Amplified, NASB, NIV and RSV **all** supply the word "offering" or "sacrifice" in Hebrews 13:11. The words "for sin" in and Hebrews10:6, 8 and 13:11 and Romans 8:3 are translated from the Greek words, *peri hamartias*. In the *Septuagint*, the Greek Old Testament, *peri hamartias* often refers to the sin offering. (Leviticus 4:3, 14, 32; 5:8, 11).

The Categories of the Offerings

Public and Private Offerings

These opening verses of Leviticus tell us of a notable attribute of these sacrifices.

> Leviticus 1:2 and 3:
> Speak unto the children of Israel, and say unto them, If any man of you bring an offering unto the LORD, ye shall bring your offering of the cattle, even of the herd, and of the flock.
> If his offering be a burnt sacrifice of the herd, let him offer a male without blemish: he shall offer it of his own voluntary will at the door of the tabernacle of the congregation before the LORD.

Verse 3 states of this sacrifice, "...he shall offer it of his own voluntary will..." This offering was to be carried out by the individual Old Covenant believer by his own initiative. Verse two says "**If** any man of you bring an offering unto the LORD..." and verse 3 says "**If** his offering be a burnt sacrifice..." Here the individual Israelites were not commanded to present a sacrifice, but rather when they wanted to offer sacrifices, these chapters stipulated how they were to be done.

Leviticus 2:1 begins: "And **when any will** offer a meat [meal] offering." When any individual wanted to offer a meal offering, chapter two commanded how it was to be done.

The section on the sin offering states, "...**if** a soul shall sin..."(4:2). Similarly, the instructions on the trespass offering open with: "**If** a soul commit a trespass..." (5:15). If and when these two offerings for sin were needed, these chapters gave instructions on how they were to be done. These offerings could be called private offerings or individual offerings presented voluntarily by an Israelite when considered necessary.

In contrast, the offerings carried out by the priests on the feasts, new moons and Sabbath days could be called "public offerings" or "national offerings" presented for the entire nation. An example of a public offering carried out for the whole nation was on the Day of Atonement. We saw in Leviticus 16 that on this most holy day two goats were to be selected for sin offerings. One goat was designated as the scapegoat and the other was to be offered on the altar.

These sin offerings on the Day of Atonement were **not** performed at a priest's own initiative; they were **not** voluntary. God decreed precisely when and how these particular offerings were to be presented.

On the other hand, Leviticus 4 provides instructions on the sin offerings. However, there is no mention of what day of the year they were to be offered. In chapter 8 of this study, we will take the time to read through Leviticus 4 to see the characteristics and functions of a sin offering. The sin offerings of Leviticus 4 were to be offered **if** and **when** they were needed, not on a certain day of the year.[9]

Another example of the individual offering is the burnt offering in Leviticus chapter one. With this burnt offering, the individual worshipper could have brought a goat (verse 10) or even a bird (verse 14) as a burnt offering. Regardless, it was done "of his own voluntary will" (Verse 3).

In contrast, the priests were commanded to carry out twice daily burnt offerings on behalf of the entire nation called the

---

[9] "**If** the priest that is anointed do sin…" (Leviticus 4:3); "And **if** the whole congregation of Israel sin…" verse 13; "**When** a ruler hath sinned…" verse 22; "…**if** any one of the common people sin…" verse 27.

The Categories of the Offerings

"continual burnt offering."[10] This public offering was always to be a lamb and meal offering, never a bird or a goat. In Numbers 28 and 29 there are numerous commands to the priests not to neglect this particular offering. These daily priestly offerings were not optional or voluntary.

National or Public Offerings	Individual or Private Offerings
Carried out by the priests by God's command for the entire nation (Leviticus 16; Numbers 28 and 29)	Voluntary; Offered when and if needed or wanted by the individual (Leviticus 1-6:7)

Sweet Savor and Sin Offerings

While the offerings of the Law could be categorized as either national or private, within the five offerings listed in Leviticus 1-7, there were two other essential categories.

These five offerings, while distinct in themselves, performed two basic functions and can be divided into two general groupings. The burnt offering, the meal offering, and the peace offering were referred to as a "sweet savour unto the Lord" (Leviticus 1:9; 2:2; 3:5). In the Hebrew language, the word for "savour" means fragrance as from incense. These three offerings were burned as incense unto God. As we shall examine in chapter 9, these offerings were, in essence,

---

[10] The ""continual burnt offering." is covered in Chapter 13 in the section, "Jesus Christ, our Continual Burnt Offering."

JESUS CHRIST OUR COMPLETE OFFERING

incense offerings representing prayer and intercession unto God.

In contrast, the sin and trespass offerings were to obtain forgiveness for and purification from sins. With the burnt, meal, and peace offerings, the Old Covenant believer approached God to fellowship with Him. With the sin and trespass offerings, the Old Covenant believer came to God as sinful and impure. The purpose of the sin and trespass offerings was to reestablish fellowship with God, obtaining purification, cleansing and forgiveness.

Two Categories of the Individual Offerings

Offerings	Category	Purpose
Burnt, Meal, Peace	**Sweet Savor** (Incense)	To approach God in fellowship To intercede and pray to God
Sin, Trespass	**Sin**	To obtain forgiveness and purification To re-establish fellowship with God

God had such love and concern for His people that He designed a detailed system of sacrifices so His covenant people could approach Him and be cleansed and forgiven. Here in Leviticus, God lovingly instituted these sacrifices so He could connect with His people and bring them into fellowship with Him. How wonderful God was to encourage His chosen nation to draw near to Him.

These offerings stood as an open invitation for the Old Testament worshipper to approach God. While these sacrifices were of some assistance in enabling people to

The Categories of the Offerings

approach God and obtain some cleansing and covering of sin, they were also a model of him who was to come: the Lord Jesus Christ.

In these sacrifices, given by revelation, God portrayed and foreshadowed the coming sacrifice of Christ. That is what made these sacrifices in the Old Testament such an integral and vital part of the Word of God. God pointed toward the manner in which true salvation would come: a sinless victim who would die in their stead, the penalty for sin paid. These multiple animal sacrifices repeatedly portrayed the one time act of the promised Christ who would, in due time, sacrifice himself for mankind.

Jesus Christ, as the consummate offering for all time, completely fulfilled both aspects of these offerings.

> Ephesians 5:2
> And walk in love, as Christ also hath loved us, and hath given himself for us an offering and a sacrifice to God for a sweetsmelling savour.

Jesus Christ's sacrifice was a sweet savour offering to God. The sweet savor offerings—the burnt offering, the meal offering, and the peace offering—all anticipated him who was to come.

> Hebrews 9:28:
> So Christ was once offered to bear the sins of many...

He also bore sins as a sin offering. The two general categories of these individual Levitical offerings portray two primary accomplishments of our redemption by Christ. The New Testament revelation declares him to be both sweet savour offering **and** sin offering.

JESUS CHRIST OUR COMPLETE OFFERING

What these Levitical offerings accomplished for the Old Covenant believer, in part and in shadow, the offering of Christ accomplished for the New Covenant believer in fullness and perfection. We have full approach and access to God **and** total cleansing from sin. These are two of the paramount realities of the New Covenant.

In this study, we will look at the offerings in reverse order of their listing in Leviticus 1-7. We'll start with the trespass offering and the sin offering. We will consider these five offerings as the sinner approached God. We will first look at the offerings for sin and then at the sweet savor offerings.

Another reason to start out with the trespass offering is because of the key statement in Isaiah 53:10 where it pointedly speaks of the coming savior as the trespass offering: "...he shalt make his soul an offering for sin [*asham*]." This unambiguous declaration serves as our point of departure into our study of the Levitical offerings.

Chapter 7

The Trespass Offering or Restitution Offering

As we have noted in a previous chapter, Isaiah 53 foretells many things of Jesus Christ's sacrifice and what it would accomplish. One salient statement serves as a springboard for our study of the offerings of the Old Covenant:

> Isaiah 53:10:
> Yet it pleased the LORD to bruise him; he hath put him to grief: when thou shalt make his soul an **offering for sin [*asham*]**, he shall see his seed, he shall prolong his days, and the pleasure of the LORD shall prosper in his hand.

The words "offering for sin" are translated from one word in Hebrew Old Testament: *asham*. This Hebrew word, *asham*, is usually translated as "trespass offering" in the Authorized King James Version. The trespass offering is one of the five primary offerings of the Old Covenant as explained in detail in Leviticus 1-7.

There are two distinct offerings for sin under the Old Testament: the sin offering (*chattath*) and the trespass

JESUS CHRIST OUR COMPLETE OFFERING

offering (*asham*). Here in Isaiah 53:10, God specifically calls Christ an *asham*, which is a trespass offering. This cogent statement calling the coming redeemer a trespass offering is a cornerstone verse which ties the accomplishments of the Christ to the Levitical sacrifices.

From here in Isaiah 53, we go to Leviticus and embark on a study of this offering, examining its distinctive characteristics, functions and significance in the Old Covenant sacrificial system. Once we understand the *asham* offering in its Old Testament context and usage, we can then go on to observe how the accomplishments of Christ are patterned in the trespass offering.

Leviticus 5 and 6 describe the various aspects of this sacrifice in detail. There are two parallel sections in these chapters: one section regarding trespasses against God, and another regarding trespasses against man.

> ## The Trespass Offering Addressed:
> **Trespasses against God:** Leviticus 5:16-19
> **Trespasses against Man:** Leviticus 6:1-7

Leviticus 5:14-16:
And the LORD spake unto Moses, saying,
If a soul commit a trespass, and sin through ignorance, in the holy things of the LORD; then he shall bring for his trespass [*asham*=trespass offering][1] unto the LORD a ram without blemish out of the flocks, with thy estimation by shekels of silver, after

---

[1] Here is an example where the word "offering" should have been supplied as is done in the Amplified, RSV and NAS.

The Trespass or Restitution Offering

> the shekel of the sanctuary, for a trespass offering [*asham*]:
> And he shall make amends for the harm that he hath done in the holy thing, and shall add the fifth part thereto, and give it unto the priest: and the priest shall make an atonement for him with the ram of the trespass offering [*asham*], and it shall be forgiven him.

If someone sinned regarding the "holy things of the Lord," he needed to bring two things to the priest. First, he was to bring a ram for a sacrifice and second, money. The ram was sacrificed and the money was paid to the priest for restitution for what that person failed to do regarding his obligations under the Mosaic Law. The monetary payment was an estimate of what he should have paid with an additional twenty percent. Then atonement was made and the trespass was forgiven.

The Trespass Offering:
Sacrifice: ram
Payment: restitution plus one fifth (20%)

The trespass offering obtained forgiveness for "harm done" to the "holy things of the Lord." Leviticus 5:14-16 addresses defrauding God of what belongs to Him—trespasses against God's property—"the holy things." In the Old Testament, anything dedicated to God could be considered His property: "a holy thing." For example, the firstborn belonged to God, hallowed, set apart, for His service.[2] The firstborn, whether of man or beast, had to be bought back from God by a redemption payment (Numbers 18:15-17). To

---

[2] Exodus 34:20 says, "…the firstborn of thy sons thou shalt redeem." Exodus 13:2, 11-16; Numbers 3:13.

JESUS CHRIST OUR COMPLETE OFFERING

deprive God of the redemption payment would be a trespass or harm done against God.

In the Authorized King James Version, the opening of verse 16 reads, "And he shall make amends..." The *New International Version* reads, "He must make restitution..." No other sacrifice under the Law demanded a restitution payment. In this aspect, the *asham* (trespass offering) was singularly unique. Restitution payment, with an added twenty percent, was the most distinctive point of this offering. As we shall see, this is where Christ is illustrated very prominently.

Another aspect of the trespass offering follows in Leviticus.

> Leviticus 5:17-19:
> And if a soul sin, and commit any of these things which are forbidden to be done by the commandments of the LORD; though **he wist [knew] it not**, yet is he guilty [has trespassed], and shall bear his iniquity.
> And he shall bring a ram without blemish out of the flock, with thy estimation, for a trespass offering [*asham*], unto the priest: and the priest shall make an atonement for him concerning his ignorance wherein he erred and **wist [knew] it not,** and it shall be forgiven him.
> It is a trespass offering [*asham*]: he hath certainly trespassed against the LORD.

Here the Israelite did that which is forbidden by the Old Testament law, but was not aware of it: "he wist [knew] it not." To receive forgiveness for trespasses committed without knowing it, a trespass offering was brought to the priest.

The Trespass or Restitution Offering

The Mosaic Law had many, many commandments. Breaches of the Law committed unknowingly would have been common and a source of concern. Regardless of the most sincere intentions, verse 19 attests, "...he hath certainly trespassed against the LORD" if a law was broken.

For example, the tenth commandment said one was not to covet anything that belonged to his neighbor.[3] The difficulty of keeping this commandment is addressed by the Apostle Paul in Romans 7.

This facet of the *asham* (trespass offering) is for the Israelite, who having done all that he knows to do from the Old Testament law, still carries guilt. Guilt from unknown trespasses was alleviated by this offering.

The Trespass Offering Addressed Property Violations Against Neighbor

In Leviticus 6, we have a parallel section to Leviticus 5:14-19. This passage does not deal with trespasses against the property of the Lord, but offenses against the property of others.

> Leviticus 6:1-7:
> And the LORD spake unto Moses, saying,
> If a soul sin, and commit a trespass against the LORD, and lie unto his neighbour in that which was delivered him to keep [entrusted to him[4]], or in fellowship [in dealing], or in a thing taken away by violence, or hath deceived his neighbour;
> Or have found that which was lost, and lieth concerning it, and sweareth falsely; in any of all these that a man doeth, sinning therein:

---

[3] Exodus 20:17.
[4] *New International Version.*

> Then it shall be, because he hath sinned, and is guilty, that he shall restore that which he took violently away, or the thing which he hath deceitfully gotten, or that which was delivered him to keep [deposit that was entrusted to him[5]], or the lost thing which he found,
>
> Or all that about which he hath sworn falsely; he shall even restore it in the principal, and shall add the fifth part more thereto, and give it unto him to whom it appertaineth, in the day of his trespass offering [*asham*].
>
> And he shall bring his trespass offering [*asham*] unto the LORD, a ram without blemish out of the flock, with thy estimation, for a trespass offering [*asham*], unto the priest:
>
> And the priest shall make an atonement for him before the LORD: and it shall be forgiven him for any thing of all that he hath done in trespassing therein.

On the day of the trespass offering, restitution of the principal in full was paid with a fifth part premium added. This was paid to the person who had been defrauded. Also, to obtain forgiveness, one was to bring a ram without blemish to the priest for a trespass offering.

While Leviticus 5:14-16 dealt with violations against the things belonging to the Lord, here in Leviticus 6:1-7 it considers five instances of violating property rights of that which belongs to a "neighbor."

1. **"...lie unto his neighbor in that which was delivered him to keep"** This relates to infringement upon a neighbor's rights in "a matter of deposit." After being

---

[5]*TANAKH The Holy Scriptures, The New Jewish Publication Society Translation According to the Traditional Hebrew Text* (New Jewish Publication Society, Philadelphia, 1985).

The Trespass or Restitution Offering

entrusted with something to keep, he has either sold it or unlawfully used it.

2. **"in fellowship"** could be translated "in dealing" (literally from the Hebrew: "to place in the hand"). This inclusive term involves deceit in any dealing or transacting with another.

3. **"a thing taken away by violence"** This refers to fraud or injustice of any kind, (e.g. to seize upon the property or possessions of others.[6])

4. **"deceived his neighbour"** This would include any matter where one would mislead another. Most of these situations specifically involve deception.

5. **"found that which was lost, and lieth concerning it, and sweareth falsely"** In this last example of offences to which the Law of the *asham* offering could be applied, a man finds something and then denies it to the rightful owner.

This list enumerates the various ways to deprive others of what is rightfully theirs. The issue confronted is violating or encroaching on the property rights of others. Leviticus 5:14-19 concerns a violation of the things of the Lord— infringing on the property rights of the Lord. The point of the trespass offering is to obtain forgiveness and restitution for these sins which were clearly a breach of the commandment: "thou shall not steal." No other offering under the Law deals directly with obtaining forgiveness for violating property rights.

The trespasses listed here in Leviticus are similar to Adam's trespass recorded in Genesis 3. Adam's sin included a

---

[6] William Wilson, *New Wilson's Old Testament Word Studies* (Grand Rapids, Michigan: Kregel, 1987) 468.

violation of property rights. Adam and Eve belonged to God; the earth belonged to God. God had entrusted the earth into Adam's care.

> Luke 4:5 and 6:
> And the devil, taking him [Jesus] up into an high mountain, shewed unto him all the kingdoms of the world in a moment of time.
> And the devil said unto him, All this power will I give thee, and the glory of them: for that is delivered unto me; and to whomsoever I will I give it.

As this verse indicates, the dominion over the kingdoms in the world had been delivered to Satan. Adam transferred the dominion and authority God had given him over the earth to Satan, God's archenemy.

While God put Adam as His under-ruler, all the things God placed under Adam's dominion and authority still ultimately belonged to God. When Adam sinned, he deprived God of what was rightfully His. For Adam to eat of the tree of knowledge of good and evil was a disobedient and unlawful act because God had commanded him not to in Genesis 2:17. This result then followed: "...by one man [Adam] sin entered into the world, and death by sin; and so death passed upon all men, for that all have sinned. (Romans 5:12).

Let's examine the violations of property rights in Leviticus 6:2 and 3 in light of their direct and detailed correlation to Adam's fall.

1. "...lie unto his neighbor in that which was delivered him to keep"

The Trespass or Restitution Offering

The world was entrusted to or "delivered to" Adam "to keep" (Genesis 1:28). In Genesis 1:29, God said to Adam "I have given you..." Genesis 2:15 states that Adam was to "dress and keep" the Garden of Eden. God had "delivered" the earth into Adam's care for him to keep. Adam then "delivered" it unto Satan. Romans 7:14 states that we are "sold under sin." Who sold humanity under sin? Adam. Adam's trespass brought sin and death into the world and upon all humanity. That which God had delivered Adam to keep, he sold and used unlawfully.

2. "in fellowship" could be translated "in dealing" (literally from the Hebrew: "to place in the hand"). According to Genesis 1:28, God entrusted or "placed in the hand" Adam with the dominion over the earth.[7] Because of Adam's trespass, the dominion and authority was transferred over to the adversary.

3. "A thing taken away by violence" "By violence" just does not mean by force, but "by fraud or injustice of any kind." For Adam to sell out all humanity and the earth was an injustice in the extreme, to God and upon Adam's progeny, the human race.

4. **"deceived his neighbor"** According to Hosea 6:7, Adam dealt treacherously with God: "But like Adam they have transgressed the covenant: there they have dealt treacherously against Me" (New American Standard).

5. "found that which was lost, and lieth concerning it, and sweareth falsely" Someone finds something and then denies its access to the rightful owner. By Adam's dishonest

---

[7] Genesis 1:28: "And God blessed them, and God said unto them, Be fruitful, and multiply, and replenish the earth, and subdue it: and have dominion over the fish of the sea, and over the fowl of the air, and over every living thing that moveth upon the earth."

disobedience, God as the rightful owner of man and the earth was deprived of His rightful use and access. Now Satan could use mankind and the world for his own purposes.

Jesus Christ offered himself as a trespass offering to God to make amends for the harm Adam had done. Christ paid the full price for Adam's sin and much more. God, as the wronged party, was fully restituted for the wrong done. When Isaiah 53:10 calls the coming Christ an *asham* offering, it is a precise and deliberate mention of the one Old Testament sacrifice that atoned and made restitution for property violations.

The Trespass Offering Addressed Treachery Toward God

Let's look at another aspect of the trespass offering mentioned here in Leviticus. To observe this distinctive characteristic, we need to look at a Hebrew word and its usage in a figure of speech.

> Leviticus 5:15:
> If a soul commit [*maal*] a trespass [*maal*], and sin through ignorance, in the holy things of the LORD; then he shall bring for his trespass unto the LORD...

> Leviticus 6:2:
> If a soul sin, and commit [*maal*] a trespass [*maal*] against the LORD...

In Leviticus 5:15 and 6:2, the Hebrew words translated "commit a trespass" are *maal maal*. The Hebrew verb, *maal*,

The Trespass or Restitution Offering

means to "act unfaithfully, treacherously."[8] This definition clarifies our understanding of the function of the trespass offering: If someone acts unfaithfully or treacherously toward God or his neighbor this offering is needed.

Also, this phrase is given more weight by a figure of speech. Both the verb and the noun are from the same Hebrew word, *maal*. This figure of repetition uses a verb and its cognate noun to draw attention to the gravity or magnitude of the trespass or treachery.[9] This same figurative expression is used in Joshua 7:1 to describe the sin of Achan. The trespass of Achan is an illustration of what Leviticus 5:15 and 6:2 is referring to.

> Joshua 7:1:
> But the children of Israel **committed [*maal*] a trespass [*maal*]** in the accursed thing: for Achan, the son of Carmi, the son of Zabdi, the son of Zerah, of the tribe of Judah, took of the accursed thing: and the anger of the LORD was kindled against the children of Israel.

In the incident in Joshua 7, Achan took items that God had instructed the children of Israel not to take from the plunder of Jericho and hid them in his tent. His covetousness led to the subsequent defeat of Israel in battle. Innocent Israelites

---

[8] Brown, Driver Briggs, 591. Also see: E.W Bullinger, *The Companion Bible*, Appendix 44, xi defines the noun form of *maal* as "treachery, unfaithfulness, breach of trust." *Exegeses Ready Research Bible* renders Levitcus 5:15, "If a soul commit treason…" Ezekiel 14:13 also repeats the word, *maal*, twice, in secession: "Son of man, when the land sinneth against me by trespassing [*maal*] grievously [*maal*]…" Here the superlative sense of the repetition is accurately translated. Ezekiel uses this figure with these Hebrew words frequently: Ezekiel 14:13, 15:8; 17:19 and 20; 20:24-28. The *"maal maal"* primarily involved breaking the Covenant by idolatry (II Chronicles 36:14 and Numbers 31:16).
[9] E.W. Bullinger, *Figures of Speech Used in the Bible*, 275. Pairing the same noun and verb together is a figure of speech adding intensity and emphasis called polyptoton.

died who had committed no sin. The consequence for his treachery and deceit was his entire family was put to death.

Years later, the children of Israel were reminded of the event:

> Joshua 22:20:
> Did not Achan the son of Zerah commit [*maal*] a trespass [*maal*] in the accursed thing, and wrath fell on all the congregation of Israel? and that man perished not alone in his iniquity.

The last phrase of Joshua 22:20 says, Achan "…perished not alone in his iniquity." Not only did his entire family die with him, but other Israelites had lost their lives in a battle following his transgression. The consequences of Achan's sin passed upon all those innocents who had not committed the treachery.

Romans 5 says death passed upon all men by Adam's sin, even those who had not sinned "after the similitude of Adam's transgression." In this sense, the treachery of Achan parallels the treachery of Adam. Innocents died because of someone else's transgression. As the last phrase of Joshua 22:20 says, Achan "…perished not alone in his iniquity." As with Achan, so much greater with Adam: "through the offense of one, many be dead."[10]

> Hosea 6:7:
> But they like men [Adam][11] have transgressed the covenant: there have they dealt treacherously against me.

---

[10] Romans 5:15.
[11] "Man" is rendered as "Adam" in the *Amplified, New American Standard* and *New International* versions.

The Trespass or Restitution Offering

The Hebrew word translated "men" in Hosea 6:7 is the same word translated "Adam" in other records. Speaking of the nation of Israel, the prophet said they have "transgressed" as Adam. Adam transgressed the covenant and betrayed God. Through the unfaithfulness and treachery of Adam, all humanity fell into sin and death. Jesus Christ's sacrifice, an *asham* (trespass offering), fulfilled the requirements to obtain forgiveness for Adam's treachery.

The trespass offering provided for forgiveness of unfaithfulness in the life of the Old Testament worshipper — whether big or small. All that we lack in faithfulness to God, God has satisfied in Christ, who was the complete trespass offering.

The *asham* sacrifice obtained forgiveness for sins against property, whether against God or a neighbor. This offering also served to alleviate guilt for committing trespasses unwittingly. We saw what distinguishes this offering from all other offerings: monetary payment. Unlike the other offerings, the trespass offering involved more than an animal sacrifice — it also involved a reparation payment to restore what was lost to the injured party plus twenty percent. That which had been taken had to be restored or an estimated value of the item had to be compensated.

Functions of the Trespass Offering:

Restored or returned; plus 20% added.
Forgave sins committed unintentionally.
Forgave property violations against God and man.
Forgave unfaithfulness and treachery toward God.

JESUS CHRIST OUR COMPLETE OFFERING

The Trespass Offering: Full Restoration and Restitution

We have seen that the trespass offering not only granted forgiveness, but also provided for restoration with a restitution payment. The offerer came to the priest with an animal for sacrifice—this was common to all offerings (except the meal offering). But in contrast to all of the other offerings of the Old Testament, with the *asham* (trespass offering), the Israelite also brought a monetary payment. The prominent distinguishing characteristic of the trespass offering was that it not only forgave, it also restored or repaid.

In this section, we will read a rather remarkable record from I Samuel where it speaks of a trespass offering involving payment or restitution. Then we will examine two Hebrew verbs that accurately express the restitution function of the trespass offering.

The record in I Samuel 4 tells of a war between the nation of Israel and the Philistines. The Israelites brought the Ark of the Covenant out into a battle against the Philistines. When the Philistines saw this most holy ark of God in the ranks of the opposing army, they were filled with alarm and fought desperately. The Philistines then emerged victorious in the battle with the Israelites and captured the ark of God. This is where the problems started for the Philistines.

> I Samuel 5:1 and 2:
> And the Philistines took the ark of God, and brought it from Ebenezer unto Ashdod.
> When the Philistines took the ark of God, they brought it into the house of Dagon, and set it by Dagon.

The Trespass or Restitution Offering

After capturing the ark, they placed it in the temple of their national god, Dagon. Being polytheistic, this may have seemed like a fairly good idea. Perhaps they thought that another god in town would be a good thing. However, it did not work out well.

> Verses 3 and 4:
> And when they of Ashdod arose early on the morrow, behold, Dagon was fallen upon his face to the earth before the ark of the LORD. And they took Dagon, and set him in his place again.
> And when they arose early on the morrow morning, behold, Dagon was fallen upon his face to the ground before the ark of the LORD; and the head of Dagon and both the palms of his hands were cut off upon the threshold; only the stump [the fish part] of Dagon was left to him.

This most sacred god of the Philistines on the first night was knocked over and lay on its face before the Ark of the Lord. The next night the idol was chopped up and then dumped on the threshold of the temple. Dagon was a fish-god, the upper half man, and the lower half fish, similar to the concept of a mermaid or merman.[12]

> Verses 5 and 6:
> Therefore neither the priests of Dagon, nor any that come into Dagon's house, tread on the threshold of Dagon in Ashdod unto this day.
> But the hand of the LORD was heavy upon them of Ashdod, and he destroyed them, and smote them

---

[12] Modern archeology has confirmed what the Scripture stated here thousands of years ago: the idol, Dagon, was half fish and half man. *New Bible Dictionary* (Grand Rapids: Michigan: Eedmans: 1973) 287.

JESUS CHRIST OUR COMPLETE OFFERING

> with emerods [tumors], even Ashdod and the coasts thereof.

After the phenomenal occurrences in the temple of Dagon, other consequences were forthcoming. A destructive plague swept the city of Ashdod with painful tumors.

> Verses 7 and 8:
> And when the men of Ashdod saw that it was so, they said, The ark of the God of Israel shall not abide with us: for his hand is sore upon us, and upon Dagon our god.
> They sent therefore and gathered all the lords of the Philistines unto them, and said, What shall we do with the ark of the God of Israel? And they answered, Let the ark of the God of Israel be carried about unto Gath.
> And they carried the ark of the God of Israel about thither.

The men of Ashdod acknowledged that the Lord of Israel had wrought this destruction on them and their chopped-up fish god. So the five lords of the Philistines got together and made a decision to ship the ark of the God of Israel off to another Philistine city, Gath. In hindsight, it looks like a sad attempt to pass off the problem to someone else, or perhaps it was simply one of those poor decisions that committees can come up with.

> Verse 9:
> And it was so, that, after they had carried it about, the hand of the LORD was against the city with a very great destruction: and he smote the men of the city, both small and great, and they had emerods [tumors] in their secret parts.

The Trespass or Restitution Offering

This second city of the Philistines did not fare well either. Whether of humble or high status, those of this city suffered and often died with "emerods in their secret parts." However, these of Gath, in keeping with precedent, were quite willing to pass on their horrific problem to another city of the Philistines.

> I Samuel 5:10-12 and 6:1:
> Therefore they sent the ark of God to Ekron. And it came to pass, as the ark of God came to Ekron, that the Ekronites cried out, saying, They have brought about the ark of the God of Israel to us, to slay us and our people
> So they sent and gathered together all the lords of the Philistines, and said, Send away the ark of the God of Israel, and let it go again to his own place, that it slay us not, and our people: for there was a deadly destruction throughout all the city; the hand of God was very heavy there.
> And the men that died not were smitten with the emerods [tumors]: and the cry of the city went up to heaven…
> And the ark of the LORD was in the country of the Philistines seven months.

Those who survived this terrible pestilence were afflicted with painful tumors. The people of Ashdod, Gath and Ekron had apparently had quite enough of these excruciating plagues. After an especially horrendous seven months, the Philistines finally got the message.

> I Samuel 6:2:
> And the Philistines called for the priests and the diviners, saying, What shall we do to the ark of the LORD? tell us wherewith we shall send it to his place.

JESUS CHRIST OUR COMPLETE OFFERING

They knew they needed to send the ark back to Israel. But the question was: How do we send it back? It is very evident that in the last seven months, they had acquired quite a lot of respect for this Ark of the Lord that they had captured from the Israelites.

> Verses 3-6:
> And they said, If ye send away the ark of the God of Israel, send it not empty; but in any wise return [*shub*] him a trespass offering [*asham*]: then ye shall be healed, and it shall be known to you why his hand is not removed from you.
> Then said they, What shall be the trespass offering [*asham*] which we shall return [*shub*] to him? They answered, Five golden emerods [tumors], and five golden mice, according to the number of the lords of the Philistines: for one plague was on you all, and on your lords
> Wherefore ye shall make images of your emerods [tumors], and images of your mice that mar the land; and ye shall give glory unto the God of Israel: peradventure he will lighten his hand from off you, and from off your gods, and from off your land.
> Wherefore then do ye harden your hearts, as the Egyptians and Pharaoh hardened their hearts? when he had wrought wonderfully among them, did they not let the people go, and they departed?

The ark of God was returned along with images of five golden tumors and five golden mice. This special trespass offering was their way of giving glory to the God of Israel. Having violated and trespassed on the sacred property of the Lord, they wanted to return it with a restitution payment in gold. While they offered no animal sacrifice, these Philistines grasped the main point of the *asham* offering: restoration and restitution.

The Trespass or Restitution Offering

Verses 7 and 8:
Now therefore make a new cart, and take two milch kine [cows], on which there hath come no yoke, and tie the kine to the cart, and bring their calves home from them:
And take the ark of the LORD, and lay it upon the cart; and put the jewels of gold, which ye return [*shub*] him for a trespass offering [*asham*], in a coffer by the side thereof; and send it away, that it may go.

As the account progressed, this plan was put in practice. The ark of God was returned to Israel along with the jewels.

The Philistines had committed a major violation of property rights against Jehovah, the God of Israel. They had deprived, robbed God of the worship due Him. The Philistines knew they should return the Ark with some form of restitution. They wanted to return the Ark with a trespass offering. This account illustrates how the *asham* (trespass offering) compensated for damages, in reparation.

One of the significant Hebrew words that expresses the distinctive function of the trespass offering is the verb: *shub*. This word is translated into the English as "return" in I Samuel 6:3, 4, and 8. This word is also used in Leviticus 6:4 "... he shall restore [*shub*] that which he took..."

> **Hebrew:** *shub* = restore, return, recompense

JESUS CHRIST OUR COMPLETE OFFERING

This Hebrew word is used in a familiar and much loved Psalm:

> Psalm 23:3:
> He restoreth [*shub*] my soul: He leadeth me in the paths of righteousness for his name's sake.

Numbers also uses this Hebrew word, *shub*, referring to restoration with the trespass offering:

> Numbers 5:6-8:
> Speak unto the children of Israel, When a man or woman shall commit any sin that men commit, to do a trespass against the LORD, and that person be guilty [*asham*];
> Then they shall confess their sin which they have done: and he shall recompense [*shub*] his trespass [*asham*] with the principal thereof, and add unto it the fifth part thereof, and give it unto him against whom he hath trespassed [*asham*].
> But if the man have no kinsman to recompense [*shub*] the trespass [*asham*] unto, let the trespass [*asham*] be recompensed [*shub*] unto the LORD, even to the priest; beside the ram of the atonement, whereby an atonement shall be made for him.

Here is a description of the trespass offering with the ram sacrificed for atonement and a restitution payment with an additional fifth added on.[13] However, in this passage, the word *asham* refers to a trespass, **not** a trespass offering as indicated by the context.

---

[13] "Atonement" and the synonym "expiation" means "the making of amends" or "paying the penalty for a wrongdoing." Walter J. Cummins, *Scripture Consulting Select Studies*, 342.

The Trespass or Restitution Offering

Here in Numbers 5, as well as in Leviticus 6 and I Samuel 6, we see the Hebrew verb, *shub*, meaning to recompense, restore, or return. Restoration is an integral part of the trespass offering. From these examples of the trespass offering, the central point of the *asham* offering is return and restitution.

Another significant Hebrew word defining the function of the trespass offering is *shalam*. The Young's Concordance defines the word *shalam* "to make whole, complete." *The New Brown Driver Briggs* lexicon defines *shalam*, "to be complete; make whole or good, restore...make compensation for injury."[14]

> **Hebrew: *shalam* =**
> **to make complete, make amends, restore**

This Hebrew word is used in Leviticus 5:16: "and he shall make amends [*shalam*] for the harm ..." and Leviticus 6:5: "... he shall even restore [*shalam*] it in the principal, and shall add the fifth part more thereto..."

The Hebrew word, *shub* translated "restore," "recompense," and "return" and the Hebrew word, *shalam*, translated "make amends" or "restore" are key words that help to understand the function of the trespass offering.

---

[14] Francis Brown, *The New Brown Driver Briggs Hebrew and English Lexicon*, (Lafayette, Indiana: Associated Publishers and Authors, 1978) 1022.

JESUS CHRIST OUR COMPLETE OFFERING

> ## Function of the Trespass Offering:
>
> ### Restore, Return, Recompense: *shub*
> Leviticus 6:4: "…he shall restore [*shub*] that which he took…"
> I Samuel 6:3: "… return [*shub*] him a trespass offering…"
> Numbers 5:6-8:"…he shall recompense [*shub*] his trespass …"
>
> ### Make complete, Make amends, Restore: *shalam*
> Leviticus 5:16: " make amends [*shalam*] for the harm …"
> Leviticus 6:5: "…even restore [*shalam*] it in the principal, and shall add the fifth part…"

He Paid it All and Much More

In Isaiah 53:10, it states the soul of the righteous servant was to be a trespass offering. Then the next verse says that God shall see the travail of his servant and be satisfied.[15] By the sacrifice of this life of the Messiah, the requirements for restitution were satisfied. Jesus Christ made complete compensation for all that Adam had defrauded from God. His sacrifice provided for the full restoration of those things that Adam had forfeited. Indeed, God was totally recompensed by the righteous servant bearing the sins of many. Our redeemer completely paid everything we owed or we lacked before God and more. All the requirements of justice have been met by the complete sacrifice of our lord and savior.

---

[15] Isaiah 53:10 and 11: "… thou shalt make his soul an offering for sin [*asham*], he shall see his seed, he shall prolong his days, and the pleasure of the LORD shall prosper in his hand. He shall see of the travail of his soul, and shall be **satisfied…**"

The Trespass or Restitution Offering

Having looked at the trespass offering as a shadow of good things to come, let's look at the reality of Christ's sacrifice. While we have already looked at various verses in Romans 5, let's view the passage in its entirety.

> Romans 5:6-21:
> For when we were yet without strength, in due time Christ died for the ungodly.
> For scarcely for a righteous man will one die: yet peradventure for a good man some would even dare to die.
> But God commendeth his love toward us, in that, while we were yet sinners, Christ died for us.
> **Much more** then, being now justified by his blood, we shall be saved from wrath through him.
> For if, when we were enemies, we were reconciled to God by the death of his Son, **much more**, being reconciled, we shall be saved by his life.
> And not only so, but we also joy in God through our Lord Jesus Christ, by whom we have now received the atonement.
> Wherefore, as by one man sin entered into the world, and death by sin; and so death passed upon all men, for that all have sinned:
> (For until the law sin was in the world: but sin is not imputed when there is no law.
> Nevertheless death reigned from Adam to Moses, even over them that had not sinned after the similitude of Adam's transgression, who is the figure [type] of him that was to come.
> But not as the offence, so also is the free gift. For if through the offence of one [Adam] many be dead, **much more** the grace of God, and the gift by grace, which is by one man, Jesus Christ, hath abounded unto many.

JESUS CHRIST OUR COMPLETE OFFERING

Verse 16: And not as it was by one that sinned [Adam], so is the gift: for the judgment was by one to condemnation, but the free gift is of many offences unto justification.

For if by one man's offence death reigned by one [Adam]; **much more** they which receive abundance of grace and of the gift of righteousness shall reign in life by one, Jesus Christ.

Verse 18: Therefore as by the offence of one [Adam] judgment came upon all men to condemnation; even so by the righteousness of one the free gift came upon all men unto justification of life.

For as by one man's disobedience many were made sinners, so by the obedience of one shall many be made righteous.

Moreover the law entered, that the offence might abound. But where sin abounded, grace did **much more** abound:

That as sin hath reigned unto death, even so might grace reign through righteousness unto eternal life by Jesus Christ our Lord.

Here in this magnificent passage of the New Testament revelation "much more" is repeated five times pertaining to Christ's work on our behalf. The *asham* offering, as a pattern depicting the savior who was to come, stipulated that an extra payment of a fifth was to be included in addition to the payment and animal sacrifice. This distinctive detail of the trespass offering points to the redeemer who would give God's people a "much more" salvation, full and complete.

Christ's sacrifice for us was not a minimal payment only, barely covering what Adam had lost. Jesus Christ offered himself as a trespass offering to God to make amends for the harm Adam had done. Jesus paid the full price for Adam's

The Trespass or Restitution Offering

sin, and he did much more. As a result of Christ's sacrifice, God's grace super-abounded toward us.

Verses 16 and 18 mention that the trespass of Adam caused judgment to pass to all men resulting in condemnation. The Greek word translated "condemnation" means a "sentence pronounced against someone." This refers to the judgment of death against Adam in Genesis 3, which resulted in the loss of spirit life.[16] This condemnation—the loss of spirit life—was then passed upon all humanity. But in abrupt contrast to this verdict of condemnation, this passage culminates: "That as sin hath reigned unto death, even so might grace reign through righteousness unto eternal life by Jesus Christ our Lord." We now have the reign of grace with the gift of righteousness bestowed upon us.

No Verdict of Condemnation

The opening verse of Romans 8 looks back to this section in Romans 5 and raises the issue of the verdict of condemnation that passed upon all men by Adam's trespass.

> Romans 8:1:
> *There is* therefore now no condemnation to them which are in Christ Jesus, who walk not after the flesh, but after the Spirit.

The last phrase of verse 1, "who walk not after the flesh, but after the Spirit" is omitted in all the critical Greek texts except one. "No condemnation" is not contingent on walking according to the spirit. No condemnation for the Christian is contingent on what Christ has accomplished as we read in Romans 5.

---

[16] Walter J. Cummins, *A Journey through the Acts and Epistles* (Franklin, Ohio: Scripture Consulting, 2006) 219.

JESUS CHRIST OUR COMPLETE OFFERING

This opening verse of Romans 8 straightforwardly states that there is no condemnation for the Christian believer. The verdict of condemnation that was passed to Adam and then upon all his progeny has been done away for the Christian believer in the Lord Jesus Christ. Christ, as the *asham* (trespass offering), restored what Adam lost and much more. We have holy spirit within, the gift of righteousness, that assures us eternal life. No verdict of condemnation has been or can be pronounced against us.

> Romans 8:33 and 34: (*Working Translation*) [17]
> Who will bring legal charges against God's chosen *ones*? God, the Justifier?
> Who can condemn *them*? Christ? *No, he is* the one who died, and rather who was raised [*from the dead*], who is also at the right *side* of God, and who also makes intercession for us.

Who will bring legal charges against us? No judgment against us shall stand. All the demands of justice have been satisfied by the life of the *asham* (trespass) offering.

The next two verses following Romans 8:1 explain how we have been set free from condemnation.

> Romans 8:1-3:
> *There is* therefore now no condemnation to them which are in Christ Jesus…
> For the law of the Spirit of life in Christ Jesus hath made me free from the law of sin and death.
> For what the law could not do, in that it was weak through the flesh, God sending his own Son in the likeness of sinful flesh, and **for sin** condemned sin in the flesh.

---

[17] Cited from the Working Translation in *A Journey through the Acts and Epistles*. Copyright © 2006 by Walter J. Cummins. All rights reserved.

The Trespass or Restitution Offering

In verse 3, the *New International Version* supplies the word offering after "for sin" reading: "...to be a sin offering."[18] As we considered in chapter six, depending on the context, the word "offering" or "sacrifices" may be supplied after the word "sin."[19]

Could Romans 8:3 read: "...God sending his own Son in the likeness of sinful flesh, and **for a sin offering** condemned sin in the flesh"? Does the context warrant supplying "offering" after the words, "for sin"?

Earlier in Romans, it speaks of how "sin in the flesh" was condemned.

> Romans 6:6:
> Knowing this, that our old man is crucified with him, that the body of sin might be destroyed, that henceforth we should not serve sin.

Our sin nature is called our "old man" and "the body of sin."

This sin nature or "sin in the flesh" was crucified with Christ. When Christ died, our sin died with him. By the offering of Jesus Christ, our sin nature was crucified, condemned and destroyed. So indeed, Christ "by a sin offering condemned sin in the flesh." Sin was condemned when Christ gave up his life as a sin offering.[20]

---

[18] *The New English Bible, The Amplified Bible*, and *New American Standard* also supply the word "offering."

[19] E.W. Bullinger, *Figures of Speech Used in the Bible*, 584. When the word "offering" is supplied it is by the figure metonymy, where "sin is put for the offering for sin."

[20] The words "for sin" in Romans 8:3 and Hebrews 10:6, 8 and 13:11 are translated from the Greek words, *peri hamartias*. In the *Septuagint*, the Greek

JESUS CHRIST OUR COMPLETE OFFERING

What a poignant parallel verse 3 makes to verse 1! Our sin nature has been condemned by the offering of Christ; the Christian has no condemnation. You and I are not condemned, but, in fact, it is sin that has been condemned. The old man nature has received a verdict of condemnation; hence the death penalty.

While we see the term "sin offering" here in Romans 8:3, the reference is best understood as the trespass offering, because Romans 8:1-3 refers back to Adam's trespass in Romans 5. Also in Isaiah 53, the righteous servant bore sin and paid the price for sin as an *asham* offering for God's people. [21]

Romans 8 opens with the declaration that there is no verdict of condemnation for those in Christ. Christ, as our trespass offering, provided for the full restoration of what Adam lost. Chapter 8 then closes with a return to this central issue.

> Romans 8:31 and 32:
> What shall we then say to these things? If God be for us, who can be against us?
> He that spared not his own Son, but delivered him up for us all, how shall he not with him also freely give us all things?

After many marvelous truths, Christ's sacrifice is again brought to the fore. If God gave up His own Son to secure

---

Old Testament, *peri hamartias* often refers to the sin offering. (Leviticus 4:3, 14, 32; 5:8, 11).

[21] In the *Septuagint*, the Greek word used for trespass offering is *plēmmeleia* (used in place of the Hebrew word, *asham*). This Greek word, *plēmmeleia*, is never used in the New Testament. So there is no equivalent word in the Greek New Testament for *asham*. So there is no direct correlation between the Hebrew Old Testament and the Greek New Testament words in this case. From the context and usage of "sin offering" here in Romans 8:3 we see that it best applies to the trespass offering.

The Trespass or Restitution Offering

our redemption and salvation, how will He not also freely give us all things?

God was the one who came up with the idea to redeem and save humanity after Adam's fall. After thousands of years, God's plan was finally completed by Christ's sacrifice. Will He now forget about us? God is surely more desirous to guide us and deliver us than we are to receive it.

What follows in Romans 8 is a rebuttal to all condemnation leveled at the Christian posed as rhetorical questions.

> Verses 33-39:
> **Who shall lay any thing to the charge of God's elect?** It is God that justifieth.
> **Who is he that condemneth?** It is Christ that died, yea rather, that is risen again, who is even at the right hand of God, who also maketh intercession for us.
> **Who shall separate us from the love of Christ?** shall tribulation, or distress, or persecution, or famine, or nakedness, or peril, or sword?
> As it is written, For thy sake we are killed all the day long; we are accounted as sheep for the slaughter.
> Nay, in all these things we are more than conquerors through him that loved us.
> For I am persuaded, that neither death, nor life, nor angels, nor principalities, nor powers, nor things present, nor things to come,
> Nor height, nor depth, nor any other creature, shall be able to separate us from the love of God, which is in Christ Jesus our Lord.

The question in verse 33: Who shall lay anything to the charge of God's elect? Who can lay an accusation against God's chosen? God, the Justifier? God, who issued the

JESUS CHRIST OUR COMPLETE OFFERING

verdict of acquittal, cannot then reissue a verdict of condemnation against us.

Next Scripture asks: who is he that condemns? Christ, who died as a trespass offering providing full restitution for our sin? Now he is resurrected and at the right hand of God making intercession for us.

What of the failings in our walk? Our shortcomings? Our sins? We have Christ pleading our case before God's throne. Who shall condemn us as unworthy? Would Christ who suffered and died so we could be worthy? Christ's accomplishments as our trespass offering can never be undone.

Finally verse 35 asks: Who shall separate us? Who or what is able to wrench us from God? No force or power has the capacity to deprive us of our access to God. Now that Christ has come and finished his work of redemption and salvation in all of the situations mentioned in verse 35, we are indeed more than conquerors through him, the Lord Jesus Christ, who loved us.

Verse 33 asks: who? Verse 34 asks: who? Verse 35 asks: who? Who in all creation has the capacity to tear us from God? What entity has the authority to bring charges against us? Or to condemn us and to separate us from God's love? No force, no event, no reality in the present or in the future has the power to separate us from the love of God, which is in Christ Jesus our Lord.

The Trespass or Restitution Offering

The Trespass Offering: A Portrayal of Christ's Accomplishments

In our examination of the trespass offering in the Old Testament we have not looked at every detail or all the examples of the *asham* (trespass offering). Rather our focus has been on the distinguishing characteristics of this offering and especially on the remarkable characteristic of the restitution payment.

The functions of the trespass offering depict what Christ achieved in his supreme sacrifice at Golgotha. The *asham* sacrifice obtained forgiveness for sins against property, whether God's or a neighbor's. It also alleviated guilt for committing trespasses unwittingly.

The trespass offering obtained forgiveness for unfaithfulness or treachery toward God. And we saw what distinguishes this offering from all other offerings: monetary payment. Unlike the other offerings, the trespass offering involved more than just an animal sacrifice—it also involved a reparation payment to restore what was lost to the injured party plus twenty percent. That which had been taken had to be restored or an estimation value of the item had to be compensated.

When Jesus Christ laid down his life as God's *asham* offering, all the wrong Adam had done to God was completely compensated. The loss that the first man perpetrated, Jesus Christ restored in full. Fulfilling the functions of the trespass offering, the savior paid the price to return what Adam forfeited plus "much more." Christ's sacrifice made whole the broken relationship between God and man.

What debt came to man in the first Adam, has been made up to the full in the Second Adam. Whether honor, service,

JESUS CHRIST OUR COMPLETE OFFERING

worship, obedience or whatever God could claim, whatever man could rob Him of, all this has He received back again in Christ.

We may often be burdened and troubled about our debts to man. How about our debts to God? In our age of grace in the New Testament we owe God service and worship and obedience. We are to be walking in obedience, as living sacrifices to God, renewing our minds.[22] Wherever we have shorted God, Christ has paid back and more. Where we have fallen short, giving God back so little in comparison of the riches of Christ He has bestowed on us, Christ, our trespass offering, has repaid and more. By his supreme act of obedience on the cross, he has discharged our unpaid debts to God "to the uttermost farthing." He is the complete restitution offering to God on our behalf. Not one of our sins or debts to God is unresolved.[23]

How many Christians today carry around feelings of guilt and sin? A deep inner sense of unworthiness and uneasiness before God can fester. Yet Jesus Christ has suffered and died as an *asham*, a trespass offering, for God's people. Isaiah 53:10 says, "Yet it pleased the LORD to bruise him; he hath put him to grief: when thou shalt make his soul an offering for sin [*asham*]..." This messianic prophecy is completely fulfilled by Jesus Christ. He is now our *asham*. Our sense of guilt was borne by him on the cross. We have no more reason to maintain a sense of sin or unworthiness before God.

---

[22] Romans 12:1 and 2: "I beseech you therefore, brethren, by the mercies of God, that ye present your bodies a living sacrifice, holy, acceptable unto God, which is your reasonable service. And be not conformed to this world: but be ye transformed by the renewing of your mind, that ye may prove what is that good, and acceptable, and perfect, will of God."

[23] Colossians 2:14 says Christ took our debts out of the way and nailed them to his cross. For more please see: Bishop K. C. Pallai, *Orientalisms of the Bible, Volume 1* (Fairborn, Ohio: Munkus Publishing Company, 1969) 125.

The Trespass or Restitution Offering

Imagine if your earthly father paid off all your student loans as a gift. Then a month later you came to him and told him that you had received another monthly bill for the same loan. You dutifully scraped together the money to pay that monthly installment. How would your father feel? You had just paid on a debt you did not owe. The same applies to Christians who carry about a sense of guilt today—they are paying on a debt that has already been fully repaid. The world still sends a bill, but the debt has been paid. We just need to inform the world that the liability has been paid in full. If the bills don't stop coming at least you know you can ignore them because they are invalid. Christ has borne our guilt and sin.

The trespass offering of the Old Testament was a detailed pattern of him who was to come, foreshadowing the savior's offering. The Old Testament revelation portrays the intricate pattern of Christ's work. We can marvel at how God planned our redemption in such detail and clarity.

Our intention in this study is not only to intellectually examine Levitical sacrifices, but to **see** Christ and his work with more clarity. This trespass offering that we examined in Leviticus is much more than an obsolete rite that passed out of practice two thousand years ago. Rather, it is a portrait of the coming redeemer, the depiction of what Jesus of Nazareth was to accomplish for you and me.

JESUS CHRIST OUR COMPLETE OFFERING

Name of Sacrifice	Hebrew Name	Functions	Distinctive Characteristic	Parallel to Christ
Trespass Offering -- Restitution Offering	Asham	-Restitution -Made amends -Restoration Forgave: -unintentional sins -property violations -unfaithfulness to God	monetary payment plus 20%	Isaiah 53:10 Romans 8:3 Romans 5: "much more"

Chapter 8

The Sin Offering or Purification Offering

Examination of the sin offering in the Bible is somewhat akin to walking into an art exhibit and noticing one painting that is much larger than the others. This painting stretches from floor to ceiling and extends the entire length of the wall. As you gaze at the massive canvas which depicts various scenes and multiple themes, you consider how the artist must have had much to say. In studying the sin offering, you should similarly consider how God had so much to teach and show His people by this offering. The sin offering is quite expansive. It portrays so many aspects of the multifaceted sacrifice of Christ.

We have looked at a very unique sin offering, the scapegoat, in chapter 4 of this study. In this chapter, we will look at the major function of the sin offering and its immense significance in looking forward to the paramount salvation Christ would accomplish. We will also look at another exceptional and rare offering called the red heifer.

JESUS CHRIST OUR COMPLETE OFFERING

The law of the sin offering is set forth in Leviticus 4. This chapter has four sections addressing how the sin offering should be applied to various categories of individuals. The first section addresses the case of the anointed priest who sins.

> Leviticus 4:1-7:
> And the LORD spake unto Moses, saying,
> Speak unto the children of Israel, saying, If a soul shall sin through ignorance against any of the commandments of the LORD concerning things which ought not to be done, and shall do against any of them:[1]
> If the priest that is anointed do sin according to the sin of the people; then let him bring for his sin, which he hath sinned, a young bullock without blemish unto the LORD for a sin offering [*chattath*].
> And he shall bring the bullock unto the door of the tabernacle of the congregation before the LORD; and shall lay his hand upon the bullock's head, and kill the bullock before the LORD.
> And the priest that is anointed shall take of the bullock's **blood**, and bring it to the tabernacle of the congregation:
> And the priest shall dip his finger in the **blood**, and sprinkle of the **blood** seven times before the LORD, before the vail of the sanctuary.
> And the priest shall put some of the **blood** upon the horns of the altar of sweet incense before the LORD, which is in the tabernacle of the congregation; and shall pour all the **blood** of the bullock at the bottom of the altar of the burnt offering, which is at the door of the tabernacle of the congregation.

---

[1] The sin offering was offered when one became aware of inadvertent sins done in ignorance. Sins done "presumptuously," despising the Word of the Lord, were not forgiven by this offering (Numbers 15:27-31).

The Sin or Purification Offering

If the anointed priest sinned, he was to present a young bull, lay his hand upon it, and kill it. Then he was to take the blood of the sacrifice and sprinkle the blood seven times in front of the curtain of the sanctuary. Then, he entered into the first compartment of the tabernacle where he put blood on the horns of the altar of incense. The horns on the altar were projections at each corner of the altar that looked like horns. And, the rest of the blood was then poured out at the base of the altar of the burnt offering which was outside of the tabernacle in front of the of the doorway.

On the Day of Atonement, the high priest went into the holy of holies and sprinkled the blood of the sin offering.[2] Conversely, in Leviticus 4, the priest only went into the first part of the tabernacle to sprinkle the blood. Regardless of where the blood was poured or sprinkled, the prominent feature of the sin offering is the blood of the sacrifice. Distinctly different from the trespass offering, the sin offering focused on the application of the blood.

> Verses 8-10:
> And he shall take off from it all the fat of the bullock for the sin offering [chattath]; the fat that covereth the inwards, and all the fat that is upon the inwards,
> And the two kidneys, and the fat that is upon them, which is by the flanks, and the caul above the liver, with the kidneys, it shall he take away,
> As it was taken off from the bullock of the sacrifice of peace offerings: and the priest shall burn them upon the altar of the burnt offering.

---

[2] Leviticus 16:15: "Then shall he kill the goat of the sin offering, that is for the people, and bring his blood within the vail [in the holy of holies], and do with that blood as he did with the blood of the bullock, and sprinkle it upon the mercy seat, and before the mercy seat:"

JESUS CHRIST OUR COMPLETE OFFERING

The fat of the sin offering was to be handled in the same way as commanded with the peace offering. When examining the peace offering in a future chapter, we will see how fat was burned as incense on the altar and its subsequent significance.

>Verses 11 and 12:
>And the skin of the bullock, and all his flesh, with his head, and with his legs, and his inwards, and his dung,
>Even the whole bullock shall he carry forth without the camp unto a clean place, where the ashes are poured out, and burn him on the wood with fire: where the ashes are poured out shall he be burnt.

The rest of the sacrifice was to be taken to a clean place outside the camp and incinerated to ashes. The fact that the sacrifice was to be burned outside the camp will become significant in our further consideration of the sin offering. However, our main focus in this part of the study is the distinguishing characteristic of the sin offering: the blood.

The next section of Leviticus 4 pertains to a sin of the "whole congregation." It again brings into view the prominent feature of the sin offering.

>Verses 13-20:
>**And if the whole congregation of Israel sin** through ignorance, and the thing be hid from the eyes of the assembly, and they have done somewhat against any of the commandments of the LORD concerning things which should not be done, and are guilty;
>When the sin, which they have sinned against it, is known, then the congregation shall offer a young

The Sin or Purification Offering

bullock for the sin [offering, *chattath*],³ and bring him before the tabernacle of the congregation.

And the elders of the congregation shall lay their hands upon the head of the bullock before the LORD: and the bullock shall be killed before the LORD.

And the priest that is anointed shall bring of the bullock's **blood** to the tabernacle of the congregation:

And the priest shall dip his finger in some of the **blood**, and sprinkle it seven times before the LORD, even before the vail.

And he shall put some of the **blood** upon the horns of the altar which is before the LORD, that is in the tabernacle of the congregation, and shall pour out all the **blood** at the bottom of the altar of the burnt offering, which is at the door of the tabernacle of the congregation.

And he shall take all his fat from him, and burn it upon the altar.

And he shall do with the bullock as he did with the bullock for a sin offering [*chattath*], so shall he do with this: and the priest shall make an atonement for them, and it shall be forgiven them.

This sin offering was for the entire congregation of Israel. When the sin became known, they were to present a sin offering. This aspect of the sin offering is also augmented in Leviticus 5:5: "And it shall be, when he shall be guilty in one of these things, that he shall confess that he hath sinned in that thing." Acknowledging that one has sinned and needs forgiveness is crucial to receiving forgiveness. As we will

---

³ As we noted in Chapter 6, on occasion the KJV omits the word "offering" when it should be supplied. The NIV, NAS and NRSV all supply the word "offering."
In the *Septuagint*, the Greek Old Testament, "for the sin" is translated from *peri hamartias* which refers to a sin offering as in Leviticus 4:3, 32; 5:8, 11.

discuss later in this chapter, Leviticus 5:5 forms a parallel to I John 1:9: "If we confess our sins, he is faithful and just to forgive us our sins, and to cleanse us from all unrighteousness."

The noticeably emphasized subject is the blood. Howbeit, verse 20 points to a function of this offering: "...priest shall make an atonement for them, and it shall be forgiven them." By this offering, those of the Old Covenant sought to overcome their alienation from God and repair a broken relationship with Him.

> Verses 22-26:
> **When a ruler hath sinned**, and done somewhat through ignorance against any of the commandments of the LORD his God concerning things which should not be done, and is guilty;
> Or if his sin, wherein he hath sinned, come to his knowledge; he shall bring his offering, a kid of the goats, a male without blemish:
> And he shall lay his hand upon the head of the goat, and kill it in the place where they kill the burnt offering before the LORD: it is a sin offering [*chattath*].
> And the priest shall take of the **blood** of the sin offering [*chattath*] with his finger, and put it upon the horns of the altar of burnt offering, and shall pour out his **blood** at the bottom of the altar of burnt offering.
> And he shall burn all his fat upon the altar, as the fat of the sacrifice of peace offerings: and the priest shall make an atonement for him as concerning his sin, and it shall be forgiven him.

When a ruler sinned, he was to present a young goat, rather than a bull, as a sin offering. The ruler would then lay his hand on the head of goat, just as stipulated, to the anointed priest or the elders of the congregation on the young bull.

The Sin or Purification Offering

The placement of the hands on the sin offering identified the offerer with the offering. This signified the transfer of sin to the bull or the goat.[4] The goat then would be sacrificed and its blood put on the horns of the altar and poured out at the bottom of the altar.

Sprinkling the blood on or around the altar is mentioned in connection with other sacrifices. However, with the sin offering, the application of the blood is spelled out in more detail and done more frequently.[5]

As mentioned in verse 20, the sin offering made "an atonement for him as concerning his sin, and it shall be forgiven him." "Atonement" denotes propitiation and reconciliation through payment.[6] In presenting the sin offering, the ruler sought forgiveness for sins and to restore a severed relationship with God.

> Verses 27-31:
> **And if any one of the common people** sin through ignorance, while he doeth somewhat against any of the commandments of the LORD concerning things which ought not to be done, and be guilty
> Or if his sin, which he hath sinned, come to his knowledge: then he shall bring his offering, a kid of the goats, a female without blemish, for his sin which he hath sinned.
> And he shall lay his hand upon the head of the sin offering [*chattath*], and slay the sin offering [*chattath*] in the place of the burnt offering.

---

[4] Leviticus 16:21.
[5] The blood is sprinkled with burnt offering (Leviticus 1:5), the peace offering (3:2) and mentioned once concerning the trespass offering (7:2).
[6] The concept of atonement will be explored in chapter 11. In Genesis 32 we will see that atonement dissolves enmity and brings reconciliation by payment, all in the context of grace.

JESUS CHRIST OUR COMPLETE OFFERING

> And the priest shall take of the **blood** thereof with his finger, and put it upon the horns of the altar of burnt offering, and shall pour out all the **blood** thereof at the bottom of the altar.
> And he shall take away all the fat thereof, as the fat is taken away from off the sacrifice of peace offerings; and the priest shall burn it upon the altar for a sweet savour unto the LORD;[7] and the priest shall make an atonement for him, and it shall be forgiven him.

If an Israelite who was not a priest or ruler sinned, he was to bring a young female goat as a sin offering. Again, special attention is paid to the blood of the sacrifice, which the priest put upon the altar horns and poured out the rest at the base of the altar. Again, verse 31 says the effect of this offering was to "make an atonement for him, and it shall be forgiven him." The sin offering functioned to grant pardon and reconcile the individual back to God.

Leviticus 4 states how four categories of individuals could present the sin offering: the anointed priest, the entire congregation, the ruler, and ordinary people.

> **Four Categories in Leviticus 4:**
> -anointed priest,
> -entire congregation
> -ruler
> -ordinary people

---

[7] The fat of all offerings was to be burned upon the altar. In our study of the peace offering we will examine the significance of the fat and why it must be burned on the altar.

The Sin or Purification Offering

Purifying by the Blood

While the key point of the trespass offering was monetary restitution for wrongs done, the distinctive focus of the sin offering in Leviticus 4 is the blood of the sacrifice. Whether the blood is sprinkled, daubed, or poured, what does this symbolize in the Old Covenant sacrificial system? In our examination of the sin offering, our immediate question is: what is the exact significance of the blood of this sacrifice?

Before looking at the Scriptures to find an answer to this query, let's first recognize that the answer to these questions is well outside our modern cultural context. Presently, there is little, if anything in our experience that relates to animal sacrifice as depicted here in Leviticus. Taking a domesticated animal that you have raised or purchased to a priest, laying your hand on the head of that animal and then having a priest kill it as a sacrifice on your behalf is not common in our society.

Therefore, to answer the question of the significance of the blood in the Old Testament sacrifices, we cannot rely on our sense of what seems logical to us, but rather on what the Word of God says. Our concern here is not with customs or mores from our times and their significance, but rather on what the Scriptures declare.

A few verses from Hebrews give some insight into the biblical significance of sprinkling blood:

> Hebrews 9:21 and 22:
> Moreover he [Moses] sprinkled with blood both the tabernacle, and all the vessels of the ministry.

JESUS CHRIST OUR COMPLETE OFFERING

And almost all things are by the law purged [cleansed, purified] with blood; and without shedding of blood is no remission.

Verse 22 declares, "…And almost all things are by the law purged with blood…" Sprinkling the blood of a sacrifice had the ceremonial effect of cleansing and purifying. The Law requires that nearly everything be purified by means of blood. When Moses sprinkled the tabernacle and the sacred vessels with the blood of a sacrifice, it signified that they were cleansed and purified.

> **The blood of a sacrifice had the ceremonial effect of cleansing and purifying.**

Ezekiel 43:19-22
And thou shalt give to the priests the Levites that be of the seed of Zadok, which approach unto me, to minister unto me, saith the Lord GOD, a young bullock for a sin offering [*chattath*].
And thou shalt take of the blood thereof, and put it on the four horns of it, and on the four corners of the settle [ledge], and upon the border round about: thus shalt thou **cleanse and purge [atone for]** it.
Thou shalt take the bullock also of the sin offering [*chattath*], and he shall burn it in the appointed[8] place of the house, without the sanctuary.

---

[8] "Appointed" is the same Hebrew word as mentioned Nehemiah 3:31: "the gate Miphkad." Young's Concordance translates Miphkad as, "the appointed place." Ernest Martin says it should be translated as the "numbering place" where the red heifer offering was burned. Ernest Martin, *Secrets of Golgotha* (Associates of Scriptural Knowledge: Portland, Oregon) 15, 34, 39. See Appendix One of this study: "Probable Location of the Crucifixion."

The Sin or Purification Offering

> And on the second day thou shalt offer a kid of the goats without blemish for a sin offering [*chattath*]; and they shall **cleanse** the altar, as they did **cleanse** it with the bullock.

In Ezekiel's vision, the blood of the sin offering was applied to the altar to "cleanse and purge it." Then on the second day, another sin offering was sacrificed to cleanse the altar. Again, we see that blood of the sin offering had a purifying and atoning effect.

> Leviticus 16:18 and 19:
> And he shall go out unto the altar that is before the LORD, and make an atonement for it; and shall take of the blood of the bullock, and of the blood of the goat, and put it upon the horns of the altar round about.
> And he shall sprinkle of the blood upon it with his finger seven times, and **cleanse it, and hallow [sanctify] it** from the uncleanness of the children of Israel.

In examining these references, we see that the sprinkling, daubing or pouring of blood, in the biblical context of sacrifices, indicates cleansing and purification. The blood in the sacrificial system was not a pollutant or a contamination as often viewed today, but rather quite the opposite; it served as a ceremonial cleansing agent.[9]

Leviticus 8:15 is also explicit about the function of the blood of the sin offering after the consecration of Aaron and his sons as priests.[10]

---

[9] Blood could also be unclean under the Law, such as an issue of blood (Leviticus 12).
[10] Exodus 29 speaks of the consecration of the priests in more detail.

JESUS CHRIST OUR COMPLETE OFFERING

> Leviticus 8:13-15:
> And Moses brought Aaron's sons, and put coats upon them, and girded them with girdles [sashes], and put bonnets [caps] upon them; as the LORD commanded Moses.
> And he brought the bullock for the sin offering [*chattath*]: and Aaron and his sons laid their hands upon the head of the bullock for the sin offering [*chattath*].
> And he slew it; and Moses took the blood, and put it upon the horns of the altar round about with his finger, and **purified** the altar, and poured the blood at the bottom of the altar, and **sanctified** it, to **make reconciliation** [atonement] upon it.

Moses put the blood of this sin offering on the horns of the new altar to purify it and then poured the blood at the base of the altar for sanctification and atonement. Verse 15 clearly states that applying the blood to the altar purified it and set it apart for God's divine service in addition to making atonement. While different from our modern cultural perceptions, the Scriptures are clear on the exact significance and function of the blood of the sin offering. As we have seen and will observe in yet more detail, the primary distinguishing characteristic of the sin offering is how its blood purified and sanctified.

Understanding the significance of sprinkling of blood of the sin offering can bring added appreciation of this verse in the New Testament.

> I Peter 1:2:
> Elect according to the foreknowledge of God the Father, through sanctification of the Spirit, unto [because of] obedience and sprinkling of the blood of

The Sin or Purification Offering

> Jesus Christ: Grace unto you, and peace, be multiplied.

This opening verse of I Peter, was addressed to those who knew the Old Testament. It hearkens back to the Mosaic revelation. "Sprinkling of the blood of Jesus Christ," is set in beautiful Levitical terminology, illustrating our purity, our cleansing, and our sanctification by the work of Jesus Christ on the tree at Golgotha.[11] This is truly a marvelous representation of our complete sanctification and purity before God.

The *Chattath*, Sin Offering, can be called Purification Offering

We have described the trespass offering as a "restitution offering" distinguished by its primary function of reparation or restoration. The sin offering can be described as a "purification offering" because its essential function is to purify or cleanse and to make atonement.

Additionally, the Hebrew word, *chattath*, which is used for the sin offering, may actually be translated in some places as "purification offering."

> Numbers 8:7 and 8:
> And thus shalt thou do unto them, to cleanse them: Sprinkle water of purifying [*chattath*] upon them, and let them shave all their flesh, and let them wash their clothes, and so make themselves clean.
> Then let them take a young bullock with his meat offering, even fine flour mingled with oil, and another

---

[11] Also see: David Bergey, *Jesus Christ Our Approach Offering*, 147.

JESUS CHRIST OUR COMPLETE OFFERING

> young bullock shalt thou take for a sin offering [*chattath*].

In verse 7, the Hebrew word, *chattath*, is translated as "purifying." The Hebrew word, *chattath*, can also carry the sense of purification as well as sin or sin offering.[12]

The *Tanakh*, the Jewish translation of the Old Testament, notes that the sin offering of Leviticus 4 is more precisely the "offering of purgation." Other scholars have also recognized the sin offering could be called the purification offering from the etymology of the Hebrew word.[13]

We have seen in the broad array of sin offerings that purification is central. For instance, the altar in Leviticus 8:15 had to be cleansed and set apart for God, but it certainly had not sinned. The new altar being common, had to be sanctified, set apart for God's service; being unclean, it had to be cleansed.

Leviticus 12 speaks of required offerings after childbirth.

> Leviticus 12:6-8:
> And when the days of her purifying are fulfilled, for a son, or for a daughter, she shall bring a lamb of the first year for a burnt offering, and a young pigeon, or a turtledove, for a **sin offering** [*chattath*], unto the door of the tabernacle of the congregation, unto the priest:

---

[12] The Hebrew root word of *chattath* is *chata*. This word, *chata*, is also translated as "cleanse" in Ezekiel 43:20, 22 and 23 and "purge" in Psalm 51:7. In the Peil conjugation, *chata*, means cleanse while in the far more common Kal conjugation, it refers to sin.

[13] Jacob Milgrom, *The Anchor Bible Leviticus 1-16* (Doubleday, New York, 1991) 253; *TANAKH*, 156. Allen Ross, *Holiness to the Lord* (Baker, Grand Rapids, MI, 2002) 124.

The Sin or Purification Offering

> Who shall offer it before the LORD, and make an atonement for her; and she shall be **cleansed from the issue of her blood**. This is the law for her that hath born a male or a female.
> And if she be not able to bring a lamb, then she shall bring two turtles [doves], or two young pigeons; the one for the burnt offering, and the other for a **sin offering** [*chattath*]: and the priest shall make an atonement for her, and she shall be clean.

After childbirth, when the days of a woman's purification were finished, offerings were to be brought to the priest for her cleansing. A lamb was to be presented as a burnt offering and a young pigeon or a dove as a sin offering. Or, if they could not afford that, "two turtles [doves], or two young pigeons; the one for the burnt offering, and the other for a sin offering."

Here, the purpose of the sin offering was cleansing or purification from an issue of blood (verse 7), not for forgiveness or expiation of sin. Under the Law, an issue of blood was considered uncleanness, not sin. The *chattath* offering after childbirth functioned as a purification offering. This offering facilitated atonement or reconciliation with God, not because of sin, but because of uncleanness.

> Luke 2:21-24:
> And when eight days were accomplished for the circumcising of the child, his name was called JESUS, which was so named of the angel before he was conceived in the womb.
> And when the days of her purification according to the law of Moses were accomplished, they brought him to Jerusalem, to present him to the Lord;

JESUS CHRIST OUR COMPLETE OFFERING

> (As it is written in the law of the Lord, Every male that openeth the womb shall be called holy to the Lord;)
> And to offer a sacrifice according to that which is said in the law of the Lord, A pair of turtledoves, or two young pigeons.

When Mary's days of purification were finished, the new parents presented Jesus to the Lord at the temple and presented these offerings: "a pair of turtledoves, or two young pigeons" specifically as Leviticus 12:8 instructed. Mary, having just given birth to the savior, certainly had no need to be forgiven or cleansed of sin by a "sin offering." She needed, according to the Law of Moses, a *chattath*, a purification offering.

Looking at the function of this offering as well as the etymology of the Hebrew word, the *chattath* offering can be called a sin offering or purification offering. Regardless of the term used to describe this offering, the overall function was cleansing or purification. At times, it purified from sin, resulting in atonement and forgiveness (Leviticus 4:20, 26, 31, 35). After the scapegoat was released into the wilderness on the Day of Atonement the Scripture states:

> Leviticus 16:30:
> For on that day shall the priest make an atonement for you, to cleanse you, that ye may be clean from all your sins before the LORD.

The effect of the *chattath* offering was to be "clean from all your sins"

At times, this offering purified from uncleanness as with the new altar (Leviticus 8:15). This offering functioned to purify a woman who had given birth to "make an atonement for

The Sin or Purification Offering

her, and she shall be clean." (Leviticus 12:8). On the Day of Atonement, the sprinkling of the blood of this offering cleansed and sanctified the holy of holies, the holy place and the altar. In chapter 16, we undertake an examination of the Day of Atonement and how this offering was front and center functioning to cleanse from sin and from uncleanness.

Whether this offering is called a sin offering or a purification offering, its overarching purpose was to cleanse from sin or cleanse from uncleanness. As we explore the New Testament we will see some remarkable parallels to Christ's work on our behalf. But first, we will look at what was the most infrequently offered sacrifice of the Old Testament.

Functions of the *Chattath* Offering

Forgiveness
Leviticus 4:20, 26, 31, 35

Cleansing
Hebrews 9:22; Ezekiel 43:20,22; Leviticus 8:15; 16:19

Sanctifying
Leviticus 8:15; 16:19

Atonement
Leviticus 4:20, 26, 31, 35; 8:15; 12:7,8; 16:6-34

The Red Heifer Sin Offering

We read in Leviticus that the main focus of the sin offerings was the application of the blood, either sprinkled, dabbed or poured. We also have considered that the blood of the sin offerings were for purification and to obtain forgiveness of

JESUS CHRIST OUR COMPLETE OFFERING

sin through atonement. We have further observed that the Hebrew word, *chattath*, could be translated as purification offering or sin offering. The distinctive characteristic of the *chattath* offering was the blood and its capacity to cleanse and forgive sins and provide reconciliation.

However, with some types of sin offerings, the blood was not the principal focus. The scapegoat, a sin offering only offered on the Day of Atonement, was unique in that it was not sacrificed by the priest. Instead, after laying his hands upon it and confessing sins, the scapegoat was led off into the wilderness bearing the sins of the nation. As we noted in chapter 4, the scapegoat formed a dramatic parallel to Christ: both bore the sins of God's people.

As we shall see, the red heifer offering is also a unique sin offering with some distinctive parallels to Christ. It is also referenced in the book of Hebrews. This unusual sin offering is described in Numbers.

> Numbers 19:1-3:
> And the LORD spake unto Moses and unto Aaron, saying,
> This is the ordinance of the law which the LORD hath commanded, saying, Speak unto the children of Israel, that they bring thee a red heifer without spot, wherein is no blemish, and upon which never came yoke:
> And ye shall give her unto Eleazar the priest, that he may bring her forth **without the camp**, and one shall slay her before his face:

This offering differed from all others in some significant particulars. First, this sacrifice was to be a heifer, a young female cow, rather than a bullock, a young male. Then it was to be sacrificed by Eleazar, Aaron's eldest surviving son

The Sin or Purification Offering

and the successor to the position of high priest. Also, the red heifer offering was to be brought outside the camp to be killed. It was not to be slaughtered on the altar before the tabernacle as the other offerings. But, what was extraordinary about this sacrifice was that it had to be a rare color: red.

A completely red cow was genetically very rare, hence the reason it was seldom offered.[14] The red heifer was the only sacrifice under the Law where this specification made it most difficult to attain. No other offering in the Old Testament was so infrequently offered. The red heifer foreshadowed Christ in how rare and precious it was. The color red points to the precious blood of Christ in its uniqueness and rarity.

> Verses 4-6:
> And Eleazar the priest shall take of her blood with his finger, and sprinkle of her blood directly before [toward the front of] the tabernacle of the congregation seven times:
> And one shall burn the heifer in his sight; her skin, and her flesh, and her blood, with her dung, shall he burn:
> And the priest shall take cedar wood, and hyssop, and scarlet, and cast it into the midst of the burning of the heifer.

After the red heifer was sacrificed "without the camp," Eleazar was to take her blood and sprinkle it in the direction

---

[14] The ancient rabbinical writings from the Mishnah claimed, "from the time of Moses to the final destruction of the Temple, only seven, or else nine, such red heifers had been offered: first by Moses, the second by Ezra, and the other five, or else seven, between the time of Ezra and that of the taking of Jerusalem by the Romans." Quoted from: Alfred Edersheim, *The Temple* (Grand Rapids, MI: Eerdmans, 1987) 355.

JESUS CHRIST OUR COMPLETE OFFERING

of the tabernacle of the congregation seven times. Then the entire offering was to be burned: "her skin, and her flesh, and her blood, with her dung."

As the entire carcass of the animal was burning, the priest was to take "cedar wood, and hyssop, and scarlet, and cast it into the midst of the burning of the heifer."

> Verses 7-9:
> Then the priest shall wash his clothes, and he shall bathe his flesh in water, and afterward he shall come into the camp, and the priest shall be unclean until the even.
> And he that burneth her shall wash his clothes in water, and bathe his flesh in water, and shall be unclean until the even.
> And a man that is clean shall gather up the ashes of the heifer, and lay them up without the camp in a clean place, and it shall be kept for the congregation of the children of Israel for a water of separation [for impurity]: it is a purification for sin.

Later the ashes of this heifer as well as the ashes of the cedar wood, and hyssop, and scarlet were collected and put in a ceremonially clean place outside the camp. Verse 9 states the purpose of this sin offering: "…it shall be kept for the congregation of the children of Israel for a water of separation [for impurity]: it is a purification for sin [*chattath*]." Water mixed with these ashes could then serve as a *chattath* — a purification offering.

This "water for impurity" is also mentioned in Numbers 8:7: "And thus shalt thou do unto them, to cleanse them: Sprinkle water of purifying [*chattath*] upon them…" Here, this solution of water and ashes is called "water of purifying" being water of a purification offering, a *chattath*.

The Sin or Purification Offering

Numbers 19 explains an important use of this purifying water:

> Numbers 19:11-13:
> He that toucheth the dead body of any man shall be unclean seven days.
> He shall purify himself with it on the third day, and on the seventh day he shall be clean: but if he purify not himself the third day, then the seventh day he shall not be clean.
> Whosoever toucheth the dead body of any man that is dead, and purifieth not himself, defileth the tabernacle of the LORD; and that soul shall be cut off from Israel: because the water of separation [for impurity] was not sprinkled upon him, he shall be unclean; his uncleanness is yet upon him.

Sprinkling this water for impurity cleansed the Israelite from one of the most vile contaminations under the Mosaic Law, contact with the dead. The purpose of this water of the purification offering was to facilitate this cleansing from this defilement of death.

Hebrews 9 mentions the ashes of the heifer:

> Hebrews 9:13 and 14:
> For if the blood of bulls and of goats, and the ashes of an heifer sprinkling the unclean, sanctifieth to the purifying of the flesh:
> How much more shall the blood of Christ, who through the eternal Spirit offered himself without spot to God, purge [cleanse, purify] your conscience from dead works to serve the living God?

JESUS CHRIST OUR COMPLETE OFFERING

The ashes of the red heifer sacrifice as well as the blood of the sin offerings of bulls and goats had the effect of purifying the ceremonially unclean. In Leviticus 4 and 16, we read how the blood of bulls and goats purified and sanctified.

Far greater, the purification offering of Jesus Christ cleanses our conscience from dead works. The "dead works" of the old man nature are cleansed by the blood of Christ, like the purifying water ritually cleansed those under the Law from the contamination of death.[15] The purifying water gave only a temporary, external, and ceremonial cleansing while pointing toward that spiritual, inward, and permanent purity that the blood of Christ was to provide. The cleansing power of the *chattath* offering of Jesus Christ was so superior that it fully cleansed us from our sins.

From God's point of view, our conscience is cleansed by the blood of Christ. Hebrews 10:17 also gives God's perspective: "And their sins and iniquities will I remember no more." However, we can still carry around a consciousness of sin unless we change our thinking to reflect God's estimation of us. We need to control our thinking to recognize the reality of our cleansed conscience by the blood of Christ.

> Hebrews 13:10-13:
> We have an altar, whereof they have no right to eat which serve the tabernacle.
> For the bodies of those beasts, whose blood is brought into the sanctuary by the high priest for sin [offerings], are burned without the camp.
> Wherefore Jesus also, that he might sanctify the people with his own blood, suffered without the gate.

---

[15] Romans 7:5 and 6 mention works that "bring forth fruit unto death," referring to the dead works under the Law.

The Sin or Purification Offering

> Let us go forth therefore unto him without the camp, bearing his reproach.

Verse 11 is a reference to the burning of the "bodies of those beasts" of the sin offerings outside the camp. According to Leviticus, after sin offerings were sacrificed on the altar, they were carried out of the camp to be burned.[16]

Note that Hebrews 13:12 says, "Wherefore Jesus also, that he might sanctify the people with his own blood, suffered without the gate." Where did Jesus lay down his life as a sacrifice? Jesus' place of death was outside of Jerusalem's gates.

All the sin offerings were to be *burned* outside the camp; however, only one was to be *sacrificed* outside the camp. Numbers 19:3 tells us, "that he may bring her forth without the camp, and one shall slay her before his face." An aspect of the red heifer offering that is distinctively unique from all other sacrifices is the location of the sacrifice.

The only offering sacrificed by the priests without the camp (or later without the gate of the temple) was the red heifer offering.[17] The other offerings were sacrificed before the

---

[16] Leviticus 4:12: "Even the whole bullock shall he carry forth **without the camp** unto a clean place, where the ashes are poured out, and burn him on the wood with fire…" Leviticus 16:27: "And the bullock for the sin offering, and the goat for the sin offering, whose blood was brought in to make atonement in the holy place, shall one carry forth **without the camp**; and they shall burn in the fire their skins, and their flesh, and their dung."

[17] The Passover offering was offered by and in individual households. But Leviticus 17:8 and 9 gives strict instructions concerning the location of other sacrifices: "And thou shalt say unto them, Whatsoever man there be of the house of Israel, or of the strangers which sojourn among you, that offereth a burnt offering or sacrifice, And bringeth it **not** unto the door of the tabernacle of the congregation, to offer it unto the LORD; even that man shall be cut off from among his people."

JESUS CHRIST OUR COMPLETE OFFERING

altar that was before the tabernacle. We have seen some rather unique parallels the red heifer offering has to Christ.[18]

The red heifer sacrifice forms a truly graphic pattern of the sacrifice of Christ with three characteristics that distinguish it from all others. First, the exact color of this offering was stipulated which made it very rare. Then, its ashes were mixed with water which expanded the use of the *chattath* offering and its cleansing capacity. Finally, the location of this sacrifice was unique in that it was slain outside the camp.

Unique Characteristics of the Red Heifer Offering:
   Rarity: red
   Location of sacrifice: without the camp
     (Hebrews 13:12)
   Water of Purifying for cleansing
     (Hebrews 9:13)

Jesus Christ, Our *Chattath* Offering

The *chattath* offering of the Law presents a panoramic exhibit of "the good things to come." A scapegoat was led out into the wilderness. Blood was sprinkled to purify the holy places and obtain forgiveness. A rare red heifer was sacrificed outside the camp. From that exceptional sacrifice

---

[18] See Appendix One: "Probable Location of the Crucifixion." Ernest Martin in *Secrets of Golgotha*, makes a case that the location where the red heifer was slain was the actual location of Christ's crucifixion. In *Archaeology of the Bible: Book by Book* , Gaalyah Cornfeld (New York: Harper and Row, 1976) 55: "…Mishna and Talmud say that the "red heifer was taken out of the Temple courts and slain on the Mount of Olives."

The Sin or Purification Offering

a solution of ashes and water was made to serve for cleansing. All these were facets of this most cardinal and expansive *chattath* offering. All these were features of the *chattath* offering that served essential functions in the Old Testament sacrificial system.

What an expansive, yet precise, tutorial this offering was of the coming Christ. As we behold this offering, it is evident the lengths God went to exhibit the range of models and patterns of he who was to come.

While we have seen references in Hebrews that correspond directly to the sin (purification) offering of Jesus Christ, let's look at another example in I John.

> I John 1:3-7:
> That which we have seen and heard declare we unto you, that ye also may have **fellowship** with us: and truly our **fellowship** is with the Father, and with his Son Jesus Christ.
> And these things write we unto you, that your joy may be full.
> This then is the message which we have heard of him, and declare unto you, that God is light, and in him is no darkness at all.
> If we say that we have **fellowship** with him, and walk in darkness, we lie, and do not the truth:
> But if we **walk** in the light, as he is in the light, we have **fellowship** one with another, and the blood of Jesus Christ his Son cleanseth us from all sin.

This passage speaks of the walk and fellowship of the believer. Our complete salvation and position as sons and daughters of God is attained when we do what it says in

JESUS CHRIST OUR COMPLETE OFFERING

Romans 10:9.[19] The moment we confess with our mouth Jesus as Lord and believe that God raised him from the dead, the full cleansing and forgiveness is ours by Christ's sacrifice. However, here in I John, in the context of walking in fellowship with God, verse 7 says, "...the blood of Jesus Christ his Son cleanseth us from all sin." The cleansing power of the *chattath* offering of Jesus Christ carries on into our walks. Even when we have fallen short in our walk, we continue to have access to the abundant forgiveness and cleansing.

> Verses 8-10:
> If we say that we have no sin, we deceive ourselves, and the truth is not in us.
> If we confess our sins, he is faithful and just to forgive us our sins, and to cleanse us from all unrighteousness.
> If we say that we have not sinned, we make him a liar, and his word is not in us.

The human capacity for self-deception is addressed in verses 8 and 10. If we deny we have sin, we deceive ourselves and "make him a liar and his word is not in us."[20] When our fellowship with God is interrupted, we are not to be in denial, but rather we are to confess our sins and God will forgive and cleanse.[21]

---

[19] Romans 10:9: "That if thou shalt confess with thy mouth the Lord Jesus, and shalt believe in thine heart that God hath raised him from the dead, thou shalt be saved."

[20] The phrase, "...we make him a liar" seems to drip with irony. Romans 3:4 is literal: "...let God be true, but every man a liar..." Also see the note in the *Working Translation* in I John 1:10.

[21] Confessing the sin was also involved with the sin offering: Leviticus 5:5: "And it shall be, when he shall be guilty in one of these things, that he shall confess that he hath sinned in that thing."

The Sin or Purification Offering

Verse 9 states God will "forgive us our sins," <u>not</u> "keep an account of our sins!" God is faithful and just to continue to forgive and to cleanse because He knows what Jesus Christ has achieved by his sacrificial offering.

This epistle continues to explain what God has accomplished through Jesus Christ.

> I John 2:1 and 2:
> My little children, these things write I unto you, that ye sin not. And if any man sin, we have an advocate with the Father, Jesus Christ the righteous:
> And he is the propitiation [atonement] for our sins: and not for ours only, but also for the sins of the whole world.

This epistle is written that we sin not, but if we sin, we have a legal advocate at God's right hand: "Jesus Christ the righteous." The defense attorney pleading our case is none other than the Son of God.

He is the propitiation not only for our sins, but for all humanity. This word, propitiation, relates to the word atonement, used in the Old Testament.[22] Christ's atoning sacrifice is payment for the sins of the entire world rather than an animal sacrifice which was repeatedly offered.

---

[22] In I John 2:2 the Greek for propitiation, *hilasmos,* is a form of *hilastērion* translated "mercyseat" in Hebrews 9:5. In the Old Testament, the Hebrew word for "mercyseat" (Strong's # 3727) is closely related to the word for "atonement" (Strong's # 3722) in Hebrew. Also see: I John 4:10: Herein is love, not that we loved God, but that he loved us, and sent his Son to be the propitiation [*hilasmos*] for our sins.

JESUS CHRIST OUR COMPLETE OFFERING

> ## The Blood of Jesus Christ:
> ### Forgives
> ### Cleanses
> ### Atones

Those of the Old Covenant had a symbol and shadow of the salvation that was to come. As Christians, we have the continuing glorious reality of the forgiveness, purification and atonement by the blood of Jesus Christ.

> I John 3:19-22:
> And hereby we know that we are of the truth, and shall assure [persuade] our hearts before him.
> For if our heart condemn [*kataginōskō*] us, God is greater than our heart, and knoweth [*ginōskō*] all things.
> Beloved, if our heart condemn [*kataginōskō*] us not, then have we confidence toward God.
> And whatsoever we ask, we receive of him, because we keep his commandments, and do those things that are pleasing in his sight.

As with chapter one, this section deals with the walk of the believer. It speaks of things that we ought to do: assure our hearts, keep His commandments addressed to us and have our actions be pleasing. It also mentions something we ought not to do: engaging in self-condemnation. God is certainly greater than any feelings of self-blame our hearts may have.

The Sin or Purification Offering

The Greek word, *ginōskō*, means "to know by experience," while *kataginōskō* literally means "to know something against," thus to find fault, condemn or blame.[23]

God knows our sins, faults and failures, but He also knows what His only begotten Son has legally accomplished. I John 1:9 states that God is faithful and just to continue to forgive and to cleanse. As verses 21 and 22 indicate, we are not to condemn ourselves. We can come before God freely with confidence to receive answers to our prayers.

II Corinthians tells us more about how Jesus Christ became our sin offering.

> II Corinthians 5:14-21:
> For the love of Christ constraineth us; because we thus judge, that if one died **for** all, then were all dead:
> And that he died **for** all, that they which live should not henceforth live unto themselves, but unto him which died **for** them, and rose again.
> Wherefore henceforth know we no man after the flesh: yea, though we have known Christ after the flesh, yet now henceforth know we him no more.
> Therefore if any man be in Christ, he is a new creature: old things are passed away; behold, all things are become new
> And all things are of God, who hath reconciled us to himself by Jesus Christ, and hath given to us the ministry of reconciliation;
> To wit, that God was in Christ, reconciling the world unto himself, not imputing their trespasses unto them; and hath committed unto us the word of reconciliation

---

[23] W. E. Vine, *Vine's Expository Dictionary of New Testament Words* (Macdonald Publishing: Mclean, Virginia) 224.

JESUS CHRIST OUR COMPLETE OFFERING

> Now then we are ambassadors for Christ, as though God did beseech you by us: we pray you in Christ's stead, be ye reconciled to God.
> For he [God] hath made him [Christ] to be sin **for** us, who knew no sin; that we might be made the righteousness of God in him.

What does verse 21 mean when it says Christ was made sin for us? Could this be a case where "sin" is put for a sin offering? Was Christ made sin or made a sin offering? We saw in chapter 6 how the context of the word "sin" determines whether it is an actual sin or a sin offering.

Verses 14 and 15 say that Christ died **for** us, in our place, as a substitute. Verse 21 revisits the theme of Christ's sacrificial substitution: "For he [God] hath made him [Christ] to be sin **for** us." He bore the penalty that was rightfully ours. This concept of substitution was illustrated time and time again by every Old Testament sacrifice. In the context, we have references to Christ's sacrificial work as the one who "died for all."

To explore exactly what it means for Jesus Christ to be "made sin for us," we need to look at Isaiah 53. Isaiah 53:4 tells us, "Surely he hath borne our grief and carried our sorrows..." and verse 12 says, "...he bare the sin of many..." The Messiah was to bear the sins and sickness of God's people.

Christ's sacrifice corresponds to the sin offering of the scapegoat of the Day of Atonement that would "bear upon him all their iniquities..." (Leviticus 16:22). This sin offering led out into the wilderness had all the sins placed upon him, just as Christ did: "...the Lord hath laid on him the iniquity of us all" (Isaiah 53:6).

The Sin or Purification Offering

Also note that Isaiah 52:14 and 15 declares, in reference to the crucifixion: "As many were astonied at thee; his visage was so marred more than any man, and his form more than the sons of men: So shall he sprinkle many nations..." As we have seen repeatedly, a distinctive emphasis of the sin offering was the sprinkling of blood.[24] Isaiah spoke of the coming Christ as a sin offering, who would bear sin as a scapegoat and also be a purification offering, cleansing the nations.

> **Christ as Sin Offering in Isaiah 52 and 53:**
> "...shall he sprinkle many nations..."(as sin offering)
>   Isaiah 52:15
> "...he bare the sin of many..." (as scapegoat)
>   Isaiah 53:12

Christ fulfilled the sin offering as Isaiah foretold. Looking at the context of II Corinthians 5:21 and the references to Christ's sacrifice in Isaiah, we see that he was made a sin offering.

Previously we saw that Isaiah 53:10 says that God shall "make his soul an offering for sin..." In the Hebrew text there is not a word for "offering." In the Hebrew, it simply reads that he was made an *asham*, a trespass. Yet translators unanimously supply the word "offering" or "sacrifice," understanding that Christ was not made an actual trespass, but rather made a trespass offering.

---

[24] The Hebrew word for "sprinkling" used in Isaiah 52:15, *nazah*, is the identical word used in Leviticus 4 and 16.

JESUS CHRIST OUR COMPLETE OFFERING

Similarly in II Corinthians 5:21, the word "offering" should be supplied like it was in Isaiah 53:10: "For he [God] hath made him [Christ] to be a sin offering for us..."[25]

> "...thou [God] shalt make his soul an offering for sin..." Isaiah 53:10
>
> "...he [God] hath made him to be sin [offering] for us." II Corinthians 5:21

With this in mind, we can grasp both components of II Corinthians 5:21: God made Christ to be a sin offering for us, so "that we might be made the righteousness of God in him."

Just as with the sacrifices of the Old Covenant, in Christ all of our sin has been transferred to an innocent substitute. Patterned after the scapegoat on the Day of Atonement, all of our iniquities and all of our transgressions and all of our sins were transferred to Jesus of Nazareth. And then in turn, all his innocence and righteousness was transferred to us. Now we have a standing before God with the status of righteousness! Our hearts may be slow to absorb this glorious reality, but God knows and remembers what He has accomplished by His Son's sacrifice. From God's viewpoint we are totally identified with Christ, sharing fully in his righteousness as he fully shared in our sin and the consequence of sin—death.

---

[25] Julia B. Hans, *Go Figure! An Introduction to Figures of Speech in the Bible*, 152. In *Figures of Speech Used in the Bible*, Bullinger says of II Corinthians 5:21: "sin is put for the offering for sin." (584). The Companion Bible note on II Corinthians 5:21 does not concur. Perhaps because this part of the Companion Bible was written posthumously by others. See: Juanita Carey, *E. W. Bullinger, A Biography* (Kregel: Grand Rapids MI, 2000) 213.

The Sin or Purification Offering

II Corinthians 5:14, "...if one died for all, then were all dead," directly correlates to verse 21 referring to our substitution and identification with Christ. Since Christ died for us all as a substitute, then we were also identified with him in his death.

Our full sharing and utter oneness with Christ is brilliantly set forth in Galatians 2:20:

> I am [was] crucified with Christ: nevertheless I live; yet not I, but Christ liveth in me: and the life which I now live in the flesh I live by the faith of [concerning] the Son of God, who loved me, and gave himself for me.

Identified with Christ, our sin nature died with him, yet we now live, not in our sin nature, but as those alive from the dead walking in newness of life.[26]

How do we now live? By believing, concerning the Son of God "who loved me, and gave himself for me." In this life we now live in the flesh, we are to believe the reality and the scope of what Christ accomplished when he gave himself for us on the cross.

The breathtaking extent and reality of our Lord Jesus Christ's towering accomplishments by his sacrifice is set forth in Hebrews.

> Hebrews 9:26 and 28:
> ...but now once in the end [*telos*] of the world [ages] hath he appeared to put away sin by the sacrifice of himself...

---

[26] Romans 6:4-6.

JESUS CHRIST OUR COMPLETE OFFERING

> So Christ was once offered to bear the sins of many; and unto them that look for him shall he appear the second time without sin unto salvation.

The first coming of Christ was so monumental it is called the "end of the ages" or the consummation of the ages. All the ages awaited the appearance of him who would redeem humanity. Looking back on his immense achievements, we now await his second appearance and the deliverance that will bring.

Name of Sacrifice	Hebrew Name	Functions	Distinctive Characteristic	Parallel to Christ
Sin Offering -- Purification Offering	chattath	Forgiving Cleansing Sanctifying Atoning	Blood applied	**Blood of Christ:** -Forgiving -Cleansing -Sanctifying -Atoning Hebrews 9:12-14; 10:22; 13:12 I Peter 1:2 II Corinthians 5:21 I John 1:7-2:2

Chapter 9

The Sweet Savor Offerings

Having considered the trespass and sin offerings, we shall next examine the sweet savor offerings. As mentioned in chapter six, the three sweet savor offerings, under the Law of Moses, were the burnt offering, meal offering, and peace offering. Before looking at them individually in upcoming chapters, it is necessary to investigate this class of offerings as a whole to see exactly what a sweet savor offering is and its significance in the Scriptures.

The importance of understanding these offerings is highlighted by the following verse in the New Testament.

> Ephesians 5:2
> And walk in love, as Christ also hath loved us, and hath given himself for us an offering and a sacrifice to God for a sweetsmelling savour.

Jesus Christ gave himself for us as a sweet, fragrant, pleasing offering to God. In light of this key verse, it would behoove us to explore biblically exactly what a sweet savor offering is. Although mentioned in the Church Epistles, to define its

JESUS CHRIST OUR COMPLETE OFFERING

precise functions we need to look at its usage earlier in the Bible.

As we will see in this chapter, a sweet savor offering is not a sin (purification) offering or a trespass (restitution) offering. The burnt offering, meal offering, and peace offering are focused on a sweet savor or aroma unto the Lord. For example, Leviticus 1:9 states: "...and the priest shall **burn** [burn as incense] all on the altar, to be a burnt sacrifice, an offering made by fire, of a **sweet savour** [fragrance] unto the LORD."

The "...offering and a sacrifice to God for a sweet smelling savour" in Ephesians 5:2 has a direct parallel to: "...sacrifice, an offering...of a sweet savour unto the LORD," the offering in Leviticus 1:9.

> **Ephesians 5:2:**
> "...an offering and a sacrifice to God for a sweet smelling savour"
> **parallels:**
> Leviticus 1:9:
> "...sacrifice, an offering...of a sweet savour unto the LORD."

The burnt, meal, and peace offerings were, in essence, *incense offerings* for a sweet fragrance unto the Lord. But before we conduct a more thorough study of how incense is the primary focus of the burnt offering, meal offering, and peace offering, let's search the Scriptures to find the function and significance of incense.

The Sweet Savor Offerings

Incense=Prayer

Prior to considering the opening three chapters of Leviticus and how they relate to incense, we will first need to firmly fix in our minds exactly what burning incense symbolizes in the Bible.

> Psalm 141:2:
> Let my prayer be set forth before thee as incense; and the lifting up of my hands as the evening sacrifice.

In the Authorized King James Version, prayer is compared to incense by a simile using "as." But in the Hebrew text, prayer is simply called "incense:" "My prayer is prepared—incense before Thee." (*Young's Literal Translation*). Here in Psalms, prayer is called incense.

> Revelation 5:8:
> And when he had taken the book, the four beasts and four and twenty elders fell down before the Lamb, having every one of them harps, and golden vials [bowls] full of odours [incense], which are the prayers of saints.

Here again, the Scriptures pointedly refer to incense as "the prayers of the saints." Here, as in Psalms, incense is a symbol of prayer.

> Revelation 8:3 and 4:
> And another angel came and stood at the altar, having a golden censer; and there was given unto him much incense, that he should offer it with the prayers of all saints upon the golden altar which was before the throne.

JESUS CHRIST OUR COMPLETE OFFERING

And the smoke of the incense, which came with the prayers of the saints, ascended up before God out of the angel's hand.

The angel held a golden censer, which is a container or vessel to hold incense. Then, in verse three, prayers of the saints and incense are offered together on the heavenly golden altar. Again, we have prayer and incense explicitly linked. As incense, the prayers of the saints ascended up to God.

Numbers records a sad event where Korah and his followers demanded that they, as Levites, had every right to approach the tabernacle, just as Aaron, the high priest, did (Numbers 16:10).[1] They were attempting to undercut, if not nullify, the office and function of the high priest. In attacking the Aaronic priesthood, the pattern of the coming one, they were attacking Christ. Korah's rebellion was a frontal assault by Satan on Christ and the salvation he would accomplish for us. The following deals with the aftermath of the rebellion of Korah.

> Numbers 16:44-48:
> And the LORD spake unto Moses, saying,
> Get you up from among this congregation, that I may consume them as in a moment. And they fell upon their faces.
> And Moses said unto Aaron, Take a censer, and put fire therein from off the altar, and put on incense, and go quickly unto the congregation, and make an atonement for them: for there is wrath gone out from the LORD; the plague is begun.
> And Aaron took as Moses commanded, and ran into the midst of the congregation; and, behold, the plague

---

[1] For more on this episode see: David Bergey, *Jesus Christ Our Approach Offering*, 141, 142, 178.

The Sweet Savor Offerings

was begun among the people: and he put on incense, and made an atonement for the people.
And he stood between the dead and the living; and the plague was stayed.

Why would incense make an atonement for the people? The incense represented the intercessory prayer of the high priest. As the high priest stood between the dead and the living, the wrath was turned away and the plague was stopped. The dire consequences of their transgressions were arrested. This episode becomes clearer when we understand that burning incense often signifies prayer.

Incense was an essential part of the Day of Atonement as described in the following record:

> Leviticus 16:12-14:
> And he shall take a censer full of burning coals of fire from off the altar before the LORD, and his hands full of sweet incense beaten small, and bring it within the vail:
> And he shall put the incense upon the fire before the LORD, that the cloud of the incense may cover the mercy seat that is upon the testimony, that he die not:
> And he shall take of the blood of the bullock, and sprinkle it with his finger upon the mercy seat eastward; and before the mercy seat shall he sprinkle of the blood with his finger seven times.

Before the high priest entered the holy of holies on the Day of Atonement, he was to "take a censer full of burning coals of fire from off the altar" and then put incense on the censer. As the high priest walked into the holy of holies the smoke from the burning incense would cover the mercy seat: "that he die not." Similar to the incense of the high priest in Numbers 19, incense symbolized prayer and intercession to

JESUS CHRIST OUR COMPLETE OFFERING

God. This cloud of incense and the prayer and intercession it represented, would turn away wrath and preserve the life of the high priest. The sweet fragrance of incense, representing prayer and intercession, turned away wrath and its consequences.

Now we can readily grasp the function of the sweet savor offerings of Leviticus 1-3, the burnt offering, meal offering, peace offering, and ultimately how Jesus Christ was our sweet savor offering.

Qatar, to Burn as Incense

In the opening chapters of Leviticus the word, "incense," is not cited in the English versions. However, when the Hebrew words are understood we will see that the burning of incense is repeatedly mentioned.

> Leviticus 1:9:
> But his inwards [entrails] and his legs shall he wash in water: and the priest shall burn [*qatar*] all on the altar, to be a burnt sacrifice, an offering made by fire, of a sweet savour unto the LORD.

The Hebrew verb, *qatar*, means to "burn as incense," but it is translated as "burn" in most English versions. The noun form of *qatar* is the Hebrew word for incense.[2]

The Hebrew word, *qatar*, could be translated "burn as incense" or more simply "cense." Cense, while not a commonly used English word, as the verb form of incense, is used in a liturgical context. For example, when a priest in an orthodox church burns incense in a pan or "censer" this is called "censing."

---

[2] The noun form of *qatar* is *qetoreth*, translated as "incense" in Psalm 141:2; Leviticus 16:12 and 13, Numbers 16:46 and 47.

The Sweet Savor Offerings

In Leviticus, chapter one, this word, *qatar*, is used three more times, describing the sacrifice of the burnt offering:

> 1:13: "burn [*qatar*=burn as incense] *it* upon the altar."
> 1:15: "burn [*qatar*=burn as incense] *it* on the altar."
> 1:17: "burn [*qatar*=burn as incense] it upon the altar."

The burnt offering was to be burned as incense on the altar, representing prayer to God.

In Leviticus 2, it occurs four times of the meal offering:

> 2:2: "burn [*qatar*=burn as incense] the memorial of it upon the altar."
> 2:9: "burn [*qatar*=burn as incense] *it* upon the altar."
> 2:11: "for ye shall burn [*qatar*=burn as incense] no leaven."
> 2:16: "burn [*qatar*=burn as incense] the memorial of it."

In chapter 2, the portion of the meal offering combined with frankincense was to be, *qatar*, burned as incense upon the altar.

In Leviticus 3, it occurs three times of the peace offering:

> 3:5: "burn [*qatar*=burn as incense] it on the altar."
> 3:11: "burn [*qatar*=burn as incense] it upon the altar."
> 3:16: "burn [*qatar*=burn as incense] them upon the altar."

With the peace offerings, the fat is separated from the sacrifice and then *qatar*, burned as incense upon the altar.[3]

---

[3] All of the fat from all the offerings sacrificed on the altar was to be, *qatar*, burned as incense, upon the altar fire: sin offerings (Leviticus 4:10,19, 26, 31,

JESUS CHRIST OUR COMPLETE OFFERING

In the first three chapters of Leviticus, the word, "burn," used 11 times, is always translated from the Hebrew word, *qatar*, meaning to "burn as incense." Clearly, these offerings are incense offerings. These sacrifices served as prayer and intercession before God on behalf of the individual.

Leviticus 4, in the context of the sin offering, uses another Hebrew word for "burn:"

> Leviticus 4:12:
> Even the whole bullock shall he carry forth without the camp unto a clean place, where the ashes are poured out, and burn [*saraph*] him on the wood with fire: where the ashes are poured out shall he be burnt [*saraph*].

The Hebrew word, *saraph*, simply means to burn or to incinerate. The sin offering was not to be offered as incense on the altar before the tabernacle. It was to be burned outside the camp in a special place set aside for that purpose.

On the Day of Atonement, Leviticus 16:27 and 28 commanded that the sin offerings of the bull and the goat be incinerated (*saraph*). Likewise, the red heifer sacrifice was also to be "*saraph*" or reduced to ashes (Numbers 19:5, 8).

These two Hebrew words, *saraph* and *qatar*, draw a sharp distinction between the two offerings for sin and the three sweet savor offerings. The sin or trespass offerings were not sweet savor offerings, to be burned as incense. The main function of the sin and trespass offering was purification and restitution. The primary point of the burnt, meal and peace

---

35); trespass offerings (Leviticus 7:7:1-5) and peace offerings (Leviticus 3). The reason why is discussed in the next the chapter on peace offering.

The Sweet Savor Offerings

offering was to approach God in intercession and prayer, turning away wrath.

Qatar **Burn as incense on the altar**	*Saraph* **Burn, incinerate in a clean place**
-All fat of peace, sin, and trespass offerings -The burnt and meal offerings[4]	Sin offerings Leviticus 4:12, 21; 16:27,28 Numbers:19:5, 8

The "sweet savour" offerings opened the door for individual Old Testament worshippers, at their own discretion, to come before God's presence. With the aid of the priests, they could approach God's dwelling place on earth, the tabernacle, to pray and intercede. With the institution of these offerings in Leviticus 1-3, each individual Israelite could draw near to God to entreat His goodness and grace and turn away wrath.

Sweet Savor: Soothing Fragrance of Rest

To establish the connection between a "sweet savor" and the incense offerings, let's return to Leviticus chapter one. Then we will examine precisely what the term "sweet savour" means from the Hebrew.

> Leviticus 1:9: ...and the priest shall **burn** [as incense] all on the altar, to be a burnt sacrifice, an offering

---

[4] As we shall see in chapter 11, only the memorial portion of the meal offering was burned as incense on the altar. In chapter 13, we will note how the <u>entire</u> burnt offering was burned as incense on the altar.

made by fire, of a **sweet** [*nichoach*] **savour** unto the LORD.

Leviticus 1:13: ...and **burn** [as incense] it upon the altar: it is a burnt sacrifice, an offering made by fire, of a **sweet** [*nichoach*] **savour** unto the LORD.

Leviticus 1:17: ...and the priest shall **burn** [as incense] it upon the altar, upon the wood that is upon the fire: it is a burnt sacrifice, an offering made by fire, of a **sweet** [*nichoach*] **savour** unto the LORD.

Both the meal and the peace offering were also burned as incense—*qatar*—upon the altar as a sweet savor unto the Lord.[5] Each time a sweet savor is mentioned in Leviticus 1-3, it is in close association with burning the offering as incense.

As we read previously, Aaron's actions with the incense halted the plague in Numbers 16. Also, the cloud of incense over the ark preserved the life of the high priest on the Day of Atonement. Hence, the sweet savor of incense functioned as intercession to God. In essence, these incense offerings were intercessory offerings unto God, which turned away wrath.

---

[5] Leviticus 2:2 "...and the priest shall **burn** [*qatar*, burn as incense] the memorial of it upon the altar, to be an offering made by fire, of a **sweet** [*nichoach*] **savour** unto the LORD:"
Leviticus 2:9: "And the priest shall take from the meat offering a memorial thereof, and shall **burn** [*qatar*, burn as incense] it upon the altar: it is an offering made by fire, of a **sweet** [*nichoach*] **savour** unto the LORD."
Leviticus 3:5: "And Aaron's sons shall **burn** [*qatar*, burn as incense] it on the altar upon the burnt sacrifice, which is upon the wood that is on the fire: it is an offering made by fire, of a **sweet** [*nichoach*] **savour** unto the LORD."
Leviticus 3:16: "And the priest shall **burn** [*qatar*, burn as incense] them upon the altar: it is the food of the offering made by fire for a **sweet** [*nichoach*] **savour**." Also in Exodus 29:18 and 25; 30:7, 8, 20.

The Sweet Savor Offerings

In light of this core characteristic of these offerings, what exactly does a "sweet savour" mean in the Hebrew language? To get a precise understanding, let's look at the first occurrence in Scripture of the term, "sweet savour."

> Genesis 8:20 and 21:
> And Noah built an altar unto the LORD; and took of every clean beast, and of every clean fowl, and offered burnt offerings on the altar.
> And the LORD smelled a sweet [*nichoach*] savour; and the LORD said in his heart, I will not again curse the ground any more for man's sake; for the imagination of man's heart is evil from his youth; neither will I again smite any more every thing living, as I have done.

After the flood, Noah sacrificed burnt offerings to God. Then it says for the first time in the Scriptures that God smelled this "sweet savour." As noted, the Hebrew word translated "sweet" is *nichoach* here and in Leviticus 1-3.

The Authorized King James Version has a marginal note on "sweet savour" that reflects the accuracy of the Hebrew text: "a savour of rest." *The New Brown Driver Briggs* lexicon agrees with this note, defining the Hebrew word for "sweet," *nichoach*, as quieting or soothing.[6] The *Gesenius* lexicon gives the definition of the word *nichoach* as "acquiescence." So as defined by the lexicons, a "sweet savour" is a fragrance of a soothing acquiescence or a quieting fragrance of rest.

In the Hebrew language, the word for "savour" means simply fragrance, smell or scent, while the word for "sweet" should be translated as quieting, soothing, or restful.

---

[6] Francis Brown, *The New Brown Driver Briggs Hebrew and English Lexicon*, 629.

A word related to *nichoach* occurs earlier in the chapter:

> Genesis 8:4:
> And the ark rested [*nuach*] in the seventh month, on the seventeenth day of the month, upon the mountains of Ararat.

Nuach, a related form of *nichoach*, is usually translated as "rest" in the Old Testament. This same Hebrew word is also used in rather puzzling prophecy in Isaiah, which we will consider briefly before returning to Genesis 8.

> Isaiah 28:11 and 12:
> For with stammering lips and another tongue will he speak to this people.
> To whom he said, This is the rest [*nuach*] wherewith ye may cause the weary to rest; and this is the refreshing: yet they would not hear.

God will speak to His people by means of languages or tongues that they will not understand. And then He says that these unknown tongues will be the place of rest where they will obtain rest and refreshing. How could God speaking to His people in an unintelligible language conceivably be "the rest?"

In our study of Isaiah 53, in chapter three of this book, we saw examples of prophecies containing sharp and puzzling contrasts. For example, how could the righteous servant of the Lord be "cut off from the land of the living" being made an offering for sin and then have his days prolonged?[7] This statement seems incomprehensible and impossible, yet this

---

[7] See Isaiah 53:8 and 10.

The Sweet Savor Offerings

prophecy was fulfilled when God raised Christ from the dead. His days were prolonged even though he had died.

In Isaiah 28 we have another puzzling statement which seems incomprehensible. How could being spoken to by God in an unintelligible language be a refreshing place of rest?

How this prophecy was fulfilled is explained in I Corinthians:

> I Corinthians 14:21 and 22:
> In the law it is written, With men of other tongues and other lips will I speak unto this people; and yet for all that will they not hear me, saith the Lord. Wherefore tongues are for a sign…

In I Corinthians 14, the rest in Isaiah 28 is described as speaking in tongues. Speaking in tongues is "the rest [*nuach*] wherewith ye may cause the weary to rest; and this is the refreshing." Rest is brought to the soul of the believer by speaking in tongues. The manifestation of the spirit which first came on the Day of Pentecost in Acts 2:1-4 would be how God would speak to His people bringing refreshing rest.

Returning to Genesis 8, we read in verse 21 where it states, "And the LORD smelled" this soothing fragrance of rest. Attributing to God a sense of smell is a vivid example of the figure of speech where God is ascribed human qualities or characteristics.[8] This figure called "condescension" draws attention to itself and intensifies the sense of the passage. The Scripture here emphasizes the pronounced impact of this sacrifice had on God. Smelling this fragrance of rest so

---

[8] E.W. Bullinger, *Figures of Speech Used in the Bible*, 871. Julia B. Hans, *Go Figure! An Introduction to Figures of Speech in the Bible*, 131-135.

JESUS CHRIST OUR COMPLETE OFFERING

touched God's heart that He said, "I will not again curse the ground any more for man's sake; for the imagination of man's heart is evil from his youth; neither will I again smite any more every thing living, as I have done." Here we see the great intercessory power these sweet savor offerings had.

The figure of speech, condescension, would apply to the sweet savor offerings of Leviticus 1-3 as well. Those sacrifices were called, "a sweet savour **unto** the LORD," suggesting that the calming fragrance of rest ascended up to God. These offerings of Leviticus 1-3 gave Israel an avenue of intercession before God.

Putting this all together we see that the burnt, meal and peace offerings were offered up to God as incense. They served as prayer and intercession with a fragrance of quiet acquiescence unto God.

Christ, Our Sweet Savor Offering

> Ephesians 5:2:
> And walk in love, as Christ also hath loved us, and hath given himself **for us** an offering and a sacrifice to God for a sweetsmelling savour.

The soothing fragrance of rest from the Levitical sacrifices looked forward to him who was to come, Jesus Christ. He would give himself for all humanity as the ultimate sweet savor sacrifice. His offering was a soothing fragrance of rest interceding to God, which turned away wrath.

In Ephesians 5:6, only four verses later, it speaks of, "…the wrath of God upon the children of disobedience." Having defined the function of the sweet savor offering, we see the precise contrast between verse 2 and verse 6. The wrath of

The Sweet Savor Offerings

God has been turned away by the intercessory offering of Christ.

Jesus Christ so loved that he gave himself as an offering of a soothing fragrance. Those sweet savor incense offerings of Leviticus 1-3, the burnt, meal and peace offerings, were just as much a foreshadowing of Christ as the sin and trespass sacrifices of Leviticus 4-6.

In fulfilling the *asham* or trespass offering, Christ restituted and restored all Adam had lost and more. In fulfilling the *chattath* or sin offering, all our sins and transgressions were laid upon him. Christ fully purified us and made us righteous. II Corinthians 5:21 declares that Christ was made, "to be sin [offering] **for us**, who knew no sin; that we might be made the righteousness of God in him."

The supreme sacrifice of Christ was not only an offering for trespasses and sins but also was for a "sweet savour." As a sweet savour offering, Jesus Christ was unto God something most precious and well-pleasing. He gave himself *for us* as a sacrifice to God: quieting, satisfying and soothing. The Son of God gave himself as an intercessory offering to God on our behalf.

Our Three-fold Intercession

The Old Testament believers, as strong in faith as they were at times, never had the complete salvation that Christ has wrought for us.

> Hebrews 7:25 and 26:
> Wherefore he is able also to save them to the uttermost that come unto God by him, seeing he ever liveth to make intercession **for them**.

JESUS CHRIST OUR COMPLETE OFFERING

> For such an high priest became us, who is holy, harmless, undefiled, separate from sinners, and made higher than the heavens;

Having given himself as a sacrifice on our behalf he now functions as the high priest. He ever lives at the right hand of God interceding for us. He is able to save them to the uttermost who approach God by him. Look at his ability at this very hour!

> Romans 8:34:
> Who is he that condemneth? *It is* Christ that died, yea rather, that is risen again, who is even at the right hand of God, who also maketh intercession **for us**.

Is Christ going to condemn us? He who died, rose again and is seated in the heavenlies at God's right hand will not condemn or accuse us! Rather, as the high priest, he intercedes to God on our behalf.

Since the Day of Pentecost in Acts 2, our Lord Jesus Christ functions as both intercessory sacrifice to God and an interceding high priest before God. The sacrificial price has been paid and now we have an active agent at the right hand of God. What grace and glory we should manifest in our lives! The impediments and any blockage between us and God have been swept aside. Any gnawing sense of guilt and regret over our sins and inadequacies should be replaced with relief and thankfulness and joy. Christ, our complete savior, has interceded as a sacrifice and continues to intercede as a high priest.

Romans 8 speaks of an additional aspect of intercession available to the believer:

The Sweet Savor Offerings

> Romans 8:26-28:
> Likewise the Spirit also helpeth our infirmities: for we know not what we should pray for as we ought: but the Spirit itself maketh intercession **for us** with groanings which cannot be uttered.
> And he that searcheth the hearts knoweth what is the mind of the Spirit, because he maketh intercession for the saints according to the will of God.
> And we know that all things work together for good to them that love God, to them who are the called according to his purpose.

Verse 26 tells us: "…the Spirit itself maketh intercession for us with groanings which cannot be uttered." When we pray in the spirit we can make intercession: for ourselves, others, and specific challenges or situations. What a privilege has been provided in this avenue of prayer! What rest and rejuvenation we can enjoy!

We have noted three remarkable aspects of intercession: Christ as an intercessory sacrifice, Christ as high priest at the right hand of God making intercession, and our ability and privilege to intercede by the spirit.[9]

Three aspects of intercession for us:

Christ as an intercessory sacrifice: Ephesians 5:2
Christ as high priest making intercession:
    Romans 8:34; Hebrews 7:25
The spirit making intercession: Romans 8:26-28

---

[9] Prayer by the spirit is defined in I Corinthians 14:13-15.

JESUS CHRIST OUR COMPLETE OFFERING

The Old Testament believers never had these resources available to them. They lacked these three facets of intercession before God. Truly we have complete salvation as well as complete intercession!

The frailties and the disappointments in the lives of Christians may appear at times. Yet we see in God's Word that which God has facilitated for us in Christ is more evident and powerful. The utter completeness of what God has accomplished for us in Christ is marvelous to behold.

Chapter 10

The Peace Offering

We have noted that the trespass offering had as the distinguishing characteristic the issue of restitution and an accompanying payment. With the sin offering, we observed that the signature trait was the function of purification. In our consideration of the peace offering, which was one of the sweet savour offerings, we will look for that one dominant characteristic that distinguishes this sacrifice from all others.

As we examine the most distinctive feature of each offering, an exact correspondence to Christ's offering comes into clear focus. Rather than engaging narrow issues of speculative typology, we intend to garner the most prominent attribute of each offering and see how it exhibited a pattern of the good things to come.

> Isaiah 53:4 and 5:
> Surely he hath borne our griefs [sickness], and carried our sorrows [pains]: yet we did esteem him stricken, smitten of God, and afflicted.
> But he was wounded for our transgressions, he was bruised for our iniquities: **the chastisement of our**

JESUS CHRIST OUR COMPLETE OFFERING

> **peace was upon him;** and with his stripes we are healed.

The phrase highlighted in bold print could be translated: "...the punishment that procured [obtained] our peace was upon him..."[1] As our substitute, this righteous servant of Jehovah bore the punishment that was rightfully ours. He took upon himself the reproach of sin so peace could be secured for us. By Christ's sacrifice, we have peace WITH God as well as the peace OF God that surpasses all understanding.[2] The Old Testament peace offering looked forward to the good things to come and has much to teach us.

> Leviticus 3:1-5:
> And if his oblation [offering] be a sacrifice of peace offering, if he offer it **of the herd**;[3] whether it be a male or female, he shall offer it without blemish before the LORD.
> And he shall lay his hand upon the head of his offering, and kill it at the door of the tabernacle of the congregation: and Aaron's sons the priests shall sprinkle the blood upon the altar round about.
> And he shall offer of the sacrifice of the peace offering an offering made by fire unto the LORD; the fat that covereth the inwards [entrails], and all the fat that is upon the inwards,
> And the two kidneys, and the fat that is on them, which is by the flanks [loins], and the caul [lobe] above the liver, with the kidneys, it shall he take away.

---

[1] Edward Young, *The Book of Isaiah Volume III* (Grand Rapids, MI: Eerdmans, 1999) 348. Also noted in *The Companion Bible*.
[2] Philippians 4:7: "And the peace of God, which passeth all understanding, shall keep your hearts and minds through Christ Jesus."
[3] "Of the herd" refers to cattle. Allen Ross, *Holiness to the Lord*, 113.

The Peace Offering

And Aaron's sons shall burn [*qatar*] it on the altar upon the burnt sacrifice, which is upon the wood that is on the fire: it is an offering made by fire, of a sweet savour unto the LORD.

A peace offering could be "of the herd," either male or female, without blemish. The Israelite would place his hand on the peace offering which symbolized identification or a full sharing with that offering. As we saw with the scapegoat of Leviticus 16, this gesture of laying the hand on the head of a sacrificial animal signified a transfer of the sin of the offerer onto an innocent sacrifice. The offering then shared fully in sin and the consequence of sin, death, looking forward to the identification we would have with Christ. This chapter is significantly more than an instruction booklet from antiquity on butchering animals.

Next the sacrifice was killed and its blood was sprinkled around the altar. Verses 3 and 4 give specific instructions on which part of the animal was to be burned on the altar. The peace offering was to be butchered in such a way that the fat of the animal was to be removed and burned as incense upon the altar. This fat from the sacrifice was censed, a soothing fragrance of rest unto the Lord. However, the passage does not say what was to be done with the rest of the sacrifice.

> Verses 7-11:
> If he offer **a lamb** for his offering, then shall he offer it before the LORD.
> And he shall lay his hand upon the head of his offering, and kill it before the tabernacle of the congregation: and Aaron's sons shall sprinkle the blood thereof round about upon the altar.
> And he shall offer of the sacrifice of the peace offering an offering made by fire unto the LORD; the fat

JESUS CHRIST OUR COMPLETE OFFERING

thereof, and the whole rump [tail[4]], it shall he take off hard by the backbone; and the fat that covereth the inwards, and all the fat that is upon the inwards,
And the two kidneys, and the fat that is upon them, which is by the flanks, and the caul above the liver, with the kidneys, it shall he take away.
And the priest shall burn [*qatar*] it upon the altar: it is the food of the offering made by fire unto the LORD.

When a lamb was presented as a peace offering the same procedure was followed. Verses 9 and 10 also give detailed directions on separating the fat from the animal. The tail was to be removed completely and the fat that covered the entrails, kidneys and around the liver was detached. The fat was then to be censed on the altar as "food of the offering made by fire unto the Lord." Again, there is no indication on what is to be done with the remainder of the carcass.

Verse 12-15:
And if his offering be **a goat**, then he shall offer it before the LORD.
And he shall lay his hand upon the head of it, and kill it before the tabernacle of the congregation: and the sons of Aaron shall sprinkle the blood thereof upon the altar round about.
And he shall offer thereof his offering, even an offering made by fire unto the LORD; the fat that covereth the inwards, and all the fat that is upon the inwards,
And the two kidneys, and the fat that is upon them, which is by the flanks, and the caul above the liver, with the kidneys, it shall he take away.

---

[4] The sheep of Palestine were often "broad-tailed." These tails of these sheep needed special care, growing to 18 inches across and weighing from 15 to as much 50 pounds, the tails being a "mere excrescense" of fat. Jacob Milgrom, *The Anchor Bible Leviticus 1-16*, 211-222, quoting Herodotus and E. Robinson.

The Peace Offering

Once again, special attention was given to how the fat of the animal is to be stripped off and burned on the altar. As we considered in the study of the sin offering, this particular process was carried out on the fat of that sacrifice as well. While the body of the sin offering was to be burned outside the camp in a clean place, the fat of the sin offering as well as the peace offering was to be removed and censed on the altar.[5]

The last two verses of the chapter explain further the significance of fat:

> Verses 16 and 17:
> And the priest shall burn [*qatar*] them upon the altar: it is the food of the offering made by fire for a sweet savour: all the fat is the LORD'S.
> It shall be a perpetual statute for your generations throughout all your dwellings, that ye eat neither fat nor blood.

Verse 15 attests that "all the fat is the LORD'S." All the fat of a sacrifice belonged to the Lord. Leviticus 3 says nothing about what is to be done with the rest of the animal, only the fat. The fat of the sacrifice was to be censed upon the altar, as fragrance of rest and quiet acquiescence unto the Lord.

Only the Best for God: Censing the Fat on the Altar

In the lands and times of the Bible, the fat of an animal was considered the most desirable part of the animal. In our society, today we may eat too much fat or the wrong kind of

---

[5] Leviticus 4:8-10, 19, 26, 31, 35.

JESUS CHRIST OUR COMPLETE OFFERING

fat. However in Bible times, the fat was the best and the choicest portion.

The fat of the sacrifice burned as incense on the altar unto the Lord was considered the most excellent part. In fact, the word for fat in Hebrew is occasionally translated as "finest" or "best."

> Psalm 81:16:
> He should have fed them also with the finest [fat] of the wheat: and with honey out of the rock should I have satisfied thee.

> Numbers 18:12:
> All the best [fat] of the oil, and all the best [fat] of the wine, and of the wheat, the firstfruits of them which they shall offer unto the LORD, them have I given thee.

The "fat of the oil" and the "fat of the wine" were the best portions. Only the best was to be offered to God. With Abel's offering in Genesis 4:4, he presented "the firstlings of his flock and of the fat thereof. And the LORD had respect unto Abel and to his offering." Cain's offering was merely "the fruit of the ground," and was not accepted by God. Abel presented the best, the choicest portions, the firstlings and the fat, as well as the shed blood of a sacrifice. (See Appendix Four).

The issue of burning the fat of the offering came up with the wicked sons of Eli. I Samuel 2 records that they disregarded this command of God that all the fat was to be burned *first* unto the Lord. They would not burn the fat on the altar until

The Peace Offering

they received their portion.[6] This violation caused the people to "abhor the offering of the Lord."

The fat portion of the offering points to Christ. The best, "the choice," of all humanity was the Lord Jesus Christ. He was a perfect man, the only begotten Son of God. The very best of all humanity was sacrificed on our behalf as a soothing fragrance of rest to God.

Sharing Fully in the Peace Offering

Leviticus 3 is not a full explanation of the peace offering. This chapter only addresses the Lord's portion of the peace offering—the fat of the sacrifice. Leviticus 3 does not give instructions on what was to be done with the rest of the offering. This chapter only details the portion that the Lord was to receive, the fat of the animal. The chapter is summed up by Leviticus 3:16: "all the fat is the Lord's." The best portion was for the Lord, meaning it was burned up on the altar as incense.

> Leviticus 7:29-34:
> Speak unto the children of Israel, saying, He that offereth the sacrifice of his peace offerings unto the LORD shall bring his oblation unto the LORD of the sacrifice of his peace offerings.
> His own hands shall bring the offerings of the LORD made by fire, the fat with the breast, it shall he bring, that the breast may be waved *for* a wave offering before the LORD.

---

[6] I Samuel 2:16 and 17: "And if any man said unto him [the priest's servant], Let them not fail to burn the fat presently, and then take as much as thy soul desireth; then he would answer him, Nay; but thou shalt give it me now: and if not, I will take it by force. Wherefore the sin of the young men was very great before the LORD: for men abhorred the offering of the LORD."

JESUS CHRIST OUR COMPLETE OFFERING

> And the priest shall burn [*qatar*] the fat upon the altar [the Lord's portion]: but the breast shall be Aaron's and his sons'.
> And the right shoulder shall ye give unto the priest *for* an heave offering of the sacrifices of your peace offerings.
> He among the sons of Aaron, that offereth the blood of the peace offerings, and the fat, shall have the right shoulder for *his* part.
> For the wave breast and the heave shoulder have I taken of the children of Israel from off the sacrifices of their peace offerings, and have given them unto Aaron the priest and unto his sons by a statute for ever from among the children of Israel.

The priest's portion of the peace offering was the breast and the right shoulder of the animal. These were given to the priests to eat. The "wave breast and the heave shoulder" meant that these portions have been transferred to God and now belonged to Him. Therefore, this portion was given to the priests.[7]

Since the fat from the animal was the Lord's portion and the priest received the breast and the right shoulder: What was done with the rest of the animal?

> Leviticus 19:5 and 6:
> And if ye offer a sacrifice of peace offerings unto the LORD, ye shall offer it at your own will.
> It shall be eaten the same day ye offer it, and on the morrow: and if ought remain until the third day, it shall be burnt in the fire.

---

[7] In chapter 14, on the wave offering we will see that waving and heaving have similar meanings, signifying a change of ownership. Once the breast was waved and the shoulder was heaved, these portions legally belonged to God and were the priest's to eat.

The Peace Offering

Verse 6 states that "it shall be eaten the same day ye offer it." The rest of the peace offering was given back to be eaten by those presenting the sacrifice.

> Deuteronomy 27:7:
> And thou shalt offer peace offerings, and shalt eat there, and rejoice before the LORD thy God.

When the remainder of the animal was given back to the offerer, he and his family and friends could eat the rest of the peace offering. Since the meat would spoil quickly and the animal was more than one person could eat, the peace offering usually involved a sacrificial meal. The family and friends of the offerer would be invited to partake of the peace offering together. They fellowshipped together, in communion with each other as they ate the offering. Sharing a fellowship meal around the peace offerings was to be a time of joy and feasting. In fact, the *New International Version* translates the Hebrew word for peace offering, *shelem*, as "fellowship offering."[8]

> Leviticus 2:13:
> And every oblation [offering] of thy meat [meal] offering shalt thou season with salt; neither shalt thou suffer the salt of the covenant of thy God to be lacking

---

[8] *The New English Bible* translates peace offering as "shared-offering;" *New Revised Standard* as "well being offering;" *Amplified* and *New American Standard* as *Authorized King James* stick with "peace offering." Hebrew scholars are not clear on the translation of *shelem*: "…the supposed basic meaning 'totality' has usually been adduced: full sacrifice, community sacrifice, concluding sacrifice, or also proceeding from "peace," the 'sacrifice of well-being'." Quote from: Ernest Jenni and Claus Westermann, *Theological Lexicon of the Old Testament* (Peabody, Mass: Hendrickson, 1997) 1345.
If *shelem* carries the sense of **"totality,"** in this offering we have a foreshadowing of the utter totality and full completeness of Christ sacrifice.

from thy meat [meal] offering: with all thine offerings thou shalt offer salt.

Chapter 2 states that "the salt of the covenant of thy God" was not to be left out of the meal offering. After that it says that "with all thine offerings thou shalt offer salt." Mark 9:49 also mentions that "every sacrifice shall be salted with salt." Under the Law every sacrifice was to be salted.

Adding salt to offerings was a form of covenant making. Each time these salted offerings were presented, the salt covenant was once again made with God. A covenant of salt indicated a lifelong promise of loyalty. These offerings were to be made with a heart of commitment and dedication to God.[9] With the peace offering, salt would have been shared between God, the priests and the people forming an indissoluble bond of allegiance.

The distinguishing characteristic of the peace offering was that a major part of the offering was given back to the offerer to eat. No other offering presented at the altar was permitted to be eaten by the Israelites.

---

[9] K. C. Pillai, *Light through an Eastern Window* (New York: Robert Speller, 1976) 24. Milgrom says salt sealed a covenant. With ancient Greeks as well as Arabs eating salt was "equivalent to an indissoluble covenant." (Numbers 18:19; II Chronicles 13:5) Jacob Milgrom, *The Anchor Bible Leviticus 1-16*, 191. According to Josephus (Ant. iii. 9,1) every sacrifice was salted. C.F. Keil and R. Delitzsch, *Commentary on the Old Testament*, translated from the German by James Martin (Grand Rapids, Michigan: Eeerdmans, reprinted 1986) Volume II, 295. Psalm 50:5 mentions a covenant made by sacrifice.

The Peace Offering

The Three Portions of the Peace Offering

1. The Lord's: The fat
2. The Priest's: The breast and the right shoulder
3. The Offerer's: The remainder

Three Varieties of the Peace Offering

As the following passage indicates, the peace offering was to be eaten by the Israelites. As Leviticus 7:19 concludes, "...and as for the flesh, all that be clean shall eat thereof." These verses also give three occasions for presenting the peace offering.

> Leviticus 7:11-19:
> And this is the law of the sacrifice of peace offerings, which he shall offer unto the LORD.
> If he offer it for a thanksgiving, then he shall offer with **the sacrifice of thanksgiving** unleavened cakes mingled with oil, and unleavened wafers anointed with oil, and cakes mingled with oil, of fine flour, fried.
> Besides the cakes, he shall offer for his offering leavened bread with the sacrifice of thanksgiving of his peace offerings.
> And of it he shall offer one out of the whole oblation for an heave offering unto the LORD, and it shall be the priest's that sprinkleth the blood of the peace offerings.

JESUS CHRIST OUR COMPLETE OFFERING

> And the flesh of the sacrifice of his peace offerings for thanksgiving shall be eaten the same day that it is offered; he shall not leave any of it until the morning.
>
> But if the sacrifice of his offering be **a vow, or a voluntary offering,** it shall be eaten the same day that he offereth his sacrifice: and on the morrow also the remainder of it shall be eaten:
>
> But the remainder of the flesh of the sacrifice on the third day shall be burnt with fire.
>
> And if any of the flesh of the sacrifice of his peace offerings be eaten at all on the third day, it shall not be accepted, neither shall it be imputed unto him that offereth it: it shall be an abomination, and the soul that eateth of it shall bear his iniquity.
>
> And the flesh that toucheth any unclean thing shall not be eaten; it shall be burnt with fire: and as for the flesh, all that be clean shall eat thereof.

This passage states the three possible varieties of the peace offering. The thanksgiving offering is to praise or thank God for His blessings in verses 12-15. Besides the sacrificial animal, bread was also to be offered.

Verse 16 mentions two other reasons for a peace offering: "But if the sacrifice of his offering *be* a vow, or a voluntary [freewill] offering..." A peace offering could involve a vow or a freewill desire to sacrifice an animal to the Lord. The vow offering was brought to fulfill a special promise to God or following the successful fulfillment of a vow.[10]

The voluntary or freewill offering suggests that it was given freely, spontaneously, with a willing mind.[11] The freewill

---

[10] Leviticus 22:21: "And whosoever offereth a sacrifice of peace offerings unto the LORD to accomplish his vow..." Numbers 15:8, I Samuel 1:21, Proverbs 7:14.

[11] *Gesenius' Hebrew and Chaldee Lexicon*, 534.

The Peace Offering

offering was not limited to a peace offering but could also be gifts or money (Exodus 35:29; Ezra 8:28).

> **Varieties of the Peace Offering:**
> -Thanksgiving
> -Completion of a vow
> -Freewill offering

In each case, the motivation for offering a sacrifice unto the Lord was to be free and voluntary.

Joy and Thanksgiving Accompanying the Peace Offering

As we read in Deuteronomy 27:7, the eating of the peace offering was to be accompanied by rejoicing: "And thou shalt offer peace offerings, and shalt eat there, and rejoice before the LORD thy God."

> Psalm 107:22:
> And let them sacrifice the sacrifices of thanksgiving, and declare his works with rejoicing.

Presenting sacrifices to God was not supposed to be an empty ritual. The "sacrifices of thanksgiving," the peace offerings, were to be offered as God's wonderful works were declared with rejoicing.

> I Samuel 11:15:
> And all the people went to Gilgal; and there they made Saul king before the LORD in Gilgal; and there they sacrificed sacrifices of peace offerings before the LORD; and there Saul and all the men of Israel rejoiced greatly.

JESUS CHRIST OUR COMPLETE OFFERING

This record from Samuel mentions great jubilation associated with the peace offering. They rejoiced greatly.

> Jeremiah 33:11:
> The voice of joy, and the voice of gladness, the voice of the bridegroom, and the voice of the bride, the voice of them that shall say, Praise the LORD of hosts: for the LORD is good; for his mercy endureth for ever: and of them that shall bring the sacrifice of praise [thanksgiving] into the house of the LORD. For I will cause to return the captivity of the land, as at the first, saith the LORD.

Jeremiah prophesied of a time to come when the voice of joy and gladness will be proclaimed by those presenting the sacrifice of thanksgiving in the temple.

The following record speaks of the reign of Hezekiah, some six centuries before Christ. Then, the people saw one of the notable true revivals of the Old Covenant revelation accompanied by restoration of temple worship, the active priesthood, and sacrifices. The following record gives further insight into the peace offering.

> II Chronicles 29:1-8:
> Hezekiah began to reign when he was five and twenty years old, and he reigned nine and twenty years in Jerusalem. And his mother's name was Abijah, the daughter of Zechariah.
> And he did that which was right in the sight of the LORD, according to all that David his father had done.
> He in the first year of his reign, in the first month, opened the doors of the house of the LORD, and repaired them.

The Peace Offering

> And he brought in the priests and the Levites, and gathered them together into the east street,
> And said unto them, Hear me, ye Levites, sanctify now yourselves, and sanctify the house of the LORD God of your fathers, and carry forth the filthiness out of the holy place.
> For our fathers have trespassed, and done that which was evil in the eyes of the LORD our God, and have forsaken him, and have turned away their faces from the habitation of the LORD [the temple], and turned their backs.
> Also they have shut up the doors of the porch, and put out the lamps, and have not burned incense nor offered burnt offerings in the holy place unto the God of Israel.
> Wherefore the wrath of the LORD was upon Judah and Jerusalem, and he hath delivered them to trouble, to astonishment, and to hissing, as ye see with your eyes.

In the first year of Hezekiah's reign, this new king launched a restoration of temple worship. Previously, the gates of the house of the Lord had been closed, the lamps had extinguished, incense was not offered as mandated by the Law and the burnt offerings were not presented.[12] The duties of the priests and Levites had been ignored so this good king brought them together and had the temple restored to order.[13]

---

[12] The wicked King Ahaz, Hezekiah's father, contributed to this state of disrepair of the temple: "And Ahaz gathered together the vessels of the house of God, and cut in pieces the vessels of the house of God, and shut up the doors of the house of the LORD, and he made him altars in every corner of Jerusalem." II Chronicles 28:24.

[13] Every priest was a Levite, of the tribe of Levi. Yet not every Levite was a priest. The priests were descended from Aaron, who was from the tribe of Levi.

JESUS CHRIST OUR COMPLETE OFFERING

> II Chronicles 29:30 and 31:
> Moreover Hezekiah the king and the princes commanded the Levites to sing praise unto the LORD with the words of David, and of Asaph the seer. And they **sang praises with gladness**, and they bowed their heads and worshipped.
> Then Hezekiah answered and said, Now ye have consecrated yourselves unto the LORD, come near and bring sacrifices and **thank offerings** into the house of the LORD. And the congregation brought in sacrifices and **thank offerings**; and as many as were of a free heart burnt offerings.

The Levites took heed to Hezekiah's commands and set about to reestablish temple worship. The Levites sang praises with joy from the psalms of David and of Asaph. Then the congregation brought in "sacrifices and thank offerings." As we observed from Leviticus, a thank offering was a peace offering where the carcass was returned to the priests and the people to eat after the fat was burned on the altar. However, the burnt offerings were completely burned on the altar.

Here again, in these verses, we see the sacrificing of the peace offerings associated with joy. Sacrifices of thanksgiving were offered as they declared God's wonderful works with rejoicing.

> Verses 35 and 36:
> And also the burnt offerings were in abundance, with the fat of the peace offerings, and the drink offerings for every burnt offering. So the service of the house of the LORD was set in order [prepared].

The Peace Offering

> And Hezekiah rejoiced, and all the people, that God had prepared the people: for the thing was done suddenly.

In this wonderful resurgence of God's Word, it mentions "the fat of the peace offerings." The fat of the peace offerings were burned as incense on the altar, while the rest of the animal was given to the priests and the offerers to eat.

In context of these offerings: "Hezekiah rejoiced, and all the people..." Joy and exultation was the correct heart and attitude to offer sacrifices of peace offerings.

> II Chronicles 30:1-3:
> And Hezekiah sent to all Israel and Judah, and wrote letters also to Ephraim and Manasseh, that they should come to the house of the LORD at Jerusalem, to keep the passover unto the LORD God of Israel.
> For the king had taken counsel, and his princes, and all the congregation in Jerusalem, to keep the passover in the second month.
> For they could not keep it at that time, because the priests had not sanctified themselves sufficiently, neither had the people gathered themselves together to Jerusalem.

Hezekiah wrote letters to the northern tribes of Ephraim and Manasseh with "all Israel and Judah" inviting them to come to Jerusalem for the Passover. Centuries prior the kingdom of Israel had fractured in two. The ten northern tribes had divided off from Judah in the south with the capital at Jerusalem. In spite of this division, Hezekiah asked those of the northern tribes to attend the Passover.

JESUS CHRIST OUR COMPLETE OFFERING

While it is clearly commanded in the Law of Moses that the Passover was to be offered in the first month, here, by the grace of God, it was done on the second month.[14]

> Verse 18-20:
> For a multitude of the people, even many of Ephraim, and Manasseh, Issachar, and Zebulun, had not cleansed themselves, yet did they eat the passover otherwise than it was written. But Hezekiah prayed for them, saying, The good LORD pardon every one
> That prepareth his heart to seek God, the LORD God of his fathers, though he be not cleansed according to the purification of the sanctuary.
> And the LORD hearkened to Hezekiah, and healed the people.

Many from the north had not properly cleansed themselves in preparation for eating the Passover meal. Yet by way of Hezekiah's prayer, they were pardoned. God heard the intercession of the king and they ate the Passover and were healed. Even in this period of the Law, God's mercy abounded!

> Verses 21-23:
> And the children of Israel that were present at Jerusalem kept the feast of unleavened bread seven days with **great gladness**: and the Levites and the priests praised the LORD day by day, singing with loud instruments unto the LORD.
> And Hezekiah spake comfortably unto all the Levites that taught the good knowledge of the LORD: and

---

[14] Exodus 12:2 and 3 stated the Passover to be carried out in the first month. However, Numbers 9:6-11 provided for Passover in the second month for individuals for uncleanness due to contact with the dead or a "journey afar off." The second month exception of Numbers 9 says nothing about priests being unprepared.

The Peace Offering

> they did eat throughout the feast seven days, **offering peace offerings**, and making confession to the LORD God of their fathers.
> And the whole assembly took counsel to keep other seven days: and they kept other seven days with **gladness.**

Following the Passover meal, the Law mandated the seven day Feast of Unleavened Bread. They kept this feast with "great gladness," singing praises to God, offering peace offerings and making confession unto God.[15]

Verse 22 mentions "...the Levites that taught the good knowledge of the LORD." Here we have a small phrase with immense significance. One of the original functions of the priests and Levites was to teach the Scriptures to the children of Israel.[16] In this revival, the Word of God was once again being set forth to God's people.

While celebrating this special and unorthodox Passover and the Feast of Unleavened Bread, the assembly also decided to extend the feast for an additional week. The Law made no provision for attaching an extra week to the feast, but having such a merry time, they decided to prolong the occasion.

This was indeed a momentous event. The kingdom of Israel after David and Solomon had been fractured for centuries. But now, tribes that had been at enmity sat down and ate together. They ate the Passover meal and now they shared in the peace offerings and received God's pardon and healing.

---

[15] They offered sacrifices and kept the feast with the right heart and true believing. The prophet, Isaiah, from this time period, in all likelihood, attended this event. He had spoken of the wrong way to keep the feasts and offer sacrifices in Isaiah 1:11-19.

[16] Leviticus 10:11; Deuteronomy 17:11; 24:8.

JESUS CHRIST OUR COMPLETE OFFERING

> Verses 24-27:
> For Hezekiah king of Judah did give to the congregation a thousand bullocks and seven thousand sheep; and the princes gave to the congregation a thousand bullocks and ten thousand sheep: and a great number of priests sanctified themselves.
> And all the congregation of Judah, with the priests and the Levites, and all the congregation that came out of Israel, and the strangers that came out of the land of Israel, and that dwelt in Judah, **rejoiced**.
> So there was **great joy** in Jerusalem: for since the time of Solomon the son of David king of Israel there was not the like in Jerusalem.
> Then the priests the Levites arose and blessed the people: and their voice was heard, and their prayer came up to his holy dwelling place, even unto heaven.

They were unprepared and a month late for the Passover. They had not cleansed themselves and then they added an extra week onto the feast. Yet their voice was heard by God "and their prayer came up to his holy dwelling place, even unto heaven." This is indeed an overwhelming endorsement.

While the letter of the Law was not followed flawlessly, the Israelites had a heart of joy and thanksgiving. This great congregation was both pardoned and healed. They sang praises to God, offered peace offerings and made confession to God. Their voices carried into the very inner sanctum of heaven! This high point of the triumphant celebration had not been seen in Jerusalem for about three centuries: "since the time of Solomon."

The Peace Offering

Sacrifices of Thanksgiving in the New Testament

The New Testament has a remarkable parallel to "sacrifices of thanksgiving" in the Old Testament.

> Hebrews 13:15 and 16:
> By him therefore let us offer the sacrifice of praise to God continually, that is, the fruit of our lips giving thanks to his name.
> But to do good and to communicate[17] forget not: for with such sacrifices God is well pleased.

The Word of God tells us that we are to continually offer the sacrifice of praise to God: "the fruit of our lips giving thanks to his name." Our "sacrifices" are not the fruits of the ground or the firstlings of our herds, but the adoration of our hearts and the devotion of our lives.

The sacrifices of praise and thanks we offer harkens back to that one sacrifice of the Law that could be a sacrifice of praise and thanksgiving — the peace offering.

I Corinthians mentions an avenue to "give thanks well:"

> I Corinthians 14:14-18:
> For if I pray in an unknown tongue, my spirit prayeth, but my understanding is unfruitful.
> What is it then? I will pray with the spirit, and I will pray with the understanding also: I will sing with the spirit, and I will sing with the understanding also.

---

[17] In the phrase, "do good and to communicate," "communicate" is the Greek, *koinōnia*, usually translated as "fellowship." This word can refer to financial giving as well, as in: Romans 12:13, 15:26; Philippians 4:15; Galatians 6:6; II Corinthians 8:4 and 9:13. Philippians 4:18 also describes giving as a sacrifice.

JESUS CHRIST OUR COMPLETE OFFERING

> Else when thou shalt bless with the spirit, how shall he that occupieth the room of the unlearned say Amen at thy **giving of thanks**, seeing he understandeth not what thou sayest?
> For thou verily **givest thanks well**, but the other is not edified.
> I thank my God, I speak with tongues more than ye all:

Verse 17 says of speaking in tongues, "thou verily givest thanks well." Paul goes on to say that "I speak with tongues more than ye all." However, he did not speak in tongues aloud in the church unless he interpreted.[18] Since the Day of Pentecost we have a profound new way to "offer the sacrifice of praise to God continually." We can pray and sing in the spirit.

The Significance of the Eating Sacrifices

To eat sacrifices seems strange to our Western minds. What conceivable connection or relevance does eating a sacrificial animal have to us as readers of the New Testament today? However, understanding this significance goes far beyond another tidbit of Levitical information or some minor typological point.

The characteristic of the peace offering that distinguished it from the other offerings of Leviticus 1-7 was that a portion of the offering was given back to the offerer to eat. As we have considered with the trespass and sin offering, no portion of these offerings were ever eaten by the one presenting the sacrifice. As we shall see in future chapters, none of the

---

[18] I Corinthians 14:13: "Wherefore let him that speaketh in an unknown tongue pray that he may interpret."

The Peace Offering

burnt offering or the meal offering was returned to the offerer to eat.[19]

Since the unique attribute of the peace offering was that a major part of the sacrificed animal was returned to the Israelite, the focal question is: what does eating of the sacrifice signify? When the offerer and his family and friends sat down to eat and fellowship around this sacrificial meal, what did it represent?

Surprisingly, a verse in I Corinthians gives the answer:

> I Corinthians 10:18:
> Behold Israel after the flesh: are not they which eat of the sacrifices partakers [*koinōnos*] of the altar?

First, let's look at this verse in light of what we know about the peace offering. It mentions "Israel after the flesh" eating sacrifices of the altar. While the Passover offering was eaten by the offerer and his household, it was not presented to the priest before the altar. Also, the priests ate of the various sacrifices, but verse 18 is speaking of Israel, not of Aaronic priests or the Levites. So this verse could only be speaking of the peace offering.

The first word of the verse, "behold" is quite notable in the context of our study of sacrifices. The verb for "behold" in the Greek is in the imperative, expressing a command or an entreaty. Here in the New Testament, God tells us to look at how those "...which eat of the sacrifices" are "partakers of the altar." This verse certainly provides a sound rationale for our study of the peace offering.

---

[19] The Passover sacrifice was eaten by the Israelites in accordance with Exodus 12, but it was **not** sacrificed on the altar before the tabernacle.

JESUS CHRIST OUR COMPLETE OFFERING

Koinōnos is related to the Greek word, *koinōnia,* meaning to "share fully" or "fellowship." The second phrase of verse 18 is a rhetorical question: "...are not they which eat of the sacrifices partakers [*koinōnos*] of the altar?" Yes indeed, those who ate sacrifices did share fully with the altar. The altar represented the sacrifices offered on it. Those who ate of the sacrifices shared fully with those sacrifices. To eat the sacrifice was to have a union with that sacrifice and the God or gods it was offered to. The intent of eating a sacrifice was to identify, to fully share with what that sacrifice represented. As I Corinthians 10:18 states, "they which eat of the sacrifices" share fully. That was the significance of eating a sacrifice.

We read earlier in Leviticus 2:13 that salt was an integral part of the offerings.[20] This verse also told us what it was for: "the salt of the covenant of thy God." Offering and eating a salted sacrifice signified an unbreakable covenant of lifetime allegiance to God. Therefore this fellowship at the altar had an even deeper meaning in that they were salted together with God by eating of the meat.

The following record in Psalms also suggests that those who ate of the sacrifices shared fully with those sacrifices.

> Psalm 106:28:
> They joined themselves also unto Baalpeor, and ate the sacrifices of the dead [lifeless gods[21]].

They were united to Baalpeor, (a form of Baal) when they ate its sacrifices. By eating the sacrifices they fully shared in what that sacrifice represented, a union with the god it was

---

[20] Leviticus 2:13: "...neither shalt thou suffer the salt of the covenant of thy God to be lacking from thy meat offering: with all thine offerings thou shalt offer salt."
[21] *New International Version.*

The Peace Offering

offered to. By eating of these sacrifices it also suggests they made an unbreakable salt covenant with these gods.

Numbers records the same event:

> Numbers 25:1-3:
> And Israel abode in Shittim, and the people began to commit whoredom with the daughters of Moab.
> And they called the people unto the sacrifices of their gods: and the people did eat, and bowed down to their gods.
> And Israel joined himself unto Baalpeor: and the anger of the LORD was kindled against Israel.

When verse 2 says "...and the people did eat," we know from Psalm 106:28 that they ate the sacrifices. By eating the sacrifices and bowing down to those gods, they joined themselves to the devil god, Baal.

In the Bible times, it was understood that when one ingested a sacrifice it was more than simply eating physical food. There was an identification and spiritual union involved. In consuming the sacrifices, there was a full communion with the one the sacrifices were offered to.[22]

---

[22] There is evidence in other sources (outside the Scriptures) that eating the sacrifices was commonly understood in ancient times to signify a full sharing or identifying with the idol:
The original significance of the eating of a sacred animal [which had been sacrificed] in the Phrygian cults [religious system] was that "it was believed that thus there took place an identification with the god himself, together with a participation in his substance and qualities." F. Cumont
Sacred meals played an important part in the Mysteries [of pagan religion] as sacraments of union with the deity...
An inscription from Kos has preserved and interesting ritual: "Aristides tells how the worshippers of Serapis [an idol] **partake in the full communion** with him by 'inviting him to the hearth as guest and host.' [emphasis added]
S. Angus, *The Mystery Religions: A Study in the Religious Background of Early Christianity* (New York: Dover, 1975) 128, 129. (Originally published under the title, *The Mystery Religions and Christianity* in 1925).

JESUS CHRIST OUR COMPLETE OFFERING

Let's look I Corinthians 10:18 along with the verses following:

> I Corinthians 10:18-21:
> Behold Israel after the flesh: are not they which eat of the sacrifices partakers [*koinōnos*] of the altar?
> What say I then? that the idol is any thing, or that which is offered in sacrifice to idols is any thing?
> But I *say*, that the things which the Gentiles sacrifice, they sacrifice to devils, and not to God: and I would not that ye should have fellowship [*koinōnia*] with devils.
> Ye cannot drink the cup of the Lord, and the cup of devils: ye cannot be partakers of the Lord's table, and of the table of devils.

Here, the Apostle Paul presents what occurs when the Gentiles sacrificed to their idols: "…the things which the Gentiles sacrifice, they sacrifice to devils, and not to God." These sacrifices were offered to devil spirits represented by the idols. Also in verse 20, to eat and drink these sacrifices offered to devil spirits symbolized a full sharing [*koinōnia*]. Hence, the intent of eating and drinking these sacrifices was to identify, to share with these idols, or—as the Apostle candidly says—devils.[23]

Among the believers at Corinth, there was a concern that eating meat sacrificed to idols was a sin because of its identification with those idols.

---

[23] In these verses, God removes the veil from the worship of idols. In our vocabulary the word "idol" is used casually and applied broadly. Sports heroes are called idols. Even a helpful mentor can be referred to as an idol. But here in the Scriptures, the term "idol" has a deeply sinister connotation. God's Word candidly states that idols represent the devil spirits behind them. This is important and applicable learning for believers of any time period.

The Peace Offering

Verses 25-31:
Whatsoever is sold in the shambles [marketplace], that eat, asking no question for conscience sake:
For the earth is the Lord's, and the fulness thereof.
If any of them that believe not bid you to a feast, and ye be disposed to go; whatsoever is set before you, eat, asking no question for conscience sake.
But if any man say unto you, This is offered in sacrifice unto idols, eat not for his sake that shewed it, and for conscience sake: for the earth is the Lord's, and the fulness thereof:
Conscience, I say, not thine own, but of the other: for why is my liberty judged of another man's conscience?
For if I by grace [thanksgiving] be a partaker, why am I evil spoken of for that for which I give thanks?
Whether therefore ye eat, or drink, or whatsoever ye do, do all to the glory of God.

Verses 25 says that whatever is sold in the market, eat without questioning whether it was sacrificed to idols or not. Temples to the various gods were plentiful in the city of Corinth. A map of Corinth from this era shows the meat markets were situated across from the temples. This would suggest that the food from the temples, which had been sacrificed to the deities, was often sold in the markets.[24]

The negatives of food sacrificed to idols can be superseded by eating to the glory of God with thanksgiving. In the above passage, it is mentioned twice that "the earth is the Lord's, and the fullness thereof." Since all belongs to Him, we can eat with thanksgiving and dedicate the food to God.[25]

---

[24] David Williams, *Paul's Metaphors, Their Context and Character* (Peabody, Mass.: Hendrickson, 1999) 29.
[25] Also see I Timothy 4:4 and 5.

JESUS CHRIST OUR COMPLETE OFFERING

In conclusion, our study of the significance of eating of sacrifices in the lands and times of the Bible is far more than an intriguing exercise in anthropology. The covenant of salt, the identification and full sharing with an offering, looked forward to the marvelous redemptive realities of the New Covenant.

Peace Offering: Double Demonstration of Identification

We can now consider the one characteristic of the peace offering that distinguished it from all the other offerings. While the peace offering was the only altar sacrifice to be eaten by the Israelites, the Old Testament sacrifices were frequently eaten:

Passover Offering:	eaten by the offerers	Exodus 12:8
Peace Offering:	eaten by the offerers and priests	Leviticus 19:6
Meal Offering:	eaten by the priests	Leviticus 6:16
Sin Offering:	eaten by the priests	Leviticus 6:26
Trespass Offering:	eaten by the priests	Leviticus 7:1-6

In Leviticus 10, Moses inquired into Aaron's conduct as high priest:

> Leviticus 10:17 and 18:
> Wherefore have ye not **eaten the sin offering** in the holy place, seeing it is most holy, and God hath given it you **to bear** [*nasa*] **the iniquity** of the congregation, to make atonement for them before the LORD?

The Peace Offering

> Behold, the blood of it was not brought in within the holy place: ye should indeed have eaten it in the holy place, as I commanded.

Aaron and his sons were to bear the iniquity of the congregation by eating the sin offering. The priest shared fully in what that sin offering represented, thus bearing the sin of God's people. By consuming the sacrifice, the priest was identified with the sin offering and the sins of the congregation were transferred to him.

The Hebrew word, *nasa*, means to bear, to take away, in the sense of lifting up and carrying away. In chapter 4 of our study, we saw how the Hebrew word, *nasa*, is used to indicate the transference of sin from one party to another in Leviticus 16:22 and Isaiah 53:4 and 12. Leviticus 10:17 also used the Hebrew word, *nasa*, to indicate a transfer of sin.

Nasa: to bear
The Priest bore sin by eating the offering
Leviticus 10:17: "...God hath given it you to bear (*nasa*) the iniquity..."
The Scapegoat bore sin by laying on of hands
Leviticus 16:22: "...the goat shall bear (*nasa*) upon him all their iniquities"
The Messiah bore our sin and sickness
Isaiah 53:4: "Surely he hath borne (*nasa*) our sicknesses..."
Isaiah 53:12: "...he bare (*nasa*) the sin of many..."

As laying hands on the sacrifice indicated identification with that sacrifice, so did eating the sacrifice. These are the two cardinal demonstrations of identification in the Old Testament sacrificial system: laying a hand on the head of the sacrifice and eating the sacrifice.

JESUS CHRIST OUR COMPLETE OFFERING

> **The Two Demonstrations of Identification in the Old Testament Sacrifices:**
> 1. Laying a hand on the head of the sacrifice
> 2. Eating the sacrifice

In addition to eating a major portion of the peace offering, the offerer was also to lay his hand on the peace offering before its death.[26] **Only** the peace offering brought these two elements of identification together. In no other altar sacrifice under the Law did the worshipper both lay his hand on as well as eat of the offering.

The dominant and most arresting characteristic of the peace offering was the double demonstration of the full sharing of the offerer and the sacrifice. The Israelite laid his hand on the head of the sacrifice and then consumed the sacrifice. Two separate acts, one clarion truth: identification with the sacrifice. The peace offering represented that which was to come: the spiritual ingestion of all that Christ is—to every believer.

The central lesson of the peace offering was that it foreshadowed our full sharing with that future, true sacrifice, Jesus Christ. The peace offering sets forth a spectacular two-fold illustration of our identification with Christ.

---

[26] Leviticus 3:1: "And if his oblation [offering] *be* a sacrifice of peace offering, if he offer *it* of the herd; whether *it be* a male or female, he shall offer it without blemish before the Lord.
Verse 2: And he shall lay his hand upon the head of his offering.
Verse 8: And he shall lay his hand upon the head of his offering and kill it before the tabernacle.
Verse 13: And he shall lay his hand upon the head of it, and kill it before the tabernacle."

The Peace Offering

Our Identification with Christ

Having gone through the God-inspired tutorial of the peace offering, let's now look at the finished work of Christ regarding our identification.

> Philippians 3:10:
> That I may know him, and the power of his resurrection, and the fellowship [*koinōnia*] of his sufferings, being made conformable unto his death;

The first part of the verse, "that I may know him, and the power of his resurrection…" sounds wonderful. But the second part of the verse—"share fully in his sufferings"—doesn't sound too pleasant! Does it mean we are to be crucified as Jesus did and suffer like him? No, this verse is using sacrificial terminology. We share fully in the power of his resurrection and his sufferings and his death in the sense of our identification with Christ.

> Romans 6:5 (*Working Translation*[27]):
> So if we have become identified with *him* in the likeness of his death, *then* we shall also certainly be *in the likeness* of his resurrection.

Just as we have been identified with Christ in the likeness of his death, we also will be in the likeness of his resurrection. This verse clarifies Philippians 3:10: "…and the fellowship of his sufferings, being made conformable unto his death." We fully share in Christ's sacrifice, in utter oneness with him. As Galatians 2:20 declares, "…I was crucified with Christ, nevertheless I live…" Without grasping the terms and

---

[27] Cited from the Working Translation in *A Journey through the Acts and Epistles*. Copyright © 2006 by Walter J. Cummins. All rights reserved.

JESUS CHRIST OUR COMPLETE OFFERING

expressions associated with sacrifice, one may stumble over the meaning of these verses.

Jesus used the language of sacrifice in the following passage:

> John 6:53-57:
> Then Jesus said unto them, Verily, verily, I say unto you, Except ye eat the flesh of the Son of man, and drink his blood, ye have no life in you.
> Whoso eateth my flesh and drinketh my blood, hath eternal life; and I will raise him up at the last day.
> For my flesh is meat indeed, and my blood is drink indeed;
> He that eateth my flesh and drinketh my blood, dwelleth in me, and I in him.
> As the living Father hath sent me, and I live by the Father: so he that eateth me, even he shall live by me.

What does he mean when he refers to eating my flesh and drinking my blood? What could this possibly signify?" Jesus was speaking in sacrificial language. He was looking forward to his once-and-for-all sacrifice and the full sharing and oneness each believer would have with him.[28]

Various professions employ terminology unique to their line of work. To those outside of these fields, the use of these sometimes obscure terms can seem a deliberate attempt to be incomprehensible. In the legal profession, their vocabulary may be called "legalese" or in the medical profession, "medicalese." However, most often these professions have the need to use precise language to describe issues exclusive to their line of work.

---

[28] Eating his flesh and drinking his blood also looks forward to "holy communion" or the "Lord's supper" of Matthew 26:26-29. Also see: David Bergey, *Our Identification with Christ's Sacrifice*, chapter 3.

The Peace Offering

The record in John 6:60 tells us that many of Jesus' disciples found it difficult to understand his sacrificial terminology: "Many therefore of his disciples, when they had heard this, said, This is an hard saying; who can hear it?" Christians today may find sacrificial references puzzling as well. While the term "sacrificalese" is not recommended, nonetheless we must recognize that some of the vocabulary of the Scriptures, whether Old or New Testament, can be in the language of sacrifice.

As we have seen, passages in the book of Leviticus serve as a guidebook to precisely define and explain the terminology of sacrifice. In Leviticus 16:22, the sins of the nation were transferred onto the scapegoat by laying on of the hands of the high priest. In Leviticus 10:17, the iniquity of the congregation was transferred to the high priest by his eating of the sin offering. These two prominent examples and many others give one a "glossary" to understand the terms and expressions associated with sacrifice.

In our examination of the peace offering of the Old Testament and the significance of edible sacrifices, we have seen how the Law serves as a tutorial of Christ's sacrifice. The Mosaic Law speaks prophetically about the full sharing the believers would have with the coming Messiah.

Just as the Old Covenant believers ingested the peace offering, so those of the New Covenant would ingest Christ. The peace offering foreshadowed the utter oneness and full union we would have with Christ. He dwells in us and we in him.

In the Old Testament, the offerers were filled with the flesh of the peace offering. We are filled with all the fullness of God in Christ. By the tutorial of the peace offering, we can see how the glorious work of Christ is accomplished in every

JESUS CHRIST OUR COMPLETE OFFERING

believer. We share fully with him! When he died, we died with him. When he arose, we arose with him. We can now walk in newness of resurrection life.

He is our Peace Offering

Ephesians 2 has a noteworthy correlation to the peace offering.

> Ephesians 2:13-16:
> But now in Christ Jesus ye who sometimes were far off are made nigh [near] by the blood of Christ.
> **For he is our peace**, who hath made both one, and hath broken down the middle wall of partition *between us;*
> Having abolished in his flesh the enmity, *even* the law of commandments *contained* in ordinances; for to make in himself of twain one new man, *so* making peace;
> And that he might reconcile both unto God in one body by the cross, having slain the enmity thereby.

What does it mean when it says of Christ: "he is our peace?" Could the word "offering" be supplied after "peace?" Could this be a reference to his sacrifice as a peace offering? In chapter 6, we noted that in the case of the words "sin" or "trespass," the word "offering" may often be supplied depending on the context.

Verse 13 mentions the blood of Christ given in sacrifice. The accomplishments of the flesh of Christ given in sacrifice are referenced in verse 15. The cross is cited in verse 16. The context of "...he is our peace..." in verse 14 is that of Christ's

The Peace Offering

sacrifice. So the context permits supplying the word, "offering," after "peace": "...for he is our peace offering."[29]

The idea of a peace offering also fits well with the subsequent phrase: "...who hath made both one..." The peace offering was a full sharing and communion in the fellowship meal. God, the priest and offerers all shared of one sacrifice. The fat was burned on the altar to God. The priest received the right shoulder and the breast. The offerer got the remainder. The thought was that of union and fellowship with all parties. The role of the peace offering was to bring them all together.

In Ephesians 2:13-16, the offering of Christ brought together God and His people, both Jew and Gentile. Gentiles who had been separated were made near. The wall was broken down; the two became one new man. Both were reconciled to God by the cross. Intertwined through these verses is the full sharing and reconciliation of God's people accomplished by Christ's perfect sacrifice.

The idea of communion and full sharing is also in the context of the peace offering in I Corinthians 10:18.

> I Corinthians 10:16-18:
> The cup of blessing which we bless, is it not the communion [*koinōnia*] of the blood of Christ?
> The bread which we break, is it not the communion [*koinōnia*] of the body of Christ [given in sacrifice]?

---

[29] "For he is our peace..." may also be the figure, metonymy (of effect), to refer to the **cause** of our peace (the effect used for the cause). Walter J. Cummins, *A Journey through the Acts and Epistles*, 409. "For he is our peace (offering)..." would be metonymy (of the subject) where one noun is put for a related noun. Whether metonymy *of effect* or *of subject*, Christ's sacrifice has certainly provided us abounding peace!

JESUS CHRIST OUR COMPLETE OFFERING

> For we *being* many are one bread, *and* one body [of the church]: for we are all partakers of that one bread.
> Behold Israel after the flesh: are not they which eat of the sacrifices [peace offerings] partakers of the altar?

Verse 17 says: "we *being* many are one" and we are "one body," and "we are all partakers." As with Ephesians 2:14-17, the big point here is oneness and a full sharing.

In Ephesians 2 and in I Corinthians 10, the Old Testament peace offering is alluded to. What a touching picture the peace offering gives us! We see a group of Old Covenant believers sitting down and feasting on the peace offering, in fellowship together. What we feast on in the New Covenant is much richer and more glorious. We share fully in the riches of His grace and all that Christ accomplished for us.

The Peace Offering

Name of Sacrifice	Hebrew Name	Functions	Distinctive Characteristic	Parallel to Christ
Peace Offering	*shelem*	**Sweet savour** Sharing fully with the sacrifice ------ -thanks-giving -vow -freewill	The sacrifice was eaten by the offerer indicating a full sharing and identification with the sacrifice.	Our Identification, Full sharing with Christ I Corinthians 10:18 Ephesians 2:14

Chapter 11

The Meal Offering or Gift Offering

The meal offering, unlike the trespass, sin, peace, and burnt offerings, had no innocent animal dying as a substitute for the offerer. There was no sprinkling of blood representing cleansing. There was no ritual of placing one's hand on the head of the sacrifice to express identification. Consequently there was no foreshadowing or representation of the coming Messiah in any of these aspects. However as we shall see, the meal offering demonstrates a clear pattern of the good things to come.

We will now examine the meal offering and its corresponding Hebrew word, *minchah*. We shall also observe how this particular offering is relevant to the coming Christ.

> Leviticus 2:1-3:
> And when any will offer a meat [meal] offering unto the LORD, his offering shall be of fine flour; and he shall pour oil upon it, and put frankincense thereon:
> And he shall bring it to Aaron's sons the priests: and he shall take thereout his handful of the flour thereof, and of the oil thereof, with all the frankincense thereof; and the priest shall burn [*qatar*, burn as incense] the memorial [portion] of it upon the altar, to

The Meal Offering or Gift Offering

be an offering made by fire, of a sweet savour unto the LORD:
And the remnant [remainder] of the meat [meal] offering shall be Aaron's and his sons': it is a thing most holy of the offerings of the LORD made by fire.

In an odd twist of English word usage, the only offering in Leviticus 1-7 with **no meat** is the "meat offering." Since our current usage of the word "meat" refers the flesh of an animal, we will call this offering a "meal" or "bread" offering."[1]

Unlike the other offerings of Leviticus 1-7, the meal offering was not an animal sacrifice. The meal offering had no shedding of blood. This is the most profound distinction between the meal offering and the burnt, peace, sin, and trespass offerings.

In verses 1-3, the uncooked meal offering consisted of fine flour and olive oil. The flour and oil would form dough when mixed together. Frankincense was added to the portion that was burned as incense on the altar. In verse 2, this portion was censed on the altar as a sweet savour to the Lord and was called the memorial portion. The remainder of the offering was given to the priest.

The ingredients of the meal offering involved extensive preparation. The cereal grain and the olive oil in this offering

---

[1] In other English translations, the *minchah* offering is also translated as "grain offering" or "cereal offering." Since in the case of the Levitical *minchah*, the Law usually stipulated flour, "meal offering" is a fitting translation.
Following are examples of the Law of the *minchah* offering specifying meal or flour: The individual meal offerings (Leviticus 2); Offering for cleansing of the leper (Leviticus 14:10); Feast of Unleavened Bread (Leviticus 23:13). Pentecost: two wave loaves of leaven bread.(Leviticus 23:17); jealousy offering (Numbers 5:15). The wave sheaf of grain of the first fruits in Leviticus 23:10 is **not** called a *minchah* offering.

required harvesting and processing.[2] The meal offering was not a portion of fruit or vegetables or grain simply picked and then presented to God in sacrifice. The flour and the oil involved cultivating the soil, harvesting the crop, and then finally, processing the grain into fine flour and the olives into oil. The meal offerings were not an offering of raw produce fresh from the field.[3]

The offering of Cain in Genesis 4:3 was merely "of the fruit of the ground." While Leviticus 2 called for "fine flour; and he shall pour oil upon it, and put frankincense thereon." In Appendix Four the larger issues with Cain's offering are addressed.

> Verses 4-7:
> And if thou bring an oblation [offering] of a meat [meal] offering baken in the oven, it shall be unleavened cakes[4] of fine flour mingled with oil, or unleavened wafers anointed with oil.
> And if thy oblation be a meat [meal] offering baken in a pan [griddle], it shall be of fine flour unleavened, mingled with oil.
> Thou shalt part it in pieces, and pour oil thereon: it is a meat [meal] offering.
> And if thy oblation be a meat [meal] offering baken in the fryingpan, it shall be made of fine flour with oil.

Verses 4-7 list the various ways the meal offering could be cooked. It could be baked in an oven or fried in a griddle. The "frying pan" of verse 7 was a deep vessel to boil the

---

[2] Ruth 2:17, Judges 6:11 and Deuteronomy 24:20.
[3] The first fruits wave offering of a barley sheaf in Leviticus 23:10-12 is not called meal offering (*minchah*).
[4] The word, "cakes," is the Hebrew word, *challah,* meaning perforated or pierced cakes.

The Meal Offering or Gift Offering

meal in oil similar to our doughnuts.[5] Interestingly, the word "cakes" in verse 4 is translated from a Hebrew word meaning perforated so this piece of bread would have had a hole or holes made in it. These various ways of preparing this offering would yield a form of bread, so this offering could be presented as a bread offering.

> Verses 8-10:
> And thou shalt bring the meat [meal] offering that is made of these things unto the LORD: and when it is presented unto the priest, he shall bring it unto the altar.
> And the priest shall take from the meat [meal] offering a memorial [portion] thereof, and shall burn [*qatar*, burn as incense] it upon the altar: it is an offering made by fire, of a sweet savour unto the LORD.
> And that which is left of the meat [meal] offering shall be Aaron's and his sons': it is a thing most holy of the offerings of the LORD made by fire.

As in verse 2, the memorial portion was burned as incense on the altar. Then the priests received the remainder of the meal offering for them to eat.

> Verse 11:
> No meat [meal] offering, which ye shall bring unto the LORD, shall be made with leaven: for ye shall burn [*qatar*, burn as incense] no leaven, nor any honey, in any offering of the LORD made by fire.

No leaven or honey was to be in any meal or bread offerings. When these ingredients are combined, they can cause

---

[5] C.F. Keil and R. Delitzsch, *Commentary on the Old Testament*, 294. Jacob Milgrom, *The Anchor Bible Leviticus 1-16*, 185.

JESUS CHRIST OUR COMPLETE OFFERING

fermentation. Biblically, leaven could represent malice, evil or corruption.[6]

> Verses 12 and 13:
> As for the oblation [offering] of the firstfruits, ye shall offer them unto the LORD: but they shall not be burnt on the altar for a sweet savour
> And every oblation [offering] of thy meat offering shalt thou season with salt; neither shalt thou suffer the salt of the covenant of thy God to be lacking from thy meat [meal] offering: with all thine offerings thou shalt offer salt.

In the previous chapter, we noted that under the Law every sacrifice was to be salted. Eating salt together in the biblical times was a way of making an indissoluble covenant. Each time these salted offerings were presented, a lifelong promise of loyalty and dedication to the God of Israel was implicit.[7]

> Leviticus 2:14-16:
> And if thou offer a meat [meal] offering of thy firstfruits unto the LORD, thou shalt offer for the meat [meal] offering of thy firstfruits green ears of corn [new grain[8]] dried by the fire, even corn [new grain] beaten out of full ears.

---

[6] See: I Corinthians 5:6-8 and Victor Paul Weirwille, *Jesus Christ, Our Passover* (New Knoxville, Ohio: American Christian Press, 1980) Appendix 2: The Biblical Significance of Leaven.

[7] K. C. Pillai, *Light through an Eastern Window*, 24. Jacob Milgrom, *The Anchor Bible Leviticus 1-16*, 191, says salt sealed a covenant. With ancient Greeks as well as Arabs eating salt was "equivalent to an indissoluble covenant." (Numbers 27:19; I Chronicles 13:5)) According to Josephus (Ant. iii. 9,1) every sacrifice was salted. C.F. Keil and R. Delitzsch, *Commentary on the Old Testament*, Volume II, 295.

[8] A*bib* in Hebrew. The first month of the year was called "new grain" or *Abib*. "Corn" refers to grain, not maize. Maize or as we call it, "corn," came from the New World.

The Meal Offering or Gift Offering

> And thou shalt put oil upon it, and lay frankincense thereon: it is a meat offering.
> And the priest shall burn [*qatar*] the memorial [portion] of it, part of the beaten corn thereof, and part of the oil thereof, with all the frankincense thereof: it is an offering made by fire unto the LORD.

One aspect of the meal offering involved the first fruits offering. As the name suggests, the first fruits were offered at the start of harvest. The new grain for the first fruits offering was to be "dried by the fire" and "beaten out" meaning it was to be roasted and crushed.[9] The first fruits offering will be discussed in chapter 15.

Minchah: Meal Offering or Gift Offering

In Leviticus 2, the Hebrew word, *minchah*, is used for the meal offering. We noted that the meal offering could be uncooked meal blended with oil, forming dough or cooked as bread. The following verses show a different usage of this Hebrew word, *minchah*.

> Genesis 4:3-5:
> And in process of time it came to pass, that Cain brought of the fruit of the ground an offering [*minchah*] unto the LORD.
> And Abel, he also brought of the firstlings of his flock and of the fat thereof. And the LORD had respect unto Abel and to his offering [*minchah*]:
> But unto Cain and to his offering [*minchah*] he had not respect. And Cain was very wroth, and his countenance fell.

---

[9] "Beaten out" is translated from the Hebrew word, *geres*, meaning crushed.

JESUS CHRIST OUR COMPLETE OFFERING

Cain's offering was of the fruit of the ground, but Abel's *minchah* was of the firstlings of the flock. So in this instance, *minchah* could mean either animal sacrifices or fruit of the ground brought as an offering.

Abel's gift offering is referenced in Hebrews 11:

> Hebrews 11:4
> By faith Abel offered unto God a more excellent sacrifice than Cain, by which he obtained witness that he was righteous, God testifying of his gifts [*dōron*=offerings]: and by it he being dead yet speaketh.

This verse gives us an equivalent Greek word to the Hebrew word, *minchah*. In the New Testament, the word, *dōron*, is an offering usually given to God or given to be used in the temple. Hebrews 11:4 refers to the offerings of Genesis 4 as "gifts." As we shall see from Genesis 32, *minchah* can be understood as a gift or present.

In Leviticus 2, we observed that this term, *minchah*, used in the context of Levitical offerings, specifies meal offerings as distinct from an animal sacrifice.[10] However, from Genesis 4, we read that this term can be used inclusively of various types of offerings indicating that the word has more than one meaning.

---

[10]Hebrews maintains this Levitical distinction of *michah/ dōron* referring to meal offerings rather than animal sacrifices in these verses: 5:1 "...that he may offer both gifts [*dōron*] and sacrifices for sins." 8:3: "For every high priest is ordained to offer gifts [*dōron*] and sacrifices..." 9:9: "Which was a figure for the time then present, in which were offered both gifts [*dōron*] and sacrifices..."

The Meal Offering or Gift Offering

A Scene of Reconciliation: The *Minchah* Offering Defined

While Leviticus 2 defined the *minchah* offering in the Mosaic sacrificial framework, let's look at a passage where this offering is defined more broadly. We will consider a record in Genesis 32 and 33 of estranged twin brothers, Jacob and Esau. Genesis 27 relates how twenty years previously Jacob had deprived his brother, Esau, of a special blessing from their father, Isaac. The following verse gives us a look at Esau's feelings after this occurred.

> Genesis 27:41:
> And Esau hated Jacob because of the blessing wherewith his father blessed him: and Esau said in his heart, The days of mourning for my father are at hand; then will I slay my brother Jacob.

As we shall see, Jacob in going to meet his brother after many years had passed, was still very apprehensive about the wrath of his alienated brother.

> Genesis 32:3-7:
> And Jacob sent messengers before him to Esau his brother unto the land of Seir, the country of Edom.
> And he commanded them, saying, Thus shall ye speak unto my lord Esau; Thy servant Jacob saith thus, I have sojourned with Laban, and stayed there until now:
> And I have oxen, and asses, flocks, and menservants, and womenservants: and I have sent to tell my lord, **that I may find grace** in thy sight.
> And the messengers returned to Jacob, saying, We came to thy brother Esau, and also he cometh to meet thee, and four hundred men with him.

JESUS CHRIST OUR COMPLETE OFFERING

> Then Jacob was greatly afraid and distressed: and he divided the people that was with him, and the flocks, and herds, and the camels, into two bands;
> And said, If Esau come to the one company, and smite it, then the other company which is left shall escape.

Jacob sent messengers ahead to speak to his brother. The record does not indicate Esau's response to the message or if he even received it. Yet Jacob was told that his brother was accompanied by a force of 400. Jacob, remembering his brother's anger years before, was "greatly afraid and distressed." Jacob prepares for the worst, an armed attack from his brother, Esau. Therefore, Jacob splits up his party so at least some may escape in the event of an assault.

> Verses 9-12:
> And Jacob said, O God of my father Abraham, and God of my father Isaac, the LORD which saidst unto me, Return unto thy country, and to thy kindred, and I will deal well with thee:
> I am not worthy of the least of all the mercies, and of all the truth, which thou hast shewed unto thy servant; for with my staff I passed over this Jordan; and now I am become two bands.
> Deliver me, I pray thee, from the hand of my brother, from the hand of Esau: for I fear him, lest he will come and smite me, and the mother with the children.
> And thou saidst, I will surely do thee good, and make thy seed as the sand of the sea, which cannot be numbered for multitude.

In this touching and powerful prayer, he reminds God of His promises to him: "Return unto thy country, and to thy kindred, and I will deal well with thee" and in verse 12: "I will surely do thee good…" In his vulnerable state, with

The Meal Offering or Gift Offering

women and small children in tow, Jacob beseeches God to deliver him out of this perilous situation.

> Verses 13-15
> And he lodged there that same night; and took of that which came to his hand a present [*minchah*] for Esau his brother;
> Two hundred she goats, and twenty he goats, two hundred ewes, and twenty rams,
> Thirty milch camels with their colts, forty kine [cows], and ten bulls, twenty she asses, and ten foals.

Jacob arranged a gift offering, a *minchah*, to give to Esau. This was a sizeable gift, well over 500 animals. Jacob's intention was to make amends with his brother and to find grace in his eyes after two decades of enmity.

> Genesis 32:16-18:
> And he delivered them into the hand of his servants, every drove [herd] by themselves; and said unto his servants, Pass over **before** me, and put a space betwixt drove and drove.
> And he commanded the foremost, saying, When Esau my brother meeteth thee, and asketh thee, saying, Whose art thou? And whither goest thou? and whose are these before thee?
> Then thou shalt say, They be thy servant Jacob's; it is a present [*minchah*] sent unto my lord Esau: and, behold, also **he is behind** us.

Jacob prayed to God for the best yet prepared for the worst: an armed attack from his brother, Esau. Hence, Jacob splits up his party so at least some may escape in the event of a violent assault. He gives explicit instructions that his brother is to be told that this large herd of animals is a gift—a *minchah*—sent to him from Jacob.

JESUS CHRIST OUR COMPLETE OFFERING

> Genesis 32:19-21:
> And so commanded he the second, and the third, and all that followed the droves [herds], saying, On this manner shall ye speak unto Esau, when ye find him.
> And say ye moreover, Behold, thy servant Jacob is **behind** us. For he said, I will appease [make atonement to] him with the present [*minchah*] that goeth before me, and afterward I will see his face; peradventure he will accept of me.
> So went the present [*minchah*] over **before him**: and himself lodged that night in the company.

Jacob gave careful instructions so that before he came into his brother's presence, Esau would have already received the gift. The *minchah* Jacob sent ahead was to make atonement to Esau and gain his brother's acceptance.

After a long night, Jacob saw his brother approaching:

> Genesis 33:1 and 2:
> And Jacob lifted up his eyes, and looked, and, behold, Esau came, and with him four hundred men. And he divided the children unto Leah, and unto Rachel, and unto the two handmaids.
> And he put the handmaids and their children foremost, and Leah and her children after, and Rachel and Joseph hindermost.

It is poignant that Jacob placed his favorite wife and son in the rear of the procession so they would have a better chance of escape in case of violence.

The Meal Offering or Gift Offering

> Verses 3 and 4:
> And he passed over before them, and bowed himself to the ground seven times, until he came near to his brother.
> And Esau ran to meet him, and embraced him, and fell on his neck, and kissed him: and they wept.

Jacob demonstrated his deference and respect to his brother by prostrating or bowing seven times. This action could also include a request for forgiveness.[11] Bowing seven times made a strong statement and emphasized the depths of his feeling, deference and plea for forgiveness.

What ensued was not a cautious or nonchalant greeting. Esau ran to meet his brother, threw his arm around his neck and kissed him. This tenderness and affection was incredible compared to the wrath and malice from years before when Jacob had fled from Esau. Now these twin brothers were no longer enemies, but reconciled. Their fractured relationship had been repaired.

> Verses 5-11:
> And he lifted up his eyes, and saw the women and the children; and said, Who are those with thee? And he said, The children which God hath graciously given thy servant.
> Then the handmaidens came near, they and their children, and they bowed themselves.
> And Leah also with her children came near, and bowed themselves: and after came Joseph near and Rachel, and they bowed themselves.
> And he said, What meanest thou by all this drove [herd] which I met? And he said, These are to **find grace in the sight** of my lord.

---

[11] Genesis 50:17 and 18.

> And Esau said, I have enough, my brother; keep that thou hast unto thyself.
> And Jacob said, Nay, I pray thee, if now I have **found grace in thy sight**, then receive my present [*minchah*] at my hand: for therefore I have seen thy face, as though I had seen the face of God and thou wast pleased [*ratsah*= to be accepted[12]] with me.
> Take, I pray thee, my blessing that is brought to thee; because God hath dealt graciously with me, and because I have enough. And he urged him, and he took it.

In verse 8, Esau asks about the large herd that had been presented to him. It appears that Esau is ignorant about the purpose of the *minchah* that Jacob had given him. But it is difficult to imagine that Jacob's careful instructions to his servants to inform Esau of this gift were not carried out (32:18 and 19). What is more likely is that Esau was engaging in the ancient social convention called constraining.[13] Out of courtesy, Esau refused the gift and would only receive it after it was urged upon him. If that was the case, then the *minchah*, gift offering of Jacob achieved the desired result. Esau's wrath was appeased. Jacob was reconciled to his brother, accepted by him, and found grace in his sight.

Jacob made amends by the payment of a gift offering to his brother. Today we might call this brothers' conflict "bad blood." Now, they were brought together, embracing in tears. What a touching picture of reconciliation to behold!

---

[12] Leviticus 1:4: And he shall put his hand upon the head of the burnt offering; and it shall be accepted [*ratsah*] for him to make atonement for him. In Leviticus 1 as in Genesis 33, the term, *ratsah*, is used in the context of atonement and offerings.

[13] Bishop K. C. Pallai, "Eastern Hospitality," *The Way Magazine*, May 1965.

The Meal Offering or Gift Offering

In the previous chapter, we stated that the vocabulary of Scripture can be in the language of sacrifice. Furthermore, passages of the Old Testament can serve as a "glossary" to define and explain sacrificial terminology.

This historical account in Genesis illustrates the meaning and function of *minchah* as a gift offering. First, a gift offering was presented to find grace in the sight of someone, as mentioned four times in this record: 32:5, 33:8, 10, and 15. Also, the *minchah* gained the offerer acceptance with the recipient (32:20, 33:10). Last, this payment of a gift offering functioned to atone (32:20). These factors unite to depict the reconciliation and harmony a *minchah*, a gift offering, can produce.

This account also gives an illustrative definition of another prominent sacrificial term.

> Genesis 32:20:
> And say ye moreover, Behold, thy servant Jacob is behind us. For he said, I will appease [make atonement, *kaphar*] him with the present [*minchah*] that goeth before me, and afterward I will see his face; peradventure he will accept of me.

The Hebrew word, *kaphar*, rendered "appease" is usually translated as "atone" or "atonement." The English word, atonement, has the original meaning of "at-one-ment:" two brought together as one.[14] Atonement means making amends by paying the penalty for a wrongdoing.[15]

---

[14] According to Snaith, this word, atonement, "goes back to the 13th century rhyming chroniclers." N. H. Snaith, *Leviticus and Numbers* (Attic Press: Greenwood, S.C., 1969) 30.

[15] For a further discussion of the meaning of this word see: Walter J. Cummins, *Scripture Consulting Select Studies*, 358-362.

JESUS CHRIST OUR COMPLETE OFFERING

On occasion, in the Authorized King James Version, the Hebrew word, *kaphar*, is rendered as reconcile.[16] Translating *kaphar* as "reconciliation" speaks to the **effect** of atonement.

Portrait of Reconciliation in Genesis 32 and 33
The Function of the *Minchah*, Gift Offering:

Find Grace	32:5, 33:8, 10, 15
Gain Acceptance	32:20; 33:10
Atone	32:20

The payment of the gift offering made atonement for Jacob. It made amends to an offended brother and found grace in his sight. The central effect of atonement is reconciliation of two parties at enmity. Genesis 33 describes a touching scene of forgiveness and the restoration of a severed relationship: the brother who had been previously aggrieved "ran to meet him, and embraced him, and fell on his neck, and kissed him: and they wept." This record gives us a poignant portrait of reconciliation that looks forward to the accomplishments of Jesus Christ, who would in due time give himself a gift offering to reconcile humanity back to God.

---

[16] Leviticus 16:20: "And when he hath made an end of reconciling [atonement, *kaphar*] the holy place..." Leviticus 8:15: "...purified the altar, and poured the blood at the bottom of the altar, and sanctified it, to make reconciliation [atonement, *kaphar*] upon it.

The Meal Offering or Gift Offering

Christ, Our Gift Offering

The historical incident of Jacob and Esau's reconciliation gives a precise depiction of the meaning of *minchah* as a gift offering. Moreover, this event forms a precise and detailed parallel to Jesus Christ and his giving of himself as a gift offering on our behalf.

In Genesis 32:16-21, we read how Jacob made sure that his gift reached his brother before he did. He gave careful and repeated instructions that the gift should "pass over before me," (verses 16 and 21) with him following behind (verses 18 and 20).

Jacob's concern about his gift offering arriving in advance has a notable parallel to Christ as our gift offering. Christ went before us, ahead of us. First, as sacrifice for us he was presented to God on our behalf. Then, as forerunner, he went into heaven in person to appeal to God on our behalf.[17] Our acceptance, atonement and access to God were all achieved in Christ, who preceded us into God's presence.

Ephesians also has parallels to Jacob's gift offering.

> Ephesians 1:6 and 7:
> To the praise of the glory of his grace, wherein he hath made us accepted in the beloved.
> In whom we have redemption through his blood, the forgiveness of sins, according to the riches of his grace;

While Jacob's gift was to "find grace," in the context of the accomplishments of Christ, these verses speak of the "glory

---

[17] Hebrews 6:20: "Whither the forerunner is for us entered, even Jesus, made an high priest for ever after the order of Melchisedec."

JESUS CHRIST OUR COMPLETE OFFERING

of his grace" and "the riches of his grace." By our savior's work, we have been made "accepted in the beloved" as Jacob was accepted by his brother. "Redemption through his blood" speaks to payment by his sacrificial offering. Payment, grace, acceptance are all elements used in the context of the gift offering in Genesis 32 and 33.

While the account in Genesis is about the reconciliation between Jacob and Esau, Romans describes our reconciliation to God by Christ's sacrifice.

> Romans 5:6-9:
> For when we were yet without strength, in due time Christ died for the ungodly.[18]
> For scarcely for a righteous man will one die: yet peradventure for a good man some would even dare to die.
> But God commendeth his love toward us, in that, while we were yet sinners, Christ died for us.
> Much more then, being now justified by his blood, we shall be saved from wrath through him.

We were all without strength. Ungodly! Sinners! Yet Jesus Christ died for us. God demonstrated His abounding love for us by setting about to mend the broken relationship while we were yet so frail, antagonistic and wicked.

> Romans 5:10 and 11:
> For if, when we were enemies, we were reconciled to God by the death of his Son, much more, being reconciled, we shall be saved by his life.

---

[18] The Greek word for "ungodly" is not merely godless, but one antagonistic and condemning toward God, destitute of reverential awe toward God, impious.
Joseph Henry Thayer, *Greek-English Lexicon of the New Testament* (Milford, MI: Baker House, 1977) 79.

The Meal Offering or Gift Offering

> And not only so, but we also joy in God through our Lord Jesus Christ, by whom we have now received the atonement [reconciliation].

"When we were enemies..." God was not the enemy of humanity; rather, man was at enmity with God. In pagan religions, the gods were thought of as angry, so they had to be appeased, placated or conciliated by some offering. In sharp contrast, the One True God of the Scriptures took the initiative to display His love by giving His Son for us. This occurred while we were yet utterly incapable and antagonistic toward Him. We were neither able nor willing. Yet to demonstrate His tenderness and affection, God gave His only begotten Son.

In a parable in Luke 15, God's love is graphically depicted when the forgiving father came to the prodigal son: "But when he was yet a great way off, his father saw him, and had compassion, and ran, and fell on his neck, and kissed him." Genesis 33 also gives an extended illustration of a loving reconciliation: "And Esau ran to meet him, and embraced him, and fell on his neck, and kissed him: and they wept..."

In both illustrations we see the portrayal of the depth and passion of God's love with joyful reconciliation with humanity. God demonstrated His immense love for us, that while we were enemies with Him, He initiated our reconciliation.

> Ephesians 2:4-9:
> But God, who is rich in mercy, for his great love wherewith he loved us,
> Even when we were dead in sins, hath quickened us together with Christ,

JESUS CHRIST OUR COMPLETE OFFERING

> And hath raised us up together, and made us sit together in heavenly places in Christ Jesus:
> That in the ages to come he might shew the exceeding riches of his grace in his kindness toward us through Christ Jesus.
> For by grace are ye saved through faith; and that not of yourselves: it is the gift [*dōron*= offering] of God:
> Not of works, lest any man should boast.

Again, as in Romans 5:8, the "great love wherewith He loved us" in verse 4 is given as THE cause of God's mercy and grace.

As noted earlier, the Greek word, *dōron*, is equivalent to the Hebrew word *minchah*. In the Old Testament the Hebrew word, *minchah*, was a meal offering or a gift presented to God or to another person. In the New Testament, the Greek word, *dōron*, occurs 19 times and refers to gifts and offerings made by man, either to God or to another.

However, there is one notable exception. Here in Ephesians 2:8, *dōron* is a gift offered by God. God Himself presents as a gift offering to humanity: the finished work of Christ and the subsequent salvation.

Jacob was capable of compiling a substantial gift offering to present to his brother to facilitate reconciliation. However, mankind was utterly incapable of offering an equivalent sacrifice to pay the price for our redemption and salvation. Since we were destitute of reverence for God, without ability and at enmity—only a gift offering from God could attain our salvation.

This gift offering was purely by grace, "that not of yourselves." There is no absolutely no room for boasting.

The Meal Offering or Gift Offering

God presented the *dōron*, the gift offering, of our salvation by Christ's work.

> II Corinthians 9:15:
> Thanks be unto God for his unspeakable gift.

The Greek word for "unspeakable" means indescribable or inexpressible. God's love and His subsequent gift of salvation for us are beyond description. Since words do not suffice, God depicts scenes of His love and acceptance for us: a son, alone and destitute comes home. The father still a long way off runs to meet him. Twin brothers, alienated for so many years, encounter each other and embrace. May our hearts be enlightened to behold what words can scarcely express.

Chapter 12

The Meal and Drink Offerings: Precursors of Communion

We have examined *minchah* in the broader sense as a gift offering in Genesis and saw how it looked forward to Christ and his work. Let's return to the Levitical context where it was defined as a meal offering.

In Leviticus 2, we read that the meal offering, *minchah*, could be flour mixed with oil and combined with frankincense. It could be uncooked as dough or cooked as various forms of bread. Also, Leviticus 2:14 said the *minchah* of the first fruits offering, the grain was to be roasted and crushed.

As we will see, the meal offering was often paired with another offering.

> Exodus 29:38-42:
> Now this is that which thou shalt offer upon the altar; two lambs of the first year day by day continually.
> The one lamb thou shalt offer in the morning; and the other lamb thou shalt offer at even [between the two evenings]:

The Meal and Drink Offerings: Precursors to Communion

> And with the one lamb a tenth deal of flour mingled with the fourth part of an hin of beaten oil; and the fourth part of an hin of wine for a **drink offering.**
>
> And the other lamb thou shalt offer at even, and shalt do thereto according to the **meat offering** [*minchah*] of the morning, and according to the **drink offering** thereof, for a sweet savour, an offering made by fire unto the LORD.
>
> This shall be a continual burnt offering throughout your generations at the door of the tabernacle of the congregation before the LORD: where I will meet you, to speak there unto thee.

Every day, twice a day, the priests were to sacrifice a lamb with a meal offering and drink offering that consisted of wine. If one counts 365 days in a year, then 730 lambs were sacrificed in one year. This statistic alone makes the lamb the most prominent animal sacrificed under the Law of Moses. Yet more importantly to our study at hand, the drink offering and meal offering were also a foremost part of the Levitical system.

There were special holy days or "feasts" in the Old Testament where the meal offering and drink offering presented together.

> Leviticus 23:37:
> These are the feasts of the LORD, which ye shall proclaim to be holy convocations, to offer an offering made by fire unto the LORD, a burnt offering, and a **meat offering** [*minchah*], a sacrifice, and **drink offerings**, every thing upon his day.

The Levitical law was not the first time the drink and meal offering were paired. Centuries before the Law, Genesis

JESUS CHRIST OUR COMPLETE OFFERING

mentions the offering of bread and wine. Genesis 14 tells of the encounter of two prominent individuals, Abraham and Melchizedek. In this account, a confederation of kings had attacked and plundered the wicked city of Sodom and took food, goods and captives. One of the captives was Lot, a relative of the eminent believer, Abram (later named Abraham). Abram attacked the army of the kings and defeated them. After the victory, Abram was met by Melchizedek, a priest of the most high God.

> Genesis 14:18 and 19:
> And Melchizedek king of Salem brought forth **bread and wine**: and he *was* the priest of the most high God. And he blessed him, and said, Blessed *be* Abram of the most high God, possessor of heaven and earth.

Melchizedek, acting in his capacity as "the priest of the most high God," presented the bread and the wine as an offering to God.

Melchizedek's significance is far greater that these few verses in Genesis 14 might otherwise suggest. Psalms 110 foretells of the coming Lord: "Thou art a priest for ever after the order of Melchizedek." Hebrews chapters 5-7 then explains how Melchizedek is a model of him who was to come. Just as Melchizedek presented an offering of bread and wine, Jesus Christ presented his own flesh and his own blood as a sacrifice on our behalf.

Returning to the Law of Moses, the book of Numbers also mentions the daily offerings and how the drink offering was paired with the meal offering:

The Meal and Drink Offerings:
Precursors to Communion

> Numbers 28:4-8:
> The one lamb shalt thou offer in the morning, and the other lamb shalt thou offer at even; [between the two evenings].
> And a tenth part of an ephah of flour for a **meat offering** [*minchah*], mingled with the fourth part of an hin of beaten oil.
> It is a continual burnt offering, which was ordained in mount Sinai for a sweet savour, a sacrifice made by fire unto the LORD.
> And the **drink offering** thereof shall be the fourth part of an hin for the one lamb: in the holy place shalt thou cause the strong wine to be poured unto the LORD for a **drink offering**.[1]
> And the other lamb shalt thou offer at even: as the **meat offering** [*minchah*] of the morning, and as the **drink offering** thereof, thou shalt offer it, a sacrifice made by fire, of a sweet savour unto the LORD.

Again, the Law commanded that once in the morning and once in the evening, a sacrifice of a lamb and the meal offering paired with a drink offering were to be presented. Due to the unrelenting repetition of these daily offerings, they take on a central dominance in the Old Testament sacrificial system.

Numbers 28 and 29 continue to enumerate that on the Sabbath days, on the day of new moons and on the feast

---

[1] How was the drink offering presented? Verse 7 says it was "poured unto the Lord" suggesting it was put on the altar fire just as the meal offering was. II Kings 16:13: "...poured his drink offering, and sprinkled the blood of his peace offerings upon the altar. According to Sir. 50:15 and Josephus (Ant. Iud. III, ix, 4) the drink offering was poured out at the foot of the altar. N. H. Snaith, *Leviticus and Numbers*. After the death of Nadab and Abihu in Leviticus 10 priests were expressly prohibited from drinking "wine nor strong drink, thou, nor thy sons with thee, when ye go into the tabernacle."

JESUS CHRIST OUR COMPLETE OFFERING

days additional offerings were to be presented, again pairing the meal and drink offering. The combination of the meal and drink offerings mentioned about 20 times in these two chapters makes a surprising parallel to the following verse in the New Testament:

> Colossians 2:16 and 17:
> Let no man therefore judge you in meat [food], or in drink, or in respect of an holyday [feast], or of the new moon, or of the sabbath days
> Which are a shadow of things to come; but the body is of Christ.

Food and drink as well as the feasts, new moons and Sabbath days were a shadow of the good things to come.

In Numbers 28 and 29, the meal and drink offerings are mentioned multiple times in connection with the feasts, the new moon and the Sabbath days so that food and drink in Colossians 2:16 suggest a sacrificial aspect. Also, it leads us to ask: why were the food and drink a shadow of things to come? How did food and drink depict the reality of the coming Christ?

> Luke 22:17-20:
> And he took the cup, and gave thanks, and said, Take this, and divide it among yourselves:
> For I say unto you, I will not drink of the fruit of the vine, until the kingdom of God shall come.
> And he took **bread**, and gave thanks, and brake it, and gave unto them, saying, This is my body which is given for you: this do in remembrance of me.

The Meal and Drink Offerings:
Precursors to Communion

> Likewise also the **cup** after supper, saying, This cup is the new testament in my blood, which is shed for you.[2]

Christ, at his last supper with his disciples before the crucifixion, refers to the bread as his body and the wine, called the "fruit of the vine," as his blood. The wine and the bread are eaten in remembrance as a memorial of Christ's sacrifice. Having read about the meal and drink offerings under the Mosaic Law, we can see that what Jesus introduced is not an entirely new concept.

With hindsight we can see precisely how the meal offering foreshadowed Christ. The *minchah* offering, as a meal offering, represented the body of Christ given in sacrifice. While the wine of the drink offering corresponded to the shed blood of our Lord and Savior Jesus Christ.

Old Testament Offering:	Parallel to Christ:
Meal offering	**Body given in sacrifice**
Drink offering	**Blood shed**

The meal offering and the drink offering of the Old Covenant were a direct precursor to the wine and bread of what is commonly called "holy communion." While the offerings of the Old looked forward in anticipation of the coming one, the bread and the cup of the New Covenant looked back in remembrance.

---

[2] Wine metaphorically representing blood is also mentioned in Genesis 49:11 and Revelation 14:20.

JESUS CHRIST OUR COMPLETE OFFERING

The meal and the drink offerings combined to form a fitting complement, portraying the sacrifice of Christ. These offerings of the Old Testament form a lovely depiction of the coming redeemer. Then, in the New Testament, the eating of the bread and the drinking of the cup were to be done in remembrance of the towering accomplishments of our savior's sacrifice.

I Corinthians 10:
Eating and Drinking Symbolizing our Identification with Christ's Sacrifice

We considered how the Levitical meal and drink offerings depicted Christ and his accomplishments. We also looked at how these offerings were a precursor to communion. In Corinthians 10 and 11, communion is dealt with in detail along with many other important points central to our study. Chapter 10 starts off with a reference to the Exodus from Egypt by the nation of Israel.

> I Corinthians 10:1 and 2:
> Moreover, brethren, I would not that ye should be ignorant, how that all our fathers were under the cloud, and all passed through the sea;
> And were all baptized unto Moses in the cloud and in the sea.

These verses refer to some rather significant accomplishments of Moses, who brought to pass God's phenomenal deliverance to the nation of Israel. In believing obedience to God's revelation, he raised his staff and the Red Sea parted. Consequently, God saved the Israelites from destruction at the hand of the Egyptian army.[3] Prior to the

---

[3] Exodus 13:21-14:31.

The Meal and Drink Offerings: Precursors to Communion

trek through the Red Sea, the children of Israel had been protected by God, being "under the cloud." These extraordinary feats were achieved by Moses and the Israelites shared wholly in God's deliverance that Moses brought to pass. In this sense, they were baptized or fully immersed into all that Moses accomplished. They all were under the cloud; they all passed through the sea; they all were baptized unto Moses. They all shared fully in his believing accomplishments, just as we all share fully in Christ's accomplishments for us. Just as they were identified with Moses, so we are identified with Christ.[4]

> I Corinthians 10:3 and 4:
> And did all **eat** the same spiritual meat [food];
> And did all **drink** the same spiritual drink:[5] for they drank of that spiritual Rock that followed them: and that Rock was Christ.

The spiritual food spoken of in verse 3 refers to the manna from heaven God provided to the Israelites in their journeys through the wilderness. Jesus spoke of what this "spiritual meat" or manna represented:

> John 6:47-52:
> Verily, verily, I say unto you, He that believeth on me hath everlasting life.
> I am that bread of life.
> Your fathers did eat manna in the wilderness, and are dead.

---

[4] Romans 6:3 and 4 also use baptism in this sense: "Know ye not, that so many of us as were baptized into Jesus Christ were baptized into his death? Therefore we are buried with him by baptism into death…"

[5] Exodus 17:6: "Behold, I will stand before thee there upon the rock in Horeb; and thou shalt smite the rock, and there shall come water out of it, that the people may drink. And Moses did so in the sight of the elders of Israel."

JESUS CHRIST OUR COMPLETE OFFERING

> This is the bread which cometh down from heaven, that a man may eat thereof, and not die.
> I am the living bread which came down from heaven: if any man eat of this bread, he shall live for ever: and the bread that I will give is my flesh, which I will give for the life of the world.
> The Jews therefore strove among themselves, saying, How can this man give us his flesh to eat?

The manna they ate represented Christ. Likewise, when they drank from the rock, it too represented the coming savior.[6] In eating the manna and drinking from the rock, the Israelites all shared in looking forward to the promised Messiah. In the same way manna and the water from the rock was miraculously sent by God which provided physical life to the Israelites, so Christ gave everlasting life to humanity.

The opening four verses of I Corinthians 10 utilized illustrations from the Old Testament to convey the concept of identification: baptized into Moses in the cloud and in the sea, drinking water that came out of the rock, and eating the manna.

> I Corinthians 10:5-15:
> But with many of them God was not well pleased: for they were overthrown in the wilderness.
> Now these things were our examples [*tupos*], to the intent we should not lust after evil things, as they also lusted.

---

[6] When it says: "that rock was Christ" or Christ says: "I am the living bread" it is a metaphor. Christ is not literally a rock or the manna, rather he is represented as such. Likewise when Christ says of the bread: "this is my body," it is metaphor. The bread of communion is no more literally Christ's body than the rock Moses struck was literally Christ or the manna was literally Christ.

The Meal and Drink Offerings:
Precursors to Communion

Neither be ye idolaters, as were some of them; as it is written, The people sat down to **eat and drink**, and rose up to play.
Neither let us commit fornication, as some of them committed, and fell in one day three and twenty thousand.
Neither let us tempt Christ [the Lord], as some of them also tempted, and were destroyed of serpents.
Neither murmur ye, as some of them also murmured, and were destroyed of the destroyer.
Now all these things happened unto them for ensamples [*tupos*] and they are written for our admonition, upon whom the ends of the world are come.
Wherefore let him that thinketh he standeth take heed lest he fall.
There hath no temptation taken you but such as is common to man: but God is faithful, who will not suffer you to be tempted above that ye are able; but will with the temptation also make a way to escape, that ye may be able to bear it.
Wherefore, my dearly beloved, flee from idolatry.
I speak as to wise men; judge ye what I say.

Verse 7 says: "The people sat down to **eat and drink**, and rose up to play." Exodus 32 tells us of the event.

Exodus 32:1-6:
And when the people saw that Moses delayed to come down out of the mount, the people gathered themselves together unto Aaron, and said unto him, Up, make us gods, which shall go before us; for as for this Moses, the man that brought us up out of the land of Egypt, we wot not what is become of him.

JESUS CHRIST OUR COMPLETE OFFERING

> And Aaron said unto them, Break off the golden earrings, which are in the ears of your wives, of your sons, and of your daughters, and bring them unto me. And all the people brake off the golden earrings which were in their ears, and brought them unto Aaron.
>
> And he received them at their hand, and fashioned it with a graving tool, after he had made it a molten calf: and they said, These be thy gods, O Israel, which brought thee up out of the land of Egypt.
>
> And when Aaron saw it, he built an altar before it; and Aaron made proclamation, and said, To morrow is a feast to the LORD.
>
> And they rose up early on the morrow, and offered burnt offerings, and brought peace offerings; and the people sat down to **eat** and to **drink**, and rose up to play.

The Israelites and Aaron utilized all the official trappings of worship: high priest, altar, feast day, and sacrifices. But they worshipped the wrong god. They ate and drank, but not of the manna or of the rock which represented the coming Christ. Rather, they "brought peace offerings; and the people sat down to eat and to drink..." This account in Exodus associates eating and drinking with sacrifices. The Israelites by eating of the peace offerings, meal offerings, and drink offerings presented to the devil god, fully shared, identified, with that god. Identifying with the Egyptian devil god is quite a shocking contrast to sharing fully in the types of the coming Christ.

> I Corinthians 10:16:
> The **cup** of blessing which we bless, is it not the communion [*koinōnia*=sharing fully] of the blood of Christ? The **bread** which we break, is it not the communion [*koinōnia*] of the body of Christ?

The Meal and Drink Offerings: Precursors to Communion

In Luke 22, Christ said the cup represented his blood and the bread represented his body. Here in I Corinthians, it states that as we drink the cup, it symbolizes a full sharing in the blood of Christ. When we eat the bread, it illustrates that we are fully identified with the body of Christ given in sacrifice.

> I Corinthians 10:17:
> For we *being* many are one bread, *and* one body: for we are all partakers of that one bread.

We are all partakers in that "one bread" which is Christ. We all share fully in him. Here, as mentioned previously in this chapter, our union, our identification with Christ is in full view.

> I Corinthians 10:18-21:
> **Behold Israel after the flesh: are not they which eat of the sacrifices partakers [koinōnia] of the altar?**
> What say I then? that the idol is any thing, or that which is offered in sacrifice to idols is any thing?
> But I *say*, that the things which the Gentiles sacrifice, they sacrifice to devils, and not to God: and I would not that ye should have fellowship [koinōnia] with devils.
> Ye cannot drink the cup of the Lord, and the cup of devils: ye cannot be partakers of the Lord's table, and of the table of devils.

The Corinthian believers were given a well-defined example of the Israelites and warned to flee idolatry. The words "examples" and "ensamples" in I Corinthians 10:6 and 11 are translated from the Greek word *tupos*. The temptations of the Israelites form a rather remarkable type or parallel to the situation in the Corinthian church.

JESUS CHRIST OUR COMPLETE OFFERING

Identification by Eating and Drinking
I Corinthians 10

Israel:	Corinthians:
Sharing in:	Sharing in:
Christ: Verses 3 and 4	Christ: Verse 16
Idols: Verse 7	Idols: Verses 20 and 21

In the Old Testament, they had eaten of the manna and drunk of the rock, and therefore were identified with the coming Christ. They also ate and drank and were identified with the idol. The believers in Corinth were cautioned that it was possible to fall into a similar trap. Just as the Israelites fully shared in both the coming Christ and idolatry, so the believers at Corinth were warned not to share fully in idolatry.

I Corinthians 11:
Proclaiming the Lord's Death till He Come.

In I Corinthians chapter 11, we're provided with additional information about holy communion:

> I Corinthians 11:23-26:
> For I have received of the Lord that which also I delivered unto you, That the Lord Jesus the same night in which he was betrayed took bread:

The Meal and Drink Offerings: Precursors to Communion

> And when he had given thanks, he brake it, and said, Take, **eat**: this is my body, which is broken for you: this do in remembrance of me.
>
> After the same manner also he took the cup, when he had supped, saying, This cup is the new testament in my blood: this do ye, as oft as ye **drink** it, in remembrance of me.
>
> For as often as ye **eat** this bread, and **drink** this cup, ye do shew [proclaim, announce] the Lord's death till he come.

As in Luke 22, eating the bread and drinking the cup was to be done in remembrance of Christ's sacrificial work. After quoting the words of Jesus in verses 24 and 25, the cardinal purpose of communion is expressed in verse 26: "…ye do shew the Lord's death till he come." The Greek word translated "shew" means to proclaim or announce. By sharing in the bread and the wine, we proclaim and declare the Lord's death.

What precisely is proclaimed about his death? As I Corinthians 10:16 states, the cup represents the full sharing of the blood of Christ. The bread represents the full sharing of the body of our Lord given in sacrifice. Our common union with Christ, our identification with him in his sacrifice, is demonstrated and memorialized as we drink the cup and eat the bread.

Two aspects of Christ's sacrifice are to be distinguished and remembered in communion: the blood and the body.

JESUS CHRIST OUR COMPLETE OFFERING

> # Remembering our Full Sharing in His Sacrifice
>
> ## The Wine represents his Blood
> ## The Bread represents his Body

What specifically is to be remembered about the blood of Jesus Christ?

In chapter 8, we noted that the sin offering specifically focused on the blood of the sacrifice. Leviticus was very clear on the functions of the blood of the sin offering. The blood of the sin offering facilitated forgiveness, cleansing, sanctifying, atonement, and reconciliation to God. After looking at the sin offering, we then considered how it foreshadowed Christ's sacrifice, portraying what the blood of Jesus Christ accomplished on our behalf.

The one overarching message of the sin offering was purification and cleansing. II Corinthians 5:21 states that God made Christ a sin offering for us, that we might be made the righteousness of God in him. When we drink of the cup, we should consider the awesome extent of our righteousness.

We can draw a straight line from the sin offerings in Leviticus that forgave, cleansed, and also atoned to I John where the blood of Christ forgives, cleanses and atones for us.

The Meal and Drink Offerings: Precursors to Communion

The Blood of Jesus Christ:
Forgives
Leviticus 4:20, 26, 31, 35_____I John 1:9
Cleanses
Leviticus 8:15; 16:19_____I John 1:7, 9
Atones
Leviticus 4:20, 26, 31, 35; 8:15; 16:6-34_____I John 2:2

Our utter purity and full righteousness was not achieved by our labors but by Christ's work on the cross. When we drink the cup we are to recall our cleansing from all unrighteousness, our forgiveness of sin and our oneness with Him. All this was achieved by his sacrifice.

> Ephesians 2:13:
> But now in Christ Jesus ye who sometimes were far off are made nigh by the blood of Christ.
>
> Colossians 1:20:
> And, having made peace through the blood of his cross, by him to reconcile all things unto himself...

The blood of Christ brought us near and reconciled us to God. What a standing we have before God! We are not far off, ruined, guilty, and helpless like the lost prodigal son who journeyed into a far country and lived with pigs.

> Hebrews 10:19:
> Having therefore, brethren, boldness to enter into the holiest by the blood of Jesus.

JESUS CHRIST OUR COMPLETE OFFERING

By the blood of the savior, given in sacrifice, we have liberty to approach the presence of God.

> Hebrews 10:22:
> Let us draw near with a true heart in full assurance of faith, having our hearts sprinkled from an evil conscience...

We are to draw near to God because our hearts are sprinkled.[7] In the Levitical context the blood was sprinkled for purification and sanctification. By his blood we have been cleansed; therefore we can approach with a purified heart. The ultimate result of the blood of Christ shed for us is our complete reconciliation with God.

By the blood of Christ we can fearlessly approach God without any sense of dread, guilt, or self-loathing. We draw near to God, not by our own merits, our own adequacy, or our own achievements. Only by the Son of God's sacrificial accomplishments do we enter into God's presence. Our welcome access to the throne of grace is by the blood of Christ's sacrifice. God's grace has abounded toward us through Christ Jesus.

> I Corinthians 11:27-29:
> Wherefore whosoever shall eat this bread, and drink this cup of the Lord, unworthily, shall be guilty of the body and blood of the Lord.
> But let a man examine himself, and so let him eat of that bread, and drink of that cup.
> For he that eateth and drinketh unworthily, eateth and drinketh damnation to himself, not discerning the Lord's body.

---

[7] David Bergey, *Jesus Christ Our Approach Offering*, 107.

The Meal and Drink Offerings: Precursors to Communion

In the Authorized King James Version, this passage is difficult to follow. First, the phase: "eateth and drinketh unworthily" raises the question of what would constitute unworthiness. Romans 5:6-10 says that we were incapable, ungodly, and sinners at enmity with God. It would be difficult to be much more unworthy than that.

The last phrase of verse 29 answers the question of what would constitute unworthiness in this context: "… not discerning the Lord's body." *The Amplified Bible* renders verse 29: "For anyone who eats and drinks without discriminating and recognizing with due appreciation…" The reason for sharing in the bread and the cup is to remember and proclaim the Lord's sacrifice. So to not discern what the body of the Lord accomplished would defeat the whole purpose.

Verse 27 is mistranslated where it says, "…shall be guilty of the body and blood of the Lord." "Guilty" should be understood from the Greek to be held liable, to be legally subject to consequences.[8] In the Gospels, it is translated, "in danger of judgment." Each person eating the bread and drinking the cup is fully responsible to recall the significance, to recognize with due appreciation, what it represents. If one does not remember the meaning of the cup and bread, they are liable or culpable, not God, for the lack of results.

The word "damnation" in verse 29 is also a less than ideal translation. Most versions render the word as "judgment." We see from verse 32, this judgment is in the sense of godly reproof: "But when we are judged, we are chastened of the Lord, that we should not be condemned [as in Romans 8:1]

---

[8] Joseph Henry Thayer, *Greek-English Lexicon of the New Testament*, 219.

JESUS CHRIST OUR COMPLETE OFFERING

with the world." These words "guilty" or in "damnation" in the Authorized King James Version could certainly distract from our understanding of this passage and the true meaning and great blessings of communion.

> I Corinthians 11:29 and 30:
> For he that eateth and drinketh unworthily, eateth and drinketh damnation [judgment] to himself, not discerning the Lord's body.
> For this cause many are weak and sickly among you, and many sleep.

Verse 30 makes a very profound statement: "For this cause many are weak and sickly among you, and many sleep." "Sleep" is a euphemism for dying.[9]

> **"...not discerning the Lord's body, for this cause many are weak and sickly among you, and many sleep."**

This verse forthrightly states what caused believers to be weak, sick and then die. They did not discern the Lord's body.

Discerning the Lord's Body

We should take a moment to consider the sheer weight and impact of this statement. Here the Scriptures give a rather pointed diagnosis as to the cause of the believers being physically weak, sick and on occasion, die.

---

[9] John 11:11-14.

The Meal and Drink Offerings:
Precursors to Communion

This statement in God's Word should be a starting point or at least an issue of deep interest for anyone concerned about health. Often people attempt to diagnosis the reason why they are sick. While there may be many factors involved, God's Word on the subject of the cause of sickness should be of concern to those of us who regard the Scriptures highly.

In the chapter on the trespass offering, we noted that by Adam's trespass he delivered the dominion of this world to Satan. While Adam's sin is the root cause of sin, death and sickness, God's Word tells us in Corinthians that not discerning the Lord's body is a reason for lack of physical wholeness among God's people.

In I Corinthians 11:29, "not discerning" is used in the sense of <u>not</u> distinguishing the significance of the Lord's body. The reason for eating the bread was to recall what the body of the Lord accomplished. Yet if one does not discern the Lord's body, the result may be a bottleneck in manifesting what God has made available.

To be forgetful, ignorant, or neglectful of the specific details of the meaning of Christ's sacrificed body may well lead to the problem stated: "For this cause many are weak and sickly among you, and many sleep."

Since discernment of what the Lord's body accomplished on our behalf is the linchpin to this passage, let's examine this subject. The following stellar verse declares quite unambiguously what the body of the savior accomplished.

> **I Peter 2:24:**
> **Who his own self bare our sins in his own body on the tree, that we, being dead to sins, should live**

JESUS CHRIST OUR COMPLETE OFFERING

> unto righteousness: by whose stripes ye were healed.

This verse contains three extraordinary phrases. All three are profoundly central to our study. Each phrase is conditional upon the one before it.

The first phrase declares a truth we have examined in previous chapters: **the Lord Jesus Christ bore our sins in his body**. The second clause, states the outcome and purpose of Christ carrying our sins: **we that are now dead to sins may live righteously**. Because Christ bore our sins in his own body on the cross, we are legally dead to sin. The verse concludes with a quote from Isaiah 53:5: **"by whose stripes ye were healed."** As we realize what Christ has accomplished, we can manifest physical wholeness.

"Who his own self bare our sins in his own body on the tree..."

Isaiah 53, anticipating the promised Christ, says:
"...the Lord laid on him the iniquity of us all." (verse 6)
"...he shall bear [*sabal*] their iniquities." (verse 11)
"...he bare [*nasa*] the sin of many..." (verse 12)

Note how Isaiah 46 also uses these Hebrew words translated as "bear" or "carry:"

> Isaiah 46:1-5:
> Bel boweth down, Nebo stoopeth, their idols were upon the beasts, and upon the cattle: your carriages were heavy loaden; they are a burden to the weary beast. They stoop, they bow down together; they

The Meal and Drink Offerings:
Precursors to Communion

> could not deliver the burden, but themselves are gone into captivity.
> Hearken unto me, O house of Jacob, and all the remnant of the house of Israel, which are borne by me from the belly, which are carried [*nasa*] from the womb:
> And even to your old age I am he; and even to hoar [gray] hairs will I carry [*sabal*] you: I have made, and I will bear [*nasa*]; even I will carry [*sabal*], and will deliver you.
> To whom will ye liken me, and make me equal, and compare me, that we may be like?

The Lord carried and bore the house of Israel and delivered them. The idols were so useless and helpless they have to be borne by beasts of burden. In contrast, God carries and delivers His people.

In the Hebrew, "to bare" means more than to take away. These words for "bear" are used with the sense of lifting up and carrying away. The righteous servant of Isaiah 53 has borne [*nasa*] our sickness and carried [*cabal*] our sorrows. God "laid on him the iniquity of us all." Christ carried away all our sins and iniquities to Golgotha where they died with him.

As I Peter 2:24 tells us, the bearing of our sins was "in his own body." In discerning between the blood and the body of our Lord's sacrifice, we should note that bearing sins was done in his body.

Previously we have discussed precisely how Christ bore our sins. He died as our substitute. We were identified with Christ, just as those of the Old Covenant were identified with their sacrifices. This identification was symbolized by

JESUS CHRIST OUR COMPLETE OFFERING

the gesture of the placing of the hand on the head of the sacrifice.

With Christ's ultimate sacrifice, we do not have a gesture or a ritual. We have a full sharing identification with Christ's sacrifice. In the bread and the cup, there is not "a remembrance again of sins" as with the laying hands on the scapegoat. Rather, God asks us to simply remember what the sacrifice of our Lord has accomplished, especially discerning his body.

Since the body of the Lord carried our sins and iniquities, the logical outcome is: "we being dead to sins, should live unto righteousness."

> "...that we, being dead to sins, should live unto righteousness..."

The following passage in Romans explains in magnificent detail how we are "dead to sin."

> Romans 6:1-5:
> What shall we say then? Shall we continue in sin, that grace may abound?
> God forbid. How shall **we, that are dead to sin**, live any longer therein?
> Know ye not, that so many of us as were baptized into Jesus Christ were baptized into his death?
> Therefore we are buried with him by baptism into death: that like as Christ was raised up from the dead by the glory of the Father, even so we also should walk in newness of life.

The Meal and Drink Offerings: Precursors to Communion

> For if we have been planted together [identified with Christ[10]] in the likeness of his death, we shall be also in the likeness of his resurrection:

Being "baptized into Jesus Christ," of verse 3 is defined in Acts 1:5 and 2:38. This refers to baptism with the holy spirit in the name of Jesus Christ. Being baptized into Jesus Christ indicates being born again of God's spirit.

So what does it mean to be "baptized into his death" or how are we "buried with him by baptism into death?" Again, God's Word uses sacrificial language to describe Christ's colossal accomplishments. Just as all the born again ones were "crucified with Christ" as Galatians 2:20 states, so we have been buried with him as well. Being "baptized into his death" suggests our full identification with Christ in his death. In the same sense as the people of Israel were "baptized into Moses" and his accomplishments, we have been baptized, fully immersed, into Christ's death and resurrection.

> Romans 6:6-11:
> Knowing this, that our old man is crucified with him, that the body of sin might be destroyed, that henceforth we should not serve sin.
> For he that is dead is freed from sin
> Now if we be dead with Christ, we believe that we shall also live with him:
> Knowing that Christ being raised from the dead dieth no more; death hath no more dominion over him.

---

[10] Romans 6:5 (*Working Translation*): "So if we have become identified with *him* in the likeness of his death, *then* we shall also certainly be *in the likeness* of his resurrection." The Working Translation in *A Journey through the Acts and Epistles*. Copyright © 2006 by Walter J. Cummins. All rights reserved.

JESUS CHRIST OUR COMPLETE OFFERING

> For in that he died, he died unto sin once: but in that he liveth, he liveth unto God.
> Likewise reckon ye also **yourselves to be dead indeed unto sin**, but alive unto God through Jesus Christ our Lord.

In verse 6, the "old man" and "body of sin" refers to our sin nature which was crucified, died and buried in Christ. Since our old man nature is utterly dead—crucified, dead and buried—we are indeed dead to sin! Because we are freed from sin, we can live righteously. As I Peter 2:24 says: "being dead to sins, should live unto righteousness."

The body of Jesus Christ was crucified, died and was buried. Three days and three nights later he was raised from the dead. We fully share and are identified in his completed sacrificial work. We are not only identified with his death, but also with his resurrection. We are to consider ourselves dead unto sin and **alive unto God.**

Just as I Peter 2:24 says we "**should live** unto righteousness," Romans 6:4 says, "we also **should walk** in newness of life." Being alive unto God, walking in newness of life, and living unto righteousness would involve manifesting the last momentous phrase of I Peter 2:24: "…**by whose stripes ye were healed."**

> **"by whose stripes ye were healed."**

This third phrase in I Peter 2:24 is a quote from Isaiah 53.

The Meal and Drink Offerings: Precursors to Communion

> Isaiah 53:4 and 5:
> Surely he hath borne our griefs [sickness], and carried our sorrows [pains]: yet we did esteem him stricken, smitten of God, and afflicted.
> But he was wounded [pierced] for our transgressions, he was bruised for our iniquities: the chastisement of our peace was upon him; **and with his stripes we are healed.**

Jesus Christ not only bore our sin, he bore the consequences of sin as well. The transgression of Adam and Eve and their subsequent death from loss of spirit life brought tremendous repercussions on humanity. Sickness and sorrows were some of the dire aftereffects.

Verse 4 declares the he not only bore our sins in his own body on the tree, he bore our sickness and pain as well. God legally transferred the sins <u>and</u> sicknesses of His people to Christ. His body was not only pierced for our transgressions and bruised for our iniquities, but the devastating consequences of sin were also laid upon him. Physical disease and mental torment was placed upon him. He carried them in his own body. So we do not need to bear them.

Verse 5 says: "…he was wounded [pierced] for our transgressions…" "Wounded" is the Hebrew word, *chalal*, meaning pierced. This prophecy was fulfilled in John 19:34: "But one of the soldiers with a spear pierced his side, and forthwith came there out blood and water." The body of the savior was pierced for our transgressions.

In Leviticus 2:4, the word "cakes" is the Hebrew word, *challah*, meaning perforated or pierced cakes. The Hebrew, *chalal*, used in Isaiah 53:5 is a related form of *challah*

JESUS CHRIST OUR COMPLETE OFFERING

translated "cakes" in Leviticus 2:4. The body of Christ was pierced as was the *minchah* of Leviticus 2. As we have seen, the meal offering forms an exact correspondence to the body of Christ given in sacrifice. Likewise, the beating of the grain in Leviticus 2:14 and 16 may parallel Christ's beatings.

In Isaiah 53:5 it says: "...the chastisement of [for] our peace was upon him; and with his stripes we are healed." The first phrase could be translated: "...the punishment that obtained our peace was upon him..."[11] As our substitute, this righteous servant of Jehovah bore the punishment that was rightfully ours. He took upon himself the reproach of sin so peace and well-being could be secured for us.

"And with his stripes we are healed" says we have healing by the beatings he suffered. By the wounds he suffered, we are made well. By the punishment his body endured, we have peace. Jesus was a substitute for sin and a substitute for sickness.

Understanding that Christ's sacrifice paid for sin as well as sickness correlates to discerning the Lord's body in I Corinthians 11. Many were weak and sick and many died because the church did not realize the scope of Christ's achievements. Apparently, they did not recognize that by the wounds he suffered, they had healing.

As a believer delves into the details of what Christ accomplished and distinguishes the significance of the Lord's body, one may grow in appreciation and application of these redemptive realities. Once we recognize the truth that "by his stripes we are healed," we can then take advantage of it.

---

[11] Edward Young, *The Book of Isaiah Volume III*, 348. Also noted in *The Companion Bible*.

The Meal and Drink Offerings: Precursors to Communion

Drinking of the cup and eating of the bread is not simply a matter of showing up and going through the motions. We should emphatically recall what the Lord's sacrifice has completed for us. We should make the distinction that while Christ bore our sin, he also bore our sickness. He carried the mental anguish as well as the physical disease. We have healing both mentally and physically by what our savior bore in the flesh. Eating the bread commemorates these superb realities.

In today's society there is a focus on health and healthcare. There is great attention on who pays for healthcare and on evaluating various courses of therapy. While it may be necessary to get the facts straight and evaluate these matters, we should never forget to properly consider what the sacrifice of the body of Christ has accomplished for us. It is vitally important to remember who paid for our healing and "by whose stripes ye were healed."

When calculating health care costs and considering what treatments to use, we should never forget to calculate the price he paid and to discern what he has accomplished for us. It is essential not to leave God and His Son's accomplishments out of the equation.[12]

Asking for God's Remembrance

Let's look at a noteworthy aspect of the meal offering that did not pertain to any animal sacrifices.

---

[12] For additional insight see Chapter 17, "Never Forget—He is God": Chris Geer, *Open My Eyes that I May See* (Glasgow, Scotland: Word Promotions, 2009).

JESUS CHRIST OUR COMPLETE OFFERING

> Leviticus 2:1-3:
> And when any will offer a meat [meal] offering unto the LORD, his offering shall be of fine flour; and he shall pour oil upon it, and put frankincense thereon:
> And he shall bring it to Aaron's sons the priests: and he shall take thereout his handful of the flour thereof, and of the oil thereof, with all the frankincense thereof; and the priest shall burn the **memorial** [*azkarah*] of it upon the altar, to be an offering made by fire, of a sweet savour unto the LORD:
> And the remnant [remainder] of the meat [meal] offering shall be Aaron's and his sons': it is a thing most holy of the offerings of the LORD made by fire.
>
> Verse 9: And the priest shall take from the meat [meal] offering a **memorial** [*azkarah*] thereof, and shall burn it upon the altar: it is an offering made by fire, of a sweet savour unto the LORD.
>
> Verse 16: And the priest shall burn the **memorial** [*azkarah*] of it, part of the beaten corn thereof, and part of the oil thereof, with all the frankincense thereof: it is an offering made by fire unto the LORD.

The "memorial" was the portion of the meal offering that was burned or censed upon the altar. Then, as verse 3 states, the remainder of the offering that was not burned on the altar was given to the priest. This "memorial portion" is a unique feature of the *minchah* offering that bears further study.

The *Gesenius* lexicon says the Hebrew word, *azkarah*, is "commending to God the remembrance of the

The Meal and Drink Offerings:
Precursors to Communion

worshipper."[13] This memorial portion served to remind God of the offerer and his prayers. Psalm 20:3 alludes to a call to God for remembrance: "may He remember all your offerings [*minchah*]..."[14] An integral part of the meal offering was its function to recall to God's mind the requests of the worshipper by means of the portion of the offering called the "memorial."

> ## The Memorial Portion of the Meal Offering: Asked for God's Remembrance

According to the Scriptures, what is the significance of God remembering or of asking God to remember? Unlike humans, God is incapable of a mental lapse of forgetfulness. So this would be the figure of speech, condescension, where human characteristics are attributed to God.[15]

In Genesis 8:1, before the flood, it says, "God remembered Noah..." Exodus 6:5 states that God said: "And I have also heard the groaning of the children of Israel, whom the Egyptians keep in bondage; and I have remembered my covenant." After remembering, He delivered Noah out of the flood and Israel out of Egypt. God's remembrance is more than a mere recollection. It also often carries the idea

---

[13] *Gesenius' Hebrew and Chaldee Lexicon*, 26. Some Hebrew scholars say *azkarah* simply refers to a "token portion" as the "memorial portion." Others disagree and say the Hebrew word, *azkarah*, for memorial is related to the Hebrew word, *zeker*, meaning remembrance. (Ross, 106). In the 3rd century BC Hebrew scholars produced a Greek translation of the Old Testament in Alexandria, Egypt called the *Septuagint*. In Leviticus 2:2, 9, 16 the *Septuagint* used the Greek word, *mnēmosunon*, for the Hebrew word, *azkarah*. This Greek word, *mnēmosunon*, means "memorial."
Also see usage of *mnēmosunon* in Acts 10:4, 31.
[14] From.the *New Revised Standard*.
[15] E.W. Bullinger, *Figures of Speech Used in the Bible*, 871.

JESUS CHRIST OUR COMPLETE OFFERING

that God will act on the basis of what is remembered and will deliver.[16] When God remembers, miraculous deliverance follows!

Another example of God's remembrance is in Acts 10, where one of the breakthrough events of the first century church is recorded: the conversion of Cornelius and his household. Rather than reading this entire exceptionally significant record, we will only look at the verses pertaining to our study.

> Acts 10:1-4:
> There was a certain man in Caesarea called Cornelius, a centurion of the band called the Italian band,
> A devout man, and one that feared God with all his house, which gave much alms to the people, and prayed to God alway.
> He saw in a vision evidently about the ninth hour of the day an angel of God coming in to him, and saying unto him, Cornelius.
> And when he looked on him, he was afraid, and said, What is it, Lord? And he said unto him, Thy prayers and thine alms are come up for a memorial [*mnēmosunon*] before God.[17]

This Greek word, *mnēmosunon*, for "memorial" is the same word used in Leviticus 2 for "memorial" in the *Septuagint*, the Greek Old Testament.

---

[16] Genesis 19:29; 30:22; Exodus 2:24 and 25; I Samuel 1:11,19. When God remembers, He acts! God's remembrance is also mention in judgment: "Babylon came in remembrance before God, to give unto her the cup of the wine of the fierceness of his wrath." (Revelation 16:19). Revelation refers to a different sense of God's remembrance with a different cup of wine than we are discussing here. Nevertheless, when God remembers, He acts.

[17] "Come up" suggests ascending to God as an offering. "memory, remembrance, memorial (as a memorial offering)." Walter J. Cummins, Working Translation in *A Journey through the Acts and Epistles*, 68.

The Meal and Drink Offerings: Precursors to Communion

Later Cornelius told Peter about this vision.

> Acts 10:30 and 31:
> And Cornelius said, Four days ago I was fasting until this hour; and at the ninth hour I prayed in my house, and, behold, a man stood before me in bright clothing,
> And said, Cornelius, thy prayer is heard, and thine alms are had in remembrance [*mnaomai*] in the sight of God.

We see from this account that "come up for a memorial before God" in verse 4 and "are had in remembrance in the sight of God" in verse 31 are equivalent statements. These verses define exactly what a memorial before God does: it comes up in remembrance before God.

In I Corinthians 11, we have seen that the cup and the bread were a memorial of Christ's accomplishments, to be done in remembrance of him. We are to recall to mind and to discern the achievements of his complete sacrifice.

We considered how the meal offering was a precursor to communion and that an integral part of this offering was a call for God's remembrance. With the understanding of the sacrificial principle of the "memorial portion" from Leviticus 2, the phrase "do in remembrance of me" suggests another layer of meaning. Since we drink the cup and eat the bread as a memorial, it also may carry the sense of invoking God's remembrance as well.

When we eat of the bread and drink from the cup, we may ask God to remember and deliver. As a memorial, communion calls on us to remember, but it calls on God to

JESUS CHRIST OUR COMPLETE OFFERING

remember as well. When God remembers, He acts in miraculous ways on behalf of His people.

When we partake of the bread we should remember what was accomplished by the body of the Savior. Also, we are well within our rights to ask God to remember as well. We should request that the bread and wine are "had in remembrance in the sight of God."

We may ask God to recall His promise that by his stripes we have healing. The memorial to Christ's sacrifice involves more than our remembrance. We call on God to remember, to act, to deliver.

In asking God to bear in mind His Son's sacrifice, perhaps we should consider that God was actually present on that afternoon when they crucified Jesus on a hill outside of Jerusalem. He would have observed the awful sight of His only begotten Son being horribly beaten, nailed to the wooden post and crucified. Still, He did not hide His face from His righteous servant as others did. While others only observed the outward events of that tragic day, He saw what the senses could not behold: His Son fully shouldered all the sins and sickness for all mankind.

God surely remembers the wounds Christ suffered for our healing. He recalls the sins and sickness laid on the savior. He was there. He remembers. Surely we can call on God to remember the price His Son paid and the promises He made when we drink the cup and eat the bread.

The Meal and Drink Offerings: Precursors to Communion

Name of Sacrifice	Hebrew Name	Functions	Distinctive Characteristics	Parallel to Christ
Meal or Bread Offering	*minchah*	Sweet savour Asking for God's remembrance	-Involved processing grain and olives into flour and oil rather than an animal sacrifice -Often paired with drink offering	The body of Christ given in sacrifice as a precursor to the bread in communion
Gift Offering	*minchah*	As gift offering: Reconciled: - Find Grace -Gain acceptance -Atone Genesis 32 and 33	Gift or present	Ephesians 1:6, 7: Christ reconciled us to God: -Riches of His Grace -Accepted in the Beloved -Atoned and redeemed

Chapter 13

Burnt Offering or Ascending Offering

Thus far, this study has considered the characteristics of the various offerings and their significance as they relate to the coming savior. As we consider the burnt offering of the Old Testament, we will see that it has some similarities to other sacrifices but also that it has unique characteristics that anticipated the coming Christ. We'll then see how Jesus Christ fulfilled that type according to God's remarkable planning and how he continues to fulfill it today.

The burnt offering has a distinctive name and functions that served as a sacrificial tutorial of the good things to come. First, let us return to Leviticus to look at the burnt offering.

> Leviticus 1:3-5:
> If his offering be a burnt sacrifice [*olah*] of the herd, let him offer a male without blemish: he shall offer it of his own voluntary will at the door of the tabernacle of the congregation before [the face of] the Lord.
> And he shall put his hand upon the head of the burnt offering [*olah*]; and it shall be accepted for him to make atonement for him.
> And he shall kill the bullock before the Lord: and the priests, Aaron's sons, shall bring the blood, and sprinkle the blood round about upon the altar that is by the door of the tabernacle of the congregation.

The Burnt or Ascending Offering

The Hebrew word, *olah,* signifies the burnt offering. The burnt offering had many similarities to the other animal sacrifices. Verse 3 stipulated this offering was to be without blemish, to be done at the initiative of the Israelite and to be presented at the door of the tabernacle. These points applied to other animal sacrifices we have examined.

As verse 4 states, the offerer was to place his hand on the head of the offering, just as with the sin offering and the peace offering. Then this sacrifice was to make atonement for the Israelite, as specifically mentioned with the trespass offering and sin offering. Like the sin offering and the peace offering, the blood of the sacrifice was to be sprinkled.

The Burnt Offering: Completely Offered unto God

Many characteristics of the burnt offering were similar to the other sacrifices we have examined. However, in the following verses we see one noteworthy difference.

> Leviticus 1:6-9:
> And he shall flay [skin] the burnt offering [*olah*], and cut it into his pieces.
> And the sons of Aaron the priest shall put fire upon the altar and lay the wood in order upon the fire
> And the priests, Aaron's sons, shall lay the parts, the head, and the fat, in order upon the wood that is on the fire which is upon the altar.
> But his inwards and his legs shall he wash in water: and the priest shall burn [*qatar*] **all** on the altar, *to be* a burnt sacrifice [*olah*], an offering made by fire, of a sweet savour unto the Lord.

JESUS CHRIST OUR COMPLETE OFFERING

This sacrifice was skinned and cut into pieces and laid upon the altar.[1] Verse 9 says: "... and the priest shall burn **all** on the altar." The entire animal was to be completely burned on the altar.

The word "whole" or "wholly" is occasionally used with the term burnt offering:[2]

> Deuteronomy 33:10: "...**whole** burnt sacrifice upon thine altar."
> I Samuel 7:9: "...a burnt offering **wholly** unto to the Lord."
> Psalm 51:19: "**whole** burnt offerings."

No portion of the offering was eaten by the offerer as were the peace and Passover sacrifices. As we noted previously, the priests were to eat of the trespass, sin, meal and peace offerings.[3] However, no part of the burnt offering was given to the priest to eat—all was consumed in the altar fire.

The sin offering was burnt, although not on the altar, but in a clean place.[4] The Hebrew word used for burning the sin offering is *saraph,* meaning to simply burn or incinerate. On the other hand, as we discussed in chapter 9, the word that referred to burning the burnt offering is the Hebrew, *qatar,* meaning to burn as incense. The burnt offering is distinguished from the other offerings in that it was wholly burned as incense to God.

---

[1] Leviticus 7:8 also says the burnt offering was to be skinned.
[2] "Whole" or "wholly" is the Hebrew adjective, kalil, meaning full or complete. *Theological Lexicon of the Old Testament,* 614; *The New Brown Driver Briggs Hebrew and English Lexicon,* 480.
[3] See chart in "Peace Offering: Double Demonstration of Identification" section in chapter 10.
[4] See chart in "*Qatar,* to burn as Incense" section in chapter 9.

The Burnt or Ascending Offering

The burnt offering entirely censed and ascended up to God as smoke; as a pleasing aroma. The distinct characteristic of the burnt offering is that it was wholly and completely offered to God.

While Leviticus 1:3-9 spoke of offering a bull, the following verses mention other animals that may be presented as a burnt offering.

> Leviticus 1:10-13:
> And if his offering be of the flocks, namely, of the sheep, or of the goats, for a burnt sacrifice [olah]; he shall bring it a male without blemish.
> And he shall kill it on the side of the altar northward before the LORD: and the priests, Aaron's sons, shall sprinkle his blood round about upon the altar.
> And he shall cut it into his pieces, with his head and his fat: and the priest shall lay them in order on the wood that is on the fire which is upon the altar:
> But he shall wash the inwards and the legs with water: and the priest shall bring it all, and burn [qatar] it upon the altar: it is a burnt sacrifice [olah], an offering made by fire, of a sweet savour unto the LORD.

Verses 3-10 mention offerings "of the herd" meaning cattle, while verses 10-13 refer to "the flocks, namely, of the sheep, or of the goats." Then the following verses, 14-17, mention a burnt offering consisting of a fowl.

> Verses 14-17:
> And if the burnt sacrifice [olah] for his offering to the LORD be of fowls, then he shall bring his offering of turtledoves, or of young pigeons.
> And the priest shall bring it unto the altar, and wring off his head, and burn [qatar] it on the altar; and the

> blood thereof shall be wrung out at the side of the altar:
> And he shall pluck away his crop with his feathers, and cast it beside the altar on the east part, by the place of the ashes:
> And he shall cleave it with the wings thereof, but shall not divide it asunder: and the priest shall burn [*qatar*] it upon the altar, upon the wood that is upon the fire: it is a burnt sacrifice [*olah*], an offering made by fire, of a sweet savour unto the LORD.

Whether a large bovine or a small bird, the worshipper could approach with a whole burnt offering as a sweet savor unto the Lord. This offering was available to Israelites in any economic strata.

The distinctive feature of this offering is that it was completely burnt on the altar as incense to God. The New Testament also points to this distinguishing characteristic.

> Hebrews 10:8:
> Above when he said, Sacrifice and offering and burnt offerings [*holokautōma*] and offering for sin thou wouldest not, neither hadst pleasure therein; which are offered by the law.

In the New Testament Greek, the word used for burnt offering is *holokautōma*, a compound word consisting of *holos*, meaning all or whole, and *kaio*, meaning "to burn." This New Testament word speaks to the distinctive feature of burnt offering: it was wholly and entirely offered unto God.

This offering looked forward to the utter totality and completeness of Christ's sacrifice for us. We behold our savior's once-and-for-all, fully accomplished sacrifice. There is nothing left undone in his sacrificial work on our behalf.

The Burnt or Ascending Offering

Since Christ performed a perfect and complete work, we are complete in him.

Olah: The Ascending Offering

Another unique feature of this offering is indicated by the meaning of the Hebrew word for the burnt offering. As noted in the above passages, *olah* is the Hebrew word for burnt offering, occurring eight times in Leviticus 1. *Olah* means "to ascend, go up" suggesting the offering going up to God in worship, not merely burning the sacrifice.[5] While every offering or portion thereof burned on the altar ascended up in smoke, the burnt offering, *olah*, is the only one so named the "ascending offering." In the "ascending offering," the actual burning is not emphasized but rather the ascending of the offering in vapor and smoke heavenward is significant.[6]

> *Olah* means "to ascend, go up"

This distinctive aspect of the ascending sacrifice is somewhat obscured by the translation of *olah* as "burnt offering." There are many words in Hebrew that literally mean to burn or incinerate. These words are not used to describe the *olah* sacrifice.[7] As mentioned, the word referring to burning the

---

[5] In the KJV, Old Testament this word, *olah*, is translated as "burnt offering" 266 times and as "burnt sacrifices" 18 times and once as "ascent."

[6] Genesis 4:3 and 4 gives the origins of sacrifice that then spread into the ancient world. According to Jacob Milgrom (*The Anchor Bible Leviticus 1-16*, 160) the ancients considered turning the offering into ascending smoke as the only way of reaching their gods.

[7] Levitical words for incinerate or burn: ***Saraph***: to burn: sin offering: Leviticus 4:12, peace offering: 7:17, 19; ***Baar*** (piel) to be consumed, burnt up: Leviticus 6:12: "...burn wood..." ***Yaqad***: burn; to set on fire. Leviticus 6:9, 13: "The fire shall ever be burning [yaqad] upon the altar; it shall never go out."
The burnt offering was *qatar*, burnt as incense, but never *saraph*, *baar* or *yaqad*.

JESUS CHRIST OUR COMPLETE OFFERING

burnt offering is the Hebrew, *qatar,* meaning to burn as incense. Leviticus 1 speaks of an offering that would ascend to God as incense to intercede on the offerer's behalf.

The following verse is the first time *olah*, the ascending offering, is mentioned by name in the Scriptures:

> Genesis 8:20 and 21:
> And Noah builded an altar unto the LORD; and took of every clean beast, and of every clean fowl, and offered[8] burnt offerings [*olah*] on the altar.
> And the LORD smelled a sweet savour; and the LORD said in his heart, I will not again curse the ground any more for man's sake; for the imagination of man's heart is evil from his youth; neither will I again smite any more every thing living, as I have done.

After the deluge of Genesis 7 and 8, Noah exited the ark and built an altar and sacrificed. This *olah* offering came up before God and it pleased Him.

In Genesis 8, as with Leviticus 1, the smoke from the ascending offerings was a "sweet savour unto the Lord." The burnt offering was an "ascending offering" which rose up to God as a soothing fragrance of acquiescence that blessed and satisfied Him. God then, lovingly and graciously, states His promise not to allow such calamity to occur again. These sacrifices had a truly powerful intercessory effect!

---

[8] The Hebrew word translated as "offered" is *alah*, the verb form of *olah*. Young's Literal renders it as: "...and causeth burnt-offerings to ascend." In Psalm 68:18 "ascended" is also *alah* in Hebrew.

The Burnt or Ascending Offering

Jesus Christ, the Complete Sacrifice that Ascended

Having learned that the literal meaning of the burnt offering is actually "ascending offering," we can see a notable parallel to the sacrifice of our savior.

> Psalm 68:18:
> Thou hast ascended on high, thou hast led captivity captive: thou hast received gifts for men...

The verb form of the Hebrew word, *olah*, is translated in this verse as "ascended." This verse from Psalms is quoted in Ephesians referring to Christ's ascension:

> Ephesians 4:8
> Wherefore he saith, When he ascended[9] up on high, he led captivity captive, and gave gifts unto men.

In Luke 24:51, speaking of the ascension states: "… he was parted from them, and carried up [*anapherō*] into heaven." The prefix of the Greek word, *anapherō* is "*ana*" meaning "up." This is of interest because *anapherō* has the thought of ascending and can be used referring to the ascending offering as it does in the following verse.

> James 2:21:
> Was not Abraham our father justified by works, when he had offered [*anapherō*] Isaac his son upon the altar?

---

[9] "Ascended" in Ephesians 4:8 is translated from the Greek word, *anabainō*. This word is used of prayers and the incense that ascended up as recorded in Revelation 8:4: "And the smoke of the incense, which came with the prayers of the saints, ascended up [*anabainō*] before God out of the angel's hand."

JESUS CHRIST OUR COMPLETE OFFERING

Abraham offered up—*anaphero*—his son as an ascending offering. In the next chapter, we will consider Abraham's offering of Isaac in detail.

This same Greek word refers to both the ascension of our Lord and the ascending of the burnt offering. The ascending sacrifice foreshadowed Christ as the complete sacrifice who ascended to God.

After Christ died, God raised him. Then he ascended into the heavens and sat down on the right hand of God.[10] He was God's ascending offering.

We have a high priest that ascended higher than the heavens and is seated at God's right hand. He has no need to offer up daily burnt offerings as required of the priests of the Old Testament. When our savior offered up himself, he was the full and final offering for God's people for all time. The ascending offering of the Old Testament portrayed Christ, the sacrifice that ascended.

Jesus Christ, our Continual Burnt Offering

There is yet another remarkable and distinctive aspect of the burnt offering that needs to be discussed. In the previous chapter on the meal offering, we read from Numbers about the daily offerings. They were to be offered twice a day and each consisted of lamb and a meal and drink offering.

> Numbers 28:3-6:
> And thou shalt say unto them, This is the offering made by fire which ye shall offer unto the LORD; two

---

[10] Hebrews 10:12: "But this man, after he had offered one sacrifice for sins for ever, sat down on the right hand of God;"

The Burnt or Ascending Offering

> lambs of the first year without spot day by day, for a **continual burnt offering**.
> The one lamb shalt thou offer in the morning, and the other lamb shalt thou offer at even; [between the two evenings].
> And a tenth part of an ephah of flour for a meat offering, mingled with the fourth part of an hin of beaten oil.
> **It is a continual burnt offering**, which was ordained in mount Sinai for a sweet savour, a sacrifice made by fire unto the LORD.

The "continual burnt offering" was the daily offering of the lamb, the meal and the wine. Carried out twice daily, this burnt offering was referred to as "continual."[11]

The burnt offering was totally censed on the altar unto God. As we observed in chapter 10 on the peace offering, the priests were to eat a portion of many of the offerings. In contrast, the daily offerings were to be continual burnt offerings completely consumed on the altar as a sweet savor unto God.

Continual Burnt Offering Offered Twice daily

Numbers 28 and 29 gave a calendar of public sacrifices to be carried out throughout the year. While laborious reading, these chapters cataloged the various offerings to take place

---

[11] The Hebrew word for "continual" is *tamid* meaning perpetual or continual. Leviticus 6:20 refers to the daily offerings: "...the tenth part of an ephah of fine flour for a meat offering perpetual [*tamid*], half of it in the morning, and half thereof at night. These daily burnt offerings were to be continual, done in perpetuity, never interrupted.

JESUS CHRIST OUR COMPLETE OFFERING

on the Sabbath days, at the new moons and on the feast days.

> Numbers 28:9 and 10:
> And on the sabbath day two lambs of the first year without spot, and two tenth deals of flour for a meat offering, mingled with oil, and the drink offering thereof:
> This is the burnt offering of every sabbath, **beside the continual burnt offering**, and his drink offering.

On every Sabbath day, there were to be supplementary offerings in addition to the daily continual burnt offering commanded in verses 3-6. Verse 10 closes with: "…**beside the continual burnt offering**, and his drink offering." Just because there were additional sacrifices to be offered on the Sabbath day did not mean that the daily offerings were to be neglected.

These chapters go on to enumerate the extra offerings to be carried out on the various holy days and during the feasts. What is of note is that after the special offerings are listed, it repeatedly appends: "…beside the continual burnt offering."

In chapters 28 and 29, the phrase "…beside the continual burnt offering" is mentioned over a dozen times.[12] In the Scriptures, this type of repetition is a figure of speech added by divine design for emphasis.

When God repeats "…beside the continual burnt offering" numerous times, the aim of this figure is not smooth

---

[12] This phrase, "…beside the continual burnt offering." occurs in the following verses: Numbers 28:10, 15, 23, 24: 31; chapter 29:11, 16, 19, 22, 25, 28, 31, 34, 38. See Julia B. Hans, *Go Figure! An Introduction to Figures of Speech in the Bible*, 69-73: The figure *Reptitio* is defined as "the repetition of the same word or words irregularly in the same passage."

The Burnt or Ascending Offering

reading, but to seize our attention. Like other figures of speech, it has one end: to catch the readers' notice. Since the continual burnt offering was so markedly emphasized in these chapters, what does it signify? What did the daily burnt sacrifice accomplish for the nation of Israel that merited this riveting figure of repetition?

In chapter 9, we explored the function of the "sweet savor" offerings, the burnt, meal, and peace offerings. We noted that the Hebrew word, *qatar*, while translated as "burned" was actually the verb form of Hebrew noun for incense.

> *Qetoreth:* **Incense (noun)**
> (Psalm 141:2; Leviticus 16:12, 13, Numbers 16:46, 47)
>
> *Qatar:* **Burn as incense; cense (verb)**
> (Leviticus 1:9, 13, 15, 17; 2:2, 9, 11, 16; 3:5, 11, 16)

These "sweet savor" offerings were in point of fact offered up as incense to God on the altar. The burnt, meal, and peace offerings were "incense offerings."

We also considered what burning incense represented in the Bible in chapter 9. One of the most dramatic examples of the role of burning incense is recorded in Numbers 16. A massive plague started to engulf and threatened to destroy the children of Israel. Then, by the instructions of Moses, Aaron quickly grabbed fire off the altar and lit the incense and ran into the middle of the camp. The pestilence was rapidly brought to a halt. This passage states that the incense made atonement for them. As the high priest stood between the dead and the living, the wrath was turned away, and then the plague was stopped. The incense represented the intercessory prayer of the high priest. As we have considered, incense has the distinctive purpose of prayer and intercession in the Scriptures.

The following verses give explicit examples of the function of the burnt (ascending) offering.

> I Samuel 7:9 and 10:
> And Samuel took a sucking lamb, and offered it for a burnt offering [*olah*, ascending offering] wholly unto the LORD: and Samuel cried unto the LORD for Israel; and the LORD heard him.
> And as Samuel was offering up the burnt offering, the Philistines drew near to battle against Israel: but the LORD thundered with a great thunder on that day upon the Philistines, and discomfited them; and they were smitten before Israel.

This ascending offering served to intercede before God.

> II Samuel 24:25:
> And David built there an altar unto the LORD, and offered burnt offerings [*olah*, ascending offering] and peace offerings. So the LORD was intreated for the land, and the plague was stayed from Israel.

These burnt offerings ascended to God, entreating Him to intervene.

Keeping this in mind, we can see the function and purpose of the "continual burnt offering." The daily offerings were to be an ever-ascending offering unto God asking Him to intervene. These daily burnt offerings functioned to intercede before God, morning and evening.

Looking at the New Covenant we can see a notable parallel:

The Burnt or Ascending Offering

Hebrews 7:22-28:

By so much was Jesus made a surety of a better testament.

And they truly were many priests, because they were not suffered to **continue** by reason of death:

But this man, because he **continueth** ever, hath an unchangeable priesthood.

Wherefore he is able also to save them to the uttermost that come unto God by him, seeing he **ever liveth to make intercession** for them.

For such an high priest became us, who is holy, harmless, undefiled, separate from sinners, and made higher than the heavens;

Who needeth not daily, as those high priests, to offer up sacrifice, first for his own sins, and then for the people's: for this he did once, when he offered up himself.

For the law maketh men high priests which have infirmity; but the word of the oath, which was since the law, maketh the Son, who is consecrated for evermore.

The high priests of the Old Covenant could not continue in their office by reason of death. In contrast, the Lord Jesus Christ continues ceaselessly in his position as high priest at God's right hand. His life and ministry of intercession on our behalf is uninterrupted. Since "he ever liveth to make intercession" for us, he can completely save us to the uttermost.

In the Law, there is no "continual **sin** offering." On the Day of Atonement once a year, the sin offerings were presented for the whole nation. But these sacrifices could not permanently remove sin. Jesus Christ's sacrifice for sin was once and for all. As the sin offering, our lord was "offered

JESUS CHRIST OUR COMPLETE OFFERING

once to bare the sins of many."[13] As the sin offering, he died once and for all, but as the ascending offering he continues to live unto God to intercede on our behalf.

The intercession of Christ for us is continual, perpetual, and forever. Christ was foreshadowed by the daily burnt offering that was offered for continual and perpetual intercession to God for the Israelites. This continual burnt offering anticipated the coming one, set higher than the heavens at God's right hand. Christ, the high priest, interceding on our behalf is able to deliver to the uttermost. Morning by morning, evening by evening, one greater than Aaron ever lives in the heavenly places to be our representative and our mediator before the Father. We are never left helpless or isolated from God.

---

[13] Hebrews 9:28.

Chapter 14

The Burnt Offering: Utterly Devoted to God

In the chapter on the peace offering, we observed that sacrifices to God was not to be an empty ritual. The peace offerings were to be offered to God with rejoicing. With the burnt offering, the frame of mind of the offerer was crucial as well. The Old Testament has some sterling examples of correct mindset of the burnt offering. We will see how our Lord Jesus Christ gave his all, demonstrating his love and unwavering commitment to God. The chapter will conclude with a consideration of how sons of God today can apply this example.

Genesis 22: Abraham's Burnt Offering

The early uses of a word in the Bible can be most revealing. The following passage gives insight into the burnt (ascending) offering, which is mentioned six times. Our look at Genesis 22 will not be comprehensive but will focus in on the burnt offering and some remarkable patterns and types of the coming Christ.[1]

---

[1] From more context on Abraham and insight into this chapter see: Christopher C. Geer, *In the Footsteps of Patriarchs, Prophets, Believers, and Kings* (Glasgow, Scotland: Word Promotions, 2006) Chapter 1.

JESUS CHRIST OUR COMPLETE OFFERING

> Genesis 22:1-4:
> And it came to pass after these things, that God did tempt [test, prove] Abraham, and said unto him, Abraham: and he said, Behold, here I am.
> And he said, Take now thy son, thine only son Isaac, whom thou lovest, and get thee into **the land of Moriah**; and offer him there for a burnt offering [*olah*=ascending offering] upon **one of the mountains which I will tell thee of**.
> And Abraham rose up early in the morning, and saddled his ass, and took two of his young men with him, and Isaac his son, and clave the wood for the burnt offering [*olah*], and rose up, and went unto **the place of which God had told him**.
> Then on the third day Abraham lifted up his eyes, and saw **the place afar off**.

God asked Abraham to take his son, Isaac, to the land of Moriah and offer him as a burnt offering, that is, to cause him to ascend as an ascending offering. Abraham was obedient to God's request and left for that location. In the passage, the multiple references to the location of the sacrifice have been emphasized with bold print for the reader. God was very specific on the exact place where the sacrifice was to be offered.

> II Chronicles 3:1:
> Then Solomon began to build the house of the LORD at Jerusalem in mount Moriah, where the LORD appeared unto David his father, in the place that David had prepared in the threshingfloor of Ornan the Jebusite.

The site of Solomon's temple, the temple mount at Jerusalem, was called Mount Moriah. Since the crucifixion

The Burnt Offering: Utterly Devoted to God

took place in close proximity to this location, the burnt offering of Genesis 22 corresponded to the location of the offering of our Lord Jesus Christ.[2] In this account, we see how God had been planning the location of where the Son of God would bear the sins of all humanity since the book of Genesis.

We have delved into the detail of Christ's work as foreshadowed in the sacrifices of the Law. Each offering had distinct aspects that corresponded to Christ's ultimate sacrifice. We can marvel at how God designed our redemption in such detail and clarity. Here in Genesis, we see how the location of the crucifixion was arranged by God so many centuries in advance.

God revealed to Abraham the location of where He would provide the sacrifice for man's redemption. It is rather paradoxical that two thousand years after the crucifixion, there is difficulty determining the exact site, while Abraham, about two thousand before, pinpointed the location (See Appendix One: "Probable Location of the Crucifixion").

> Genesis 22:5-14:
> And Abraham said unto his young men, Abide ye here with the ass; and I and the lad will go yonder and worship, and come again to you.
> And Abraham took the wood of the **burnt offering** [olah], and laid it upon Isaac his son; and he took the

---

[2] Ernest Martin explained that the term "Moriah" refers not to a single mountain, but to a mountain range that included the Mount of Olives as well as the temple mount. In the area of Jerusalem, the highest mountain was the Mount of Olives. Normally the highest peak in an area would be selected as an altar. Also since Abraham saw the mountain afar off (verse 4) it would have been the highest peak. Therefore, Abraham's sacrifice most likely took place on the Mount of Olives. See Ernest Martin, *Secrets of Golgotha* (Associates of Scriptural Knowledge: Portland, Oregon) chapter 13 and my Appendix One: "Probable Location of the Crucifixion."

fire in his hand, and a knife; and they went both of them together.

And Isaac spake unto Abraham his father, and said, My father: and he said, Here am I, my son. And he said, Behold the fire and the wood: but where is the lamb for a **burnt offering** [olah]?

And Abraham said, My son, God will provide himself a lamb for a **burnt offering** [olah]: so they went both of them together.

And they came to the place which God had told him of; and Abraham built an altar there, and laid the wood in order, and bound Isaac his son, and laid him on the altar upon the wood.

And Abraham stretched forth his hand, and took the knife to slay his son.

And the angel of the LORD called unto him out of heaven, and said, Abraham, Abraham: and he said, Here am I.

And he said, Lay not thine hand upon the lad, neither do thou any thing unto him: for now I know that thou fearest God, seeing thou hast not withheld thy son, thine only son from me.

And Abraham lifted up his eyes, and looked, and behold behind him a ram caught in a thicket by his horns: and Abraham went and took the ram, and offered [alah] him up for a **burnt offering** [olah] in the stead of his son.

And Abraham called the name of that place Jehovahjireh: as it is said to this day, In the mount of the LORD it shall be seen [provided].

In this passage, we see the obedience of both the father and the son. Abraham, by God's direction, sets off with Isaac knowing God will provide a burnt offering. Isaac, a full grown man, obeys his father and allows himself to be bound and laid upon the altar. Then, as Abraham stretches forth his

The Burnt Offering: Utterly Devoted to God

hand to kill his son, he obeys the voice that bids him to stop. After that, he offers a ram caught in the thicket in place of his son.

Abraham called the name of that place, "Jehovahjireh," meaning that in this mountain, "the Lord shall see" or "the Lord shall provide." What was the Lord going to see and provide? In this location, on this mountain, God was to provide for the salvation and redemption of humanity. Abraham said in verse 8, "...God [Elohim] will provide himself a lamb for a burnt offering." Then in verse 14, Abraham declared: "Jehovah will provide." Also, it should be noted that the Hebrew word for Moriah in verse 2, means "Jah will provide."[3]

God Provides	
Jah provides	verse 2
Elohim provides	verse 8
Jehovah provides	verse 14

The focal point is that God will supply the sacrifice in this location.

> Verses 15-18:
> And the angel of the LORD called unto Abraham out of heaven the second time,
> And said, By myself have I sworn, saith the LORD, for because thou hast done this thing, and hast not withheld thy son, thine only son:
> That in blessing I will bless thee, and in multiplying I will multiply thy seed as the stars of the heaven, and

---

[3] Robert Young, *Analytical Concordance to the Bible* (Grand Rapids: Michigan, Eerdmans, 1976) 669.

> as the sand which is upon the sea shore; and thy seed shall possess the gate of his enemies;
> And in thy seed shall all the nations of the earth be blessed; because thou hast obeyed my voice.

God says in verse 16: "...for now I know that thou fearest God, seeing thou hast not withheld thy son, thine only son from me." The reverence Abraham had for God's words and his subsequent obedience is staggering. We see evidence that the offerer presenting the burnt offering was to have an unreserved commitment to God.

Abraham's Accounting

While Genesis 22:15-18 gives insight into God's intentions, the following verses in the New Testament shed light on Abraham's perspective.

> Galatians 3:8
> And the scripture, foreseeing that God would justify the heathen through faith, preached before the gospel unto Abraham, saying, In thee shall all nations be blessed.

Galatians 3:8 makes the astounding statement that the good news of Christ was announced beforehand to Abraham. God not only told Abraham that "in thee shall all nations be blessed" but He told him how all humanity would be justified by believing in the coming redeemer.[4] Evidently Genesis does not tell us everything God told Abraham.[5]

---

[4] What Abraham knew would **not** include the Mystery as declared in Ephesians chapter 3.
[5] Geer, *Footsteps*, 92.

The Burnt Offering: Utterly Devoted to God

Christ said: "Your father Abraham rejoiced to see my day: and he saw it, and was glad" (John 8:56). God showed Abraham, by revelation, a day when the savior would come. Abraham must have known a lot about the coming Christ.

> Hebrews 11:17-19:
> By faith Abraham, when he was tried, offered up Isaac: and he that had received the promises offered up his only begotten son,
> Of whom it was said, That in Isaac shall thy seed be called:
> Accounting that God was able to raise him up, even from the dead; from whence also he received him in a figure [parable].

Abraham accounted that God was going to raise Isaac from the dead. For him to believe that Isaac would be raised from the dead, as Hebrews 11:19 tells us, Abraham must have also known that the promised savior would be raised from the dead as well. This fits with Galatians 3:8 which states that Abraham knew the gospel.

In Genesis 22, Abraham rejoiced with that day of redemption in view and was willing to sacrifice his own beloved son knowing he would be raised from the dead. Abraham was so committed to God's plan of redemption that he would even offer up his own son.

One of the leading pastimes in our country is spectator sports. People love to watch sports without participating. Genesis 22 demonstrated that Abraham was willing to go beyond being a mere spectator to God's plan of redemption. He was ready to be an actual involved participant. Abraham was willing to obey God to the uttermost.

JESUS CHRIST OUR COMPLETE OFFERING

What does it mean when it says Abraham received Isaac back from the dead in a "parable" in Hebrews 11:19? A parable is the placing of two things side by side for the purpose of comparison. A parable is an extended simile containing likenesses, comparing resemblances to teach a spiritual truth.[6]

Jesus frequently taught in parables in the Gospels. The parable of the prodigal son and the forgiving father in Luke 15 compares or parallels God's love and forgiveness to that of the father in the parable. We have seen that the sacrifices of the Old Testament parallel to Christ's sacrifice, with likenesses and resemblances. Abraham received Isaac back from the dead, paralleling how God would in the future raise His only begotten Son from the dead.

Genesis 22:4 says: "...on the third day Abraham lifted up his eyes, and saw the place afar off." On the third day of the journey, Abraham saw the mountain where the sacrifice was to be made. During the three days that elapsed from the time Abraham set out to offer Isaac as a burnt offering, he was as good as dead to him. For three days, Abraham believed that God was able to raise him from the dead once the sacrifice had taken place. Abraham received Isaac back from the dead after the third day, paralleling how God would raise His only begotten Son from the dead after three days and three nights.

Isaac serves as a model of Christ in many other respects. In Genesis 21:12, before the events of Genesis 22, God had told Abraham, "in Isaac shall thy seed be called." Hebrews 11:18

---

[6] The word "figure" in Hebrews 11:19 is a translation of the Greek word, *parabolē*, meaning an illustration, comparison or parable; a placing of two things side by side for the purpose of comparison. E. W. Bullinger in *Figures of Speech Used in the Bible,* 751. Also see: Joseph Henry Thayer, *Greek-English Lexicon of the New Testament*, 479.

The Burnt Offering: Utterly Devoted to God

also mentions this promise. Galatians 3:16 tells us to whom exactly "thy seed" refers to:

> Galatians 3:16:
> Now to Abraham and his seed were the promises made. He saith not, And to seeds, as of many; but as of one, And to thy seed, which is Christ.

Isaac is a most expressive pattern of Christ in the Old Testament. Isaac was the only begotten son, the promised seed of a miraculous conception.[7] He was taken to one of the mountains of Moriah—to the likely site of the future crucifixion—to be sacrificed. Isaac willingly allowed himself to be offered. There is no indication of any argument or struggle.

Abraham proceeded to sacrifice his son, accounting that God was able to raise him from dead. But just before he was to be offered, an angel of the Lord stopped him and a ram was supplied "in his stead."

Isaac was a type of Christ, willing to voluntarily lay down his life as a burnt offering in obedience to his father. Then in a most stunning fashion, God provides a ram, a burnt offering as a substitute for Isaac. This ram is also an outstanding parallel to Christ. God—and He alone—supplied it. Also, this ram was a substitute as was Christ, offered in place of Isaac. In the fullness of time, God would offer His only begotten Son, not Abraham's.

The account in Genesis 22 closes with God's declaration of many promises to Abraham, "because thou hast done this thing, and hast not withheld thy son, thine only son." Verse 18 closes this pledge: "And in thy seed shall all the nations

---

[7] Romans 4:17-21 and Genesis 18:1-19; 21:1-8 tell about Isaac's miraculous conception and birth.

JESUS CHRIST OUR COMPLETE OFFERING

of the earth be blessed; because thou hast obeyed my voice." Because Abraham obeyed with such devotion and commitment, God swore that He would bring to pass His promises.

In this poignant example of the burnt offering, Abraham was so completely obedient to God that he did not withhold his only son. This devotion on the part of Abraham displays one of the foremost characteristics of the burnt offering. Just as that entire burnt offering was totally devoted to God, so the entire being of the offerer was also to be totally devoted also.

To be fully burnt upon the altar before the Lord gave this offering a uniquely forceful emphasis of full commitment to do God's will. Just as the *olah* sacrifice ascended entirely to God, so the heart of the offerer was to be entirely devoted to God.

Jephthah's Burnt Offering

In Judges there is an account of another burnt offering that is often misunderstood.

> Judges 11:30 and 31:
> And Jephthah vowed a vow unto the LORD, and said, If thou shalt without fail deliver the children of Ammon into mine hands,
> Then it shall be, that whatsoever cometh forth of the doors of my house to meet me, when I return in peace from the children of Ammon, shall surely be the LORD'S, and I will offer it up for a burnt offering.

The Burnt Offering: Utterly Devoted to God

Jephthah made a commitment to God that, if victorious, whatever came out of his house would first "surely be the Lord's" and second, would be offered up as a burnt offering.

> Verses 32-36:
> So Jephthah passed over unto the children of Ammon to fight against them; and the LORD delivered them into his hands.
> And he smote them from Aroer, even till thou come to Minnith, even twenty cities, and unto the plain of the vineyards, with a very great slaughter. Thus the children of Ammon were subdued before the children of Israel.
> And Jephthah came to Mizpeh unto his house, and, behold, his daughter came out to meet him with timbrels and with dances: and she was his only child; beside her he had neither son nor daughter.
> And it came to pass, when he saw her, that he rent his clothes, and said, Alas, my daughter! thou hast brought me very low, and thou art one of them that trouble me: for I have opened my mouth unto the LORD, and I cannot go back.
> And she said unto him, My father, if thou hast opened thy mouth unto the LORD, do to me according to that which hath proceeded out of thy mouth; forasmuch as the LORD hath taken vengeance for thee of thine enemies, even of the children of Ammon.

After this phenomenal victory, Jephthah arrives home and his daughter comes out to meet him. He was very distressed because of his vow. As much as it pained Jephthah, his daughter insisted that they should do as he promised God.

JESUS CHRIST OUR COMPLETE OFFERING

> Verses 37-40:
> And she said unto her father, Let this thing be done for me: let me alone two months, that I may go up and down upon the mountains, and bewail my virginity, I and my fellows.
> And he said, Go. And he sent her away for two months: and she went with her companions, and bewailed her virginity upon the mountains.
> And it came to pass at the end of two months, that she returned unto her father, who did with her according to his vow which he had vowed: and she knew no man. And it was a custom in Israel,
> That the daughters of Israel went yearly to lament [talk to] the daughter of Jephthah the Gileadite four days in a year.

When this passage is read, it is commonly assumed that this poor child was killed and then burned up as a sacrifice. However, the question arises: if she was to be slain as an offering, why would she want to bewail her virginity? Her virginity would not be at issue here, but her imminent death! Why the concern about remaining unmarried if she was soon to be killed? Verse 39 says he "did with her according to his vow which he had vowed: and she knew no man." Again, if the vow was for her to be killed and sacrificed as a burnt offering, why does it mention "she knew no man," which suggests she would remain unmarried and childless?

According to Bishop K. C. Pillai, there were two kinds of burnt offerings. One was to be killed and consumed on the altar. The other was to dedicate oneself to serve God in the temple for the rest of one's life, remaining unmarried and childless.[8] In ancient times, it was a shame and a disgrace for a woman to be unmarried and childless.

---

[8] From the teachings of Bishop K.C. Pillai in Christopher C Geer, *Appreciating Oriental Insights in the Bible*, Student's Study Guide to Set 1, 33-35. Other

The Burnt Offering: Utterly Devoted to God

"Bewailed her virginity" indicates that she was preparing to work at the house of God and suffer the shame of being childless. Upon entering the service of God, her head would be shaved and she would put on a veil.[9]

Verse 40 says the daughters of Israel went four days a year to "lament" the daughter of Jephthah the Gileadite. The word lament simply means to "talk" in the Hebrew. The *Young's Literal Translation* more accurately renders Judges 11:40: "From time to time the daughters of Israel go to talk to the daughter of Jephthah the Gileadite, four days in a year." Four days a year, her friends would pay her a visit to celebrate her commitment and devotion to God.[10]

This wonderful woman was not slain and entirely incinerated on the altar. Rather, Jephthah's daughter was a burnt offering in the sense that she fully dedicated herself to obey God exclusively. She abandoned marriage and family and served in the house of God. Her whole life was to ascend to God in service.

> I Corinthians 13:3:
> And though I bestow all my goods to feed the poor, and though I give my body to be burned, and have not charity, it profiteth me nothing.

---

scholars also hold the view that Jephthah's daughter was not sacrificed, but served God. See: C.F. Keil and R. Delitzsch, *Commentary on the Old Testament*, 388-395.

[9] During this period the "house of God" was at Shiloh (Joshua 18:1, 8, 19:51; Judges 18:31). I Samuel 2:22 and Exodus 38:8 mention "the women that assembled at the door of the tabernacle." These women devoted themselves to serve at the house of God, as did Jephthah's daughter.

[10] *American Standard Version, World English Bible* and Darby's say: "celebrate" not "lament." Also see note in Bullinger's *Companion Bible*.

JESUS CHRIST OUR COMPLETE OFFERING

Where this verse states that "I give my body to be burned," we may think of the Christian martyrs being burned at the stake for their faith in the Middle Ages. However, in the biblical context, this burning may not indicate physical destruction but suggests giving oneself in full devotion and obedience to God.

Jesus Christ: He Gave His All

The accounts of Genesis 22 and Judges 11 demonstrated that the burnt offering expressed complete commitment and obedience to God. The entire burnt offering was to be fully consumed. Likewise, the heart and motivation of the offerer of the burnt offering should be fully devoted to carry out God's will.

Jesus Christ was the ultimate exemplar of one who devoted himself utterly to do God's will. The following passage tells of the time immediately before his arrest and subsequent crucifixion.

> Matthew 26:36-39:
> Then cometh Jesus with them unto a place called Gethsemane, and saith unto the disciples, Sit ye here, while I go and pray yonder.
> And he took with him Peter and the two sons of Zebedee, and began to be sorrowful and very heavy.
> Then saith he unto them, My soul is exceeding sorrowful, even unto death: tarry ye here, and watch with me.
> And he went a little further, and fell on his face, and prayed, saying, O my Father, if it be possible, let this cup pass from me: nevertheless not as I will, but as thou wilt.

The Burnt Offering: Utterly Devoted to God

After the last supper, Jesus went to the Garden of Gethsemane in the vicinity of the Mount of Olives to pray. He was under intense pressure knowing his arrest was imminent. He was aware of the tortures and crucifixion that awaited him. Jesus prayed that, if possible, "this cup might pass from me." Yet, his statement, "not as I will, but as thou wilt" in verse 39, demonstrates his devotion and commitment to obey God.

> Verses 40-45:
> And he cometh unto the disciples, and findeth them asleep, and saith unto Peter, What, could ye not watch with me one hour?
> Watch and pray, that ye enter not into temptation: the spirit indeed is willing, but the flesh is weak.
> He went away again the second time, and prayed, saying, O my Father, if this cup may not pass away from me, except I drink it, thy will be done.
> And he came and found them asleep again: for their eyes were heavy.
> And he left them, and went away again, and prayed the third time, saying the same words.
> Then cometh he to his disciples, and saith unto them, Sleep on now, and take your rest: behold, the hour is at hand, and the Son of man is betrayed into the hands of sinners.

Three times Jesus entreated God concerning his dire situation. His devotion to obey God is stunning. His final decision was: "thy will be done." At this point, he determined by his free will to lay down his life as the one-time perfect sacrifice for mankind. Just as the burnt offering that wholly ascended up to God, our Lord wholly gave himself to carry out God's will.

JESUS CHRIST OUR COMPLETE OFFERING

It is noteworthy that in Luke 22:37, right before Jesus departs for Gethsemane, he quotes from Isaiah 53: "For I say unto you, that this that is written must yet be accomplished in me, And he was reckoned among the transgressors: for the things concerning me have an end."

"And he was reckoned among the transgressors..." is a quote from Isaiah 53:12. He said of this prophecy in Isaiah, "must yet be accomplished in me." He knew full well he was to be the suffering servant of the Lord—the righteous man whose "visage marred more than any man" (Isaiah 52:14). He was the one to be despised, rejected, stricken, smitten, afflicted, pierced, crushed. On him would be "laid the iniquity of us all"(Isaiah 53:6). Jesus knew the suffering and death he faced. Yet, he "humbled himself, and became obedient unto death, even the death of the cross."[11]

What happened in the garden of Gethsemane must be called the greatest act of obedience to God in human history. Just as that whole burnt offering was totally devoted to God, Jesus devoted his whole being to do God's will. Just as the *olah* sacrifice ascended entirely to God, so our Lord was determined to obey God to the uttermost. Jesus Christ completely gave himself as the burnt offering.

Our savior's unreserved commitment to do God's will is mentioned in the following verses.

> Hebrews 10:4-7:
> For it is not possible that the blood of bulls and of goats should take away sins.
> Wherefore when he [Christ] cometh into the world, he saith, "Sacrifice and offering thou wouldest [desired] not, but a body hast thou prepared me:

---

[11] Philippians 2:8.

The Burnt Offering: Utterly Devoted to God

> In burnt offerings and sacrifices for sin thou hast had no pleasure.
> Then said I, Lo, I come (in the volume of the book it is written of me,) **to do thy will**, O God." [quotation marks added]

Jesus Christ declared that he came to do God's will. Sacrifices and offerings were not what God desired or had pleasure in. The blood of those sacrifices was powerless to fully remove sin and to pay the ultimate price to secure man's redemption and salvation.

Christ, quoting from Psalm 40, declared: "in the volume of the book it is written of me." The "volume of the book" could refer to the entire volume of the Scriptures.[12] Indeed, the main theme of the Word of God is the Lord Jesus Christ and his towering accomplishments. The Levitical sacrifices and offerings were only one aspect of how the Scriptures taught of the coming Christ.

> Verses 8-10:
> Above [in verses 5-7] when he said, Sacrifice and offering and burnt offerings and offering for sin thou wouldest [desired] not, neither hadst pleasure therein; which are offered by the law;
> Then said he, Lo, I come **to do thy will**, O God. He taketh away the first, that he may establish the second.
> By the which **will** we are sanctified through the offering of the body of Jesus Christ once for all.

God designed the blood of bulls and goats as well as the meal and wine offerings of the Mosaic Law to foreshadow the ultimate sacrifice to come. As Hebrews 9:10 says, these

---

[12] Walter J. Cummins and Daniel J. Bader, *Volume 2, A Journey through the Acts and Epistles* (Franklin, Ohio: Scripture Consulting, 2013) 47.

JESUS CHRIST OUR COMPLETE OFFERING

rituals were "imposed on them until" a new order was established. All the sacrifices and offerings were a temporary means to teach and show God's people about the full and perfect sacrifice to come.

Every one of these offerings of the Law was insufficient to accomplish God's plans. God wanted an equivalent substitute to pay the full price for mankind's redemption. By taking heed to God's will, Christ abolished the Old Covenant with all its offerings and sacrifices and established a New Covenant. Verse 10 further explains that by offering himself, Christ sanctified us once and for all.

As verses 7 and 9 state, Jesus came to do God's will. By his own voluntary will he placed himself at God's disposal to carry out the written Word of God as the Messiah. As the gospel records enumerate in detail, he fulfilled the prophecies and types of the Old Testament Scripture concerning himself. He knew what the volume of the book said regarding the coming one. Christ believed the Word of God specifically about himself, and then he carried it out.

To understand the eternal repercussions of the moment of decision in the garden of Gethsemane, let's look at Romans.

> Romans 5:19:
> For as by one man's disobedience many were made sinners, so by the obedience of one shall many be made righteous.

By the disobedience of Adam in the Garden of Eden all humanity fell into sin and death. But by the obedience of Christ to become our sacrifice, "many shall be made righteous." In a garden, Adam decided to disobey God; in a very different garden, the Son of Man made the ultimate decision to obey God.

The Burnt Offering: Utterly Devoted to God

Romans 5:21 says: "That as sin hath reigned unto death, even so might grace reign through righteousness unto eternal life by Jesus Christ our Lord." Instead of a reign of sin and death, grace reigns. This is a rather abrupt reversal! The entire fulcrum of human history shifted and changed direction by the sacrifice of Christ. Sin and death was replaced with grace and righteousness.

Hebrews 9:26 says, "…but now once in the end of the world [ages] hath he appeared to put away sin by the sacrifice of himself." Christ's obedience and subsequent sacrifice was so monumental it is called the end of the ages or the consummation of the ages. The ages of sin and death ended when Jesus Christ "put away sin by sacrifice of himself."

When our lord paid the price by his sacrifice, the whole course of human history was altered. This focal event of human history was more than a victory for God—it reversed the momentum for all mankind. Look at the eternal benefits to God's people when Jesus Christ decided to give his life in the garden of Gethsemane!

As a whole burnt offering was entirely offered to God, Jesus offered his entire being to do God's will. He completely fulfilled the purpose of the burnt offering. He gave his all.

Living Sacrifices Alive from the Dead

We considered that Abraham set out by God's instructions to offer his son, Isaac, as a burnt offering to God. He accounted that God was able to raise his son from the dead after being sacrificed. Abraham believed that Isaac would be raised up from the dead to be a living sacrifice. Jephthah's daughter was willing to dedicate herself to a lifetime of service as a living sacrifice.

JESUS CHRIST OUR COMPLETE OFFERING

Jesus Christ offered himself to God as a sacrifice for sin forever. God then raised him from the dead to life eternal to be a living sacrifice. Romans 6:10 states of Christ: "For in that he died, he died unto sin once: but in that he liveth, he liveth unto God." Seated at God's right hand, "he liveth unto God" as high priest and intercessor. Then Romans 12:1 says we are to be "living sacrifices."

The following section in Romans explains our service as living sacrifices.

> Romans 6:8,11-13:
> Now if **we be dead with Christ, we believe that we shall also live with him...**
> ...Likewise reckon ye also yourselves to **be dead indeed unto sin, but alive unto God** through Jesus Christ our Lord.
> Let not sin therefore reign in your mortal body, that ye should obey it in the lusts thereof.
> Neither yield [present] ye your members as instruments of unrighteousness unto sin: but yield [present] yourselves unto God, as **those that are alive from the dead,** and your members as instruments of righteousness unto God.

As emphasized by the bold print, these verses in Romans mention three times that we are dead yet alive.

> **"...dead indeed unto sin, but alive unto God..."**

The Burnt Offering: Utterly Devoted to God

In what sense are we alive from the dead? Galatians 2:20 says, "…I was crucified with Christ, nevertheless I live…," declaring that we are identified with Christ's sacrifice.

In Romans 6:5, it states: "So if we have become identified with *him* in the likeness of his death, *then* we shall also certainly be *in the likeness* of his resurrection."[13] Speaking in sacrificial terminology, since we fully share in Christ's sacrifice, in utter oneness with him, we are alive from the dead. Therefore, we should serve God as living sacrifices fully committed to Him.

Romans 6:11 tell us something that we should carry out as those alive from the dead: "…reckon ye also yourselves to be dead indeed unto sin." The Greek word translated "reckon" is the same word translated "accounting" in Hebrews 11:19: "Accounting that God was able to raise him up, even from the dead…" Abraham accounted that God was able to raise Isaac from the dead. We are to "account" ourselves as dead to sin and alive to God.

As we saw, Abraham's did not casually mental assent but rather gave a full-hearted believing action on God's revelation. Likewise, we should act on what God has revealed and step onto the higher plane of our life in Christ Jesus.

In Romans 6:11, God tells us to consider the reality of our identification with Christ. Our sin nature was crucified, died and buried in Christ. We are to transform our thinking to align with what God has accomplished by Christ's sacrificial work.

---

[13] Cited from the Working Translation in *A Journey through the Acts and Epistles*. Copyright © 2006 by Walter J. Cummins. All rights reserved.

JESUS CHRIST OUR COMPLETE OFFERING

The following verses provide further instruction on how to live as those dead to sins.

> Romans 6:16 and 17:
> Know ye not, that to whom ye yield yourselves servants to **obey**, his servants ye are to whom ye **obey**; whether of sin unto death, or of **obedience** unto righteousness?
> But God be thanked, that ye were the servants of sin, but ye have **obeyed** from the heart that form of doctrine which was delivered you.

An essential factor in the burnt offering was obedience to God. Just as the burnt offering was completely and entirely consumed on the altar, one was to be completely committed to obey God. Our service as living sacrifices alive from the dead is to obey God by heeding the teaching of His Word.

> Romans 12:1:
> I beseech you therefore, brethren, by the mercies of God, that ye present your bodies a living sacrifice, holy, acceptable unto God, which is your reasonable [divine] service.

As living sacrifices, we are to be fully devoted to God and to do His will. The next verse in Romans tells us how to carry out God's will as living sacrifices:

> Romans 12:2:
> And be not conformed to this world: but be ye transformed by the renewing of your mind, that ye may prove what is that good, and acceptable, and perfect, will of God.

We are not asked to shave our heads and enter into a lifetime of temple service. We are not asked to present our

The Burnt Offering: Utterly Devoted to God

firstborn as a burnt offering. We are not asked to die on the cross for the sins of humanity. Rather, God implores us to transform ourselves by the renewing of the mind, to live for God in sacrificial service. As a living sacrifice, wholly dedicated to God, we should not be conformed to the world, but rather transformed by renewing our minds in order to "prove what is that good, and acceptable, and perfect, will of God."

Just as Christ offered himself in complete and total obedience to God, we ought to offer ourselves in full obedience as servants of righteousness. Considering all that our Lord Jesus Christ went through to obtain our salvation, we certainly ought to present ourselves freely, joyfully and wholly to God as living sacrifices.

To account or consider ourselves dead to sin gets to a core purpose of our study. If our study of Old Testament sacrifices and how they parallel Christ never goes beyond an academic appreciation, it is largely a waste of time. May we take into account what Christ has done, internalize it, and apply it to our thinking and lives.

JESUS CHRIST OUR COMPLETE OFFERING

Name of Sacrifice	Hebrew Name	Functions	Distinctive Characteristic	Parallel to Christ
Burnt Offering or Ascending Offering	*olah*	Sweet savor Intercession Atonement Dedication	a complete sacrifice, entirely burned up on the altar	-Our complete Sacrifice -Complete obedience unto death -The Sacrifice that Ascended
"Continual Burnt Offering"		Intercession	Offered Twice daily	"…he ever liveth to make intercession" Hebrews 7:25

Chapter 15

The Wave Offering or Elevation Offering

Leviticus 1:1 recorded that God summoned Moses out of the tabernacle and gave him precise revelation on five offerings: the burnt offering, the meal offering, the peace offering, the sin offering, and the trespass offering. While we have considered these primary offerings, there is yet another distinctive category called the wave or heave offerings. While "wave" or "heave" sounds peculiar to our ears, these offerings have a unique and thrilling parallel to Christ's accomplishments. In examining the wave offering we will see parallels to Christ's resurrection as well as to our redemption and salvation.

The wave offering is mentioned in the context of the peace offering in the following record.

> Leviticus 7:28-34:
> And the LORD spake unto Moses, saying,
> Speak unto the children of Israel, saying, He that offereth the sacrifice of his peace offerings unto the LORD shall bring his oblation [offering] unto the LORD of the sacrifice of his peace offerings.
> His own hands shall bring the offerings of the LORD made by fire, the fat with the breast, it shall he bring,

that the breast may be **waved** [*nuph*] **for a wave offering** [*tenuphah*] before the LORD.
And the priest shall burn the fat upon the altar: but the breast shall be Aaron's and his sons'.
And the right shoulder shall ye give unto the priest *for* an **heave offering** [*terumah*] of the sacrifices of your peace offerings.
He among the sons of Aaron, that offereth the blood of the peace offerings, and the fat, shall have the right shoulder for *his* part.
For the **wave breast and the heave shoulder** have I taken of the children of Israel from off the sacrifices of their peace offerings, and have given them unto Aaron the priest and unto his sons by a statute for ever from among the children of Israel.

We have seen previously that the peace offering was split three ways: the fat was burned up on the altar to the Lord, the priest received the breast and right shoulder and the offerer received the remainder.

Verse 30 said the breast that the priest received was to be "waved for a wave offering before the LORD." The Hebrew word for wave offering is *tenuphah*, while the verb form is *nuph*.

The next verse tells us what the wave offering signified: "...the breast shall be Aaron's and his sons." Once the offering was waved, it belonged to the priest. Verse 32 mentioned that the right shoulder was a "heave offering." As a result of being a heave offering, the shoulder was given to the priest as his portion.

Verse 34 reiterates that the "wave breast and the heave shoulder" was to be given to Aaron and his descendents. Once the breast was "waved" and the shoulder was

The Wave or Elevation Offering

"heaved," these portions belonged to the priests. Waving and heaving have essentially the same function. These offerings signified a change of ownership.

"Waving" or "heaving" was a formal procedure that indicated transfer of ownership. To wave or heave was a ritual that signified that the item was given to God and in turn, the priests.

What motion was involved in the waving of a wave offering? What did the gesture of "waving" or "heaving" entail? The usage of the Hebrew verb, *nuph,* in the following verses suggests the nature of the gesture of the *tenuphah* or wave offering.

> Exodus 20:25: "…lift up [*nuph*] thy tool upon it…"
> Deuteronomy 23:25: "…thou shalt not move [*nuph,* lift] a sickle…"

Sometimes *nuph* is translated as shake or wave but *nuph* usually means to lift, elevate or raise.[1] The act of waving the offering may have involved the priest extending or raising the offering. Whether this gesture of elevating the offering to God was actually utilized, this offering symbolized a lifting up to God, set apart and dedicated to Him.

The *New Revised Version* and the *Tanakh* version of the Old Testament translates wave offering as "elevation offering."

---

[1] Deuteronomy 27:5: "…not lift up [*nuph*] any iron tool upon them…" Joshua 8:31: "…altar of whole stones, over which no man hath lift up [*nuph*] any iron." Isaiah 10:15: "…as if the rod should shake [*nuph*] itself against them that lift it up…" In Isaiah 13:2 *nuph* ("shake") refers to being lifted up; Isaiah 19:16: *nuph* should be translated as raised not "shake." Jacob Milgrom, *The Anchor Bible Leviticus 1-16,* 469-470.

JESUS CHRIST OUR COMPLETE OFFERING

> **Leviticus 7:30**
> "…the breast may be waved for a wave offering…"
> *Authorized King James Version*
> "**…the breast may be raised as an elevation offering…**"
> *New Revised Standard Version*
> "**…the breast to be elevated as an elevation offering…**"
> *Tanakh* **translation**

The heave offering could also be called an elevation offering since the Hebrew verb for "heave" is *rum,* meaning "to make high, lift up high."[2] The wave and heave offerings are in effect, synonymous. Both signify an elevation to God.

With this in mind, let's look at other instances of the wave (elevation) offering.

> Exodus 35:21 and 22:
> And they came, every one whose heart stirred him up, and every one whom his spirit made willing, and they brought the LORD'S offering to the work of the tabernacle of the congregation, and for all his service, and for the holy garments.
> And they came, both men and women, as many as were willing hearted, and brought bracelets, and earrings, and rings, and tablets, all jewels of gold: and every man that offered [*nuph*] *offered* an offering [*tenuphah*] of gold unto the LORD.

While not evident in the Authorized King James Version, this gold jewelry was presented as a wave (elevation) offering for the construction of the tabernacle. To wave or

---

[2] Robert Young, *Analytical Concordance to the Bible*, 470. The Hebrew word for "heave offering" is *terumah*.

The Wave or Elevation Offering

elevate signified a legal transfer of ownership. These gifts were now separated to God, and belonged to Him.

In the following passage, the entire tribe of the Levites was presented to God as a wave (elevation) offering.[3] This record in Numbers 8 gives more explanation on the purpose of this offering.

> Numbers 8:9-14:
> And thou shalt bring the Levites before the tabernacle of the congregation: and thou shalt gather the whole assembly of the children of Israel together:
> And thou shalt bring the Levites before the LORD: and the children of Israel shall put their hands upon the Levites:
> And Aaron shall offer [*nuph*] the Levites before the LORD for an offering [*tenuphah*] of the children of Israel, that they may execute the service of the LORD.
> And the Levites shall lay their hands upon the heads of the bullocks: and thou shalt offer [*nuph*] the one for a sin offering, and the other for a burnt offering, unto the LORD, to make an atonement for the Levites.
> And thou shalt set the Levites before Aaron, and before his sons, and offer them for an offering [*tenuphah*] unto the LORD.
> Thus shalt thou separate the Levites from among the children of Israel: and the Levites shall be mine.

Verse 14 says: "...the Levites shall be mine" and they were to be made separate from the rest of the tribes. The wave offering declared that the Levites were set apart and belonged to God. Once someone or something was waved before God, they or it were His, transferred to His ownership.

---

[3] To understand the context of this passage, we should note that the tribe of Levi was exchanged for the firstborn. (Exodus 13:2; 34:19 and 20; Numbers 3 and 8).

JESUS CHRIST OUR COMPLETE OFFERING

>Verses 15 and 16:
>And after that shall the Levites go in to do the service of the tabernacle of the congregation: and thou shalt cleanse them, and offer [*nuph*] them for an offering [*tenuphah*].
>For they are wholly given unto me from among the children of Israel; instead of such as open every womb, even instead of the firstborn of all the children of Israel, have I taken them unto me.

The Levites were set apart for the service of the tabernacle. The tribe of Levi was shifted to God's domain. This example of a wave offering (elevation) here in Numbers 8:14 and 16 fits with all other uses of the wave offering throughout the Old Testament.

When the Israelites brought peace offerings, and the breast was waved and the shoulder was heaved, these portions belonged to the priests. When the gold and bronze that the Israelites donated to the construction of the Tabernacle were waved, it signified a transfer of ownership. That gold and bronze were now separated to God and belonged to Him (Exodus 35:22; 38:24, 29). Whenever an offering was waved before the Lord, it became His property, separated to His use, transferred into His domain.

Significance of Wave or Heave Offering:
Set apart, dedicated to God
Change of ownership
Transferred into God's domain

The Wave or Elevation Offering

The First Fruits Offerings: Belonged to the Lord

Another category of offerings in the Old Testament is the first fruits. The first time offerings are mentioned in the Bible, it refers to a first fruits offering.

> Genesis 4:3 and 4:
> And in process of time it came to pass, that Cain brought of the fruit of the ground an offering unto the LORD.
> And Abel, he also brought of the firstlings of his flock and of the fat thereof. And the LORD had respect unto Abel and to his offering:

Abel brought the "firstlings of his flock" which indicates an offering of the first fruits. The presentation of the first fruits of the flock is an early principle of sacrifice which originated here in Genesis and then spread into the ancient world. According to scholars, most peoples of antiquity had the custom of presenting the first fruits to the deity they worshipped.[4]

When Abel presented the firstlings of the flock to God, it implied that the first fruits belonged to God and were to be offered to Him. Whether of the herds or of the harvest, the first fruits were considered God's property. The first fruits offering looked forward to the abundant harvest to follow.

The first fruits of plunder taken in war were also considered God's property.[5] Moses commanded in Numbers 31 that a portion of the plunder went to the priests and Levites. He

---

[4] Ceslas Spicq, *Theological Lexicon of the New Testament*, Volume I, 145. He quotes Thucydides, Herodotus, and Plutarch referring to the first fruits.
[5] The secular sources also say that the first fruits of plunder belonged to God or gods. Spicq, Volume 1, 148.

JESUS CHRIST OUR COMPLETE OFFERING

said one-five hundredth of the plunder of the soldiers was to be given "unto Eleazar the priest for an heave offering of the Lord" (Numbers 31:29).

The consequences of Achan's actions in Joshua 7 were so dire because he had taken what belonged to God, the first fruits of battle.[6]

> Leviticus 2:12:
> As for the oblation [offering] of the firstfruits, ye shall offer them unto the LORD: but they shall **not** be burnt on the altar...

Note that this verse says that the offering of the first fruits was to be presented to the Lord, but **not** burned on the altar. Where did the offerings of the first fruits go?

> Numbers 18:8,11-14:
> And the LORD spake unto Aaron, Behold, I also have given thee the charge of mine **heave offerings** of all the hallowed things of the children of Israel; unto thee have I given them by reason of the anointing, and to thy sons, by an ordinance for ever...
> ...And this is thine; the **heave offering** of their gift, with all the **wave offerings** of the children of Israel: I have given them unto thee, and to thy sons and to thy daughters with thee, by a statute for ever: every one that is clean in thy house shall eat of it.
> All the best of the oil, and all the best of the wine, and of the wheat, the **firstfruits** of them which they shall offer unto the LORD, them have I given thee.

---

[6] In stark contrast to Achan, after his victory, Abram gave Melchizedek tithes in Genesis 14. However, the first fruits portion was not a one tenth portion as indicated by Numbers 31:27 and 28.

The Wave or Elevation Offering

> And whatsoever is first ripe [**firstfruits**] in the land, which they shall bring unto the LORD, shall be thine; every one that is clean in thine house shall eat of it. Every thing devoted in Israel shall be thine.

The heave offerings and wave offerings as well as the first fruits were set apart and transferred to the priests. In this passage addressed to Aaron and his descendents, God states three times: "I have given thee." The wave, heave and the first fruits offerings were dedicated to God and were, in turn, given to the priests, the Aaronites.

> **First Fruits Offerings and Heave and Wave offerings: Given to the priests**

As we will see in the next sections, at times Scripture expressly states that the first fruits were waved. And at times it does not say they were waved. But whether wave offering, heave offering, or first fruits, the end result was the same: they were dedicated to God and became His property, and given to the priests.[7]

Waving the Sheaf of the First Fruits

The first fruits offerings of the Law attract our attention because of the following verses in the New Testament:

---

[7] The tithes of Israel also belonged to the priests. Numbers 18:24-28 says they were presented as heave offerings. The tithe and first fruit are not equivalent terms although occasionally mentioned together (Numbers 18:12-28; Nehemiah 10:35-39).

JESUS CHRIST OUR COMPLETE OFFERING

> I Corinthians 15:20 and 23:
> But now is Christ risen from the dead, and become the firstfruits [offering[8]] of them that slept…
> …But every man in his own order: Christ the firstfruits [offering]; afterward they that are Christ's at his coming.

These verses in I Corinthians 15 raise the question: How would such a momentous event as the resurrection of Jesus Christ have a direct parallel to an Old Testament offering? Why would the sacrificial term, "firstfruits," be related so explicitly to Christ being raised from the dead? It would be well worth our time to see what connection this offering has to the resurrection of our Lord Jesus Christ. An extraordinary parallel emerges when we consider the precise timing of the yearly waving of the first fruits.

There were three feasts ordained by God in the Law of Moses. Our focus is on the first harvest festival, the Feast of Unleavened Bread that lasted seven days.

> Leviticus 23:4-8:
> These are the feasts of the LORD, even holy convocations, which ye shall proclaim in their seasons.
> In the fourteenth day of the first month at even [between the evenings] is the LORD'S passover.
> And on the fifteenth day of the same month is the feast of unleavened bread unto the LORD: seven days ye must eat unleavened bread.

---

[8] As we have read in the Old Testament, the first fruits entails an offering. Therefore, the word "offering" should be supplied after firstfruits in I Corinthians 15:20 and 23. Also see: Walter J. Cummins, *The Working Translation in A Journey through the Acts and Epistles*, 322.

The Wave or Elevation Offering

> In the first day ye shall have an holy convocation: ye shall do no servile work therein.
> But ye shall offer an offering made by fire unto the LORD seven days: in the seventh day is an holy convocation: ye shall do no servile work therein.

On the 14th day of the first month, the Passover sacrifice was killed and eaten "between the evenings," meaning between 3pm and sunset.[9] Then on the next day, the Feast of Unleavened Bread started and lasted for seven days.

In our discussion of the Passover in chapter 5, we noted that Christ laid down his life on the exact date and the specific time of day that the Passover sacrifice was offered. On the next day after the Passover was the first day of the Feast of Unleavened Bread. As verses 6 and 7 state, the 15th was a "holy convocation" or special high day.[10]

> Leviticus 23:9-14:
> And the LORD spake unto Moses, saying,
> Speak unto the children of Israel, and say unto them, When ye be come into the land which I give unto you, and shall reap the harvest thereof, then ye shall bring a sheaf of the firstfruits of your harvest unto the priest:

---

[9] Flavius Josephus. *The Complete Works of Josephus*, trans. William Whiston, 588: "...Passover, when they slay their sacrifices, from the ninth hour [3pm] to the eleventh [5pm]."

[10] John 19:31 refers to the holy convocation on the 15th: "The Jews therefore, because it was the preparation, that the bodies should not remain upon the cross on the sabbath day, **(for that sabbath day was an high day,)** besought Pilate that their legs might be broken, and that they might be taken away." At sunset the Sabbath, the "holy convocation," would begin opening the feast.

JESUS CHRIST OUR COMPLETE OFFERING

> And he shall wave [*nuph*] the sheaf before the LORD, to be accepted for you: **on the morrow after the sabbath** the priest shall wave [*nuph*] it.[11]
>
> And ye shall offer that day when ye wave [*nuph*] the sheaf an he lamb without blemish of the first year for a burnt offering unto the LORD.
>
> And the meat offering thereof shall be two tenth deals [*ephah*] of fine flour mingled with oil, an offering made by fire unto the LORD *for* a sweet savour: and the drink offering thereof *shall be* of wine, the fourth *part* of an hin.
>
> And ye shall eat neither bread, nor parched corn, nor green ears, **until the selfsame day** that ye have brought an offering unto your God: it *shall be* a statute for ever throughout your generations in all your dwellings.

Once a year on this day during this Feast of Unleavened Bread, there was a special first fruits offering waved to the Lord. On "the morrow after the Sabbath" during the Feast of Unleavened Bread, the sheaf of the first fruits was presented to the Lord. Since the weekly Sabbath falls on what we call Saturday, "the morrow after" would have been on the first day of the week, our Sunday.

Waving the sheaf of the Firstfruits:
"on the morrow after the Sabbath"
occurred on the first day of the week

---

[11] Was this Sabbath the festival high day Sabbath on the 15th **or** the weekly Sabbath? It had to be the **weekly Sabbath**. Why? Feast of Weeks or Pentecost is counted from this Sabbath for seven weeks. If one counts from the high day Sabbath on the 15th usually the first "week" would **not** be a full week. Milgrom in his 2700 page commentary on Leviticus says it was the weekly Sabbath (volume 3, page 2059). So also does Victor Paul Weirwille in *Jesus Christ, Our Passover*, 322.

The Wave or Elevation Offering

Leviticus 23:14 says that on this first day of the week they were not to eat of the new produce <u>until</u> they presented an offering unto God.[12] If this refers to the people of Israel presenting their first fruits offerings to the priests, then this would have been quite a busy day for the priests and the people of Israel.

> Numbers 28:17, 23 and 24:
> And in the fifteenth day of this month is the feast...
> Ye shall offer these beside the burnt offering **in the morning**, which is for a continual burnt offering. After this manner ye shall offer daily, throughout the seven days...

The Hebrew word for morning refers to daybreak or at dawn.[13] The "continual burnt offering," as always, was to be offered at the beginning of the day, at or soon after sunrise. Following the daily offering at sunrise, the waving of the sheaf commenced.

---

[12] Leviticus 23:15: "Do not partake (from the new crop) of any bread or parch or fresh grain until the very day you have brought your God's offering..." as translated by Jacob Milgrom, *The Anchor Bible Leviticus 23-27* (Doubleday, New York, 2000) 1948.

[13] *Gesenius', Hebrew and Chaldee Lexicon*, 137.

JESUS CHRIST OUR COMPLETE OFFERING

The Resurrection: Christ, the First Fruits Offering

The "morrow after the Sabbath," during the Feast of Unleavened Bread, has enormous significance with regard to the resurrection of our Lord Jesus Christ:

> Mark 16:1 and 2:
> And when the **sabbath was past**, Mary Magdalene, and Mary the mother of James, and Salome, had bought sweet spices, that they might come and anoint him.
> And **very early in the morning the first day of the week**, they came unto the sepulchre at the rising of the sun.

> Luke 24:1:
> Now upon the **first day of the week, very early in the morning,** they came unto the sepulchre, bringing the spices which they had prepared, and certain others with them.

The gospel records declare that by the first day of the week, our Sunday, Jesus arose.[14]

Christ first showed himself alive on the first day of the week, on "the morrow after the Sabbath." Around the time he made his first resurrection appearances, the priest would be waving the first fruits to God as Leviticus 23:11 commanded.

In John 20, Mary Magdalene came to the empty tomb "early when it was yet dark" (verse 1) and met the Lord:

---

[14] See Victor Paul Wierwille, *Jesus Christ Our Passover*, Introduction.

The Wave or Elevation Offering

> John 20:16 and 17:
> Jesus saith unto her, Mary. She turned herself, and saith unto him, Rabboni; which is to say, Master.
> Jesus saith unto her, Touch me not; for I am not yet ascended to my Father: but go to my brethren, and say unto them, I ascend unto my Father, and your Father; and *to* my God, and your God.

John 20:17 is not a reference to his ascension into heaven which was yet forty days away.[15] We have seen that the offering of the first fruits was waved or elevated to God at daybreak. Since it was yet dark, Christ had not yet presented himself to God as the first fruits from the dead.

According the Law, the priest raised the first fruits to God on the first day of the week at sunrise during the Feast of Unleavened Bread. Just as he fulfilled the law as the Passover sacrifice that year, he also fulfilled the law as the wave offering of the first fruits. Jesus presented himself to God as raised from the dead.

The Passover offering spoke prophetically about the timing of the crucifixion. Likewise, the wave offering of the first fruits on the day after the Sabbath spoke prophetically about the timing of the resurrection of Christ. On the next morning after Christ's resurrection, the first fruits offering was waved and the Lord Jesus Christ presented himself to God as the first fruits from the dead. Just as I Corinthians 5:7 mentions Christ our Passover sacrificed for us, so I Corinthians 15:23 refers to Christ the first fruits from the dead. Both Passover and first fruits were offerings under the Law. One heralded the timing of his crucifixion, the other, his resurrection!

---

[15] See Victor Paul Wierwille, *Jesus Christ, Our Passover*, 319-322.

JESUS CHRIST OUR COMPLETE OFFERING

"Christ being raised from the dead dieth no more; death hath no more dominion over him" (Romans 6:9). I Corinthians 15:44 states of the resurrection: "It is sown a natural body; it is raised a spiritual body. There is a natural body, and there is a spiritual body."

The first fruits waved or elevated to God represented a transfer from the domain of man into God's domain, a move into God's realm. When Christ arose he did so with a spiritual body. Therefore, He was utterly transferred into God's domain.

The Timing of Christ's Resurrection:

Presenting the Firstfruits:
"on the morrow after the Sabbath"
Leviticus 23:11

Resurrection appearance of our Lord:
"in the morning the first *day* of the week"
Mark 16:2

Wave Offering of the Leaven Loaves on Feast of Pentecost

A most unusual wave offering occurred on another harvest feast, fifty days after the first fruits offering.

> Leviticus 23:15-17:
> And ye shall count unto you from the morrow after the sabbath, from the day that ye brought the sheaf of the wave offering; seven sabbaths shall be complete:

The Wave or Elevation Offering

> Even unto the **morrow after the seventh sabbath** shall ye number fifty days; and ye shall offer a new meat offering unto the LORD.
> Ye shall bring out of your habitations two wave [*tenuphah*] loaves of two tenth deals: they shall be of fine flour; they shall be **baken with leaven**; they are the firstfruits unto the LORD.

This one day feast was called the day of Pentecost in the New Testament.[16] The Law stipulated that a meal offering, consisting of two loaves baked with leaven, should be waved to the Lord. This wave offering was also a first fruits offering that was not to be burnt on the altar but given to the priests.

The Day of Pentecost:
Offer two wave loaves baked <u>with leaven</u> on "...the morrow after the seventh Sabbath..."

Seven weeks before Pentecost is the Feast of **Unleavened Bread.** Exodus 12:15 and 13:7 commanded that before Passover and the Feast of Unleavened Bread, all leaven be removed from the homes of the Israelites. This symbolism is carried over to I Corinthians 5:7 where Christ is called our Passover. In this context, Paul exhorts the Corinthian Church to clean house—to get rid of the "leaven of malice and wickedness."

The first fruits wave offering of these two loaves on the Feast of Pentecost was commanded to contain leaven. However,

---

[16] Also called "day of firstfruits:" (Numbers 28:26) and the "feast of weeks" (Deuteronomy 16:9 and 10).

JESUS CHRIST OUR COMPLETE OFFERING

Leviticus 2:11 stated that no bread or meal offering containing leaven could ever be burned on the altar. Leaven often represented malice and wickedness. Therefore, one consistent requirement of the meal offerings under the Law was that they contain no leaven.[17] It was a stunning variation for God to command that on this feast day, these two loaves were to contain leaven.

This leaven bread offering elevated to God on the day of Pentecost cannot represent or foreshadow the perfect offering of Christ.[18] Leavened bread or meal was never an acceptable offering on the altar. Rather, these two leavened loaves foreshadowed the people who the coming Messiah would redeem. Unlike the redeemer, these who would be redeemed are not free from all malice and wickedness.

The Feast of Pentecost of Leviticus 23 looked forward to Acts 2:1: "when the day of Pentecost was fully come..." In Leviticus 23:17, the two leavened loaves presented as a wave offering on Pentecost, foreshadowed the Church. On Pentecost in Acts 2, God's great wave offering was the Church. The shadow became the reality.

The last phrase of Leviticus 23:17 states of the two leavened loaves: "they are the firstfruits unto the LORD." There is an interesting reference to "firstfruits" in the New Testament.

> James 1:18:
> Of his own will begat he us with the word of truth, that we should be a kind of firstfruits of his creatures.

---

[17] The one exception is a peace offering for thanksgiving that was a heave offering, meaning that it was given to the priest to eat, not burned on the altar. (Leviticus 7:11-14 and Amos 4:5).

[18] Christ was "without sin" (Hebrews 4:15) and he "knew no sin" (II Corinthians 5:21).

The Wave or Elevation Offering

This epistle speaks of those whom God begat, that is, those who are born again by the new birth of spirit as a "kind of firstfruits." Being born by the word of truth, they became a kind of first fruits of God's created beings.[19]

Whether of the herds or of the harvest, the first fruits were to be dedicated to God and became His property. Likewise, as first fruits, the born-again ones belong to God, they are His property. Belonging to God, therefore, they should devote themselves to serve Him. They are no longer "sold under sin," belonging to this world or the god of this world.[20] By the sacrificial accomplishments of our Lord Jesus Christ, born-again sons of God are under God's dominion and under His protection.

> Romans 15:16:
> That I should be the minister of Jesus Christ to the Gentiles, ministering the gospel of God, that the offering up of the Gentiles might be acceptable, being sanctified [*hagiazo*] by the Holy Ghost [*pneuma hagion*].

Here, the Apostle Paul writes of the offering up or sacrificing of the Gentiles as acceptable. Why and how are these former Gentiles made acceptable? Because they are sanctified by *pneuma hagion*, the gift of holy spirit. The word "sanctified" is the Greek word, *hagiazo*, meaning "to make holy." The Gentile Christians were an acceptable offering to God because they were made holy by the gift of holy spirit. We are acceptable and we are worthy because of Christ's sacrifice and the gift of holy spirit.[21]

---

[19] Romans 16:5 and I Corinthians 16:15 refer to specific groups of born again ones as "firstfruits." Considering the book of James is addressed to the "twelve tribes which are scattered abroad," James 1:18 may be referring to this specific group of born again ones as "firstfruits."
[20] Romans 7:14; II Corinthians 4:4; Ephesians 2:1-3.
[21] Also see: David Bergey, *Jesus Christ Our Approach Offering*, 144-148.

JESUS CHRIST OUR COMPLETE OFFERING

As the Church of God, we are called out from two leavened loaves, the Jews and Gentiles. Christ "came and preached peace to you which were afar off [Gentiles], and to them that were nigh [Jews]. For through him we both have access by one Spirit unto the Father."[22]

While the leaven bread offering was a type for what came to pass on Pentecost in Acts 2, there was a limit to what it foreshadowed. No type or shadow of the Old Testament ever depicted that the offering up of Gentiles would be acceptable, being sanctified by holy spirit, fellow heirs of the same body and sharing fully in the promise in Christ by the gospel with the people of Israel. This was the mystery "hidden in God" from the beginning.[23] Here we see the limitations of the types and shadows of the Law. They never glimpsed the Mystery: "That the Gentiles should be fellowheirs, and of the same body, and partakers of his promise in Christ by the gospel" (Ephesians 3:6). The breathtaking scope of the Great Mystery, in which all the peoples of the earth would share fully in the promise of the Gospel, was never set forth in prophecy or type in the Old Testament revelation.

Elevated into His Kingdom

As we are seeing, the wave offerings of the Old Testament have remarkable parallels to the redemptive realities we have in Christ.

---

[22] Ephesians 2:17 and 18.
[23] Ephesians 3:9. For more explanation of the mystery of the Church see Walter J. Cummins, *Riches of God's Grace in the New Covenant,* Chapter 8.

The Wave or Elevation Offering

Colossians 1:13: (*New American Standard*)
For He delivered us from the domain of darkness, and transferred us to the Kingdom of His beloved Son.

We have been transferred into God's realm by the work of Jesus Christ.

The wave (elevation) offering signified a legal change of ownership. The offering once waved then belonged to God, set apart for His purposes. The wave (elevation) offering illustrated the future salvation when God's people were legally transferred to God by the work of Jesus Christ.

We belong to God by the work of Jesus Christ. We are His purchased possession (Ephesians 1:14); "...Ye are not your own...For ye are bought with a price..." (I Corinthians 6:19, 20). The wave (elevation) offering is a shadow of one of the great redemptive realities of Scripture—the transfer of God's people to Him.

This legal transfer to God by the accomplishments of Jesus Christ has immense practical ramifications for our day-to-day living. Since we belong to God, Satan has no legal rights over our mind or body. We can pray in the name of Jesus Christ that sickness, doubt and darkness depart.

Few would be idle or passive if someone came on their property and defaced the front lawn. Immediate action would be taken. Words would be exchanged. The response would be neither slow nor timid. In like manner, since we are God's property, we should not hesitate to demand that darkness have no part of our lives.

Indeed, this is a marvelous redemption our God has wrought for us by the accomplishments of our Lord Jesus

JESUS CHRIST OUR COMPLETE OFFERING

Christ. He has "delivered us from the domain of darkness, and transferred us to the Kingdom of His beloved Son." God has separated us and rescued us from the power of darkness. Galatians 1:4 says that Jesus Christ "gave himself for our sins that he might rescue us from the present evil age..."[24] Even while still living in this evil day, God has rescued us and delivered us. What a miraculous change of our status and position! We now walk in the kingdom of God as sons and daughters of the Highest.

> **We are rescued from the present evil age**
> **We are delivered from the domain of darkness**
> **We are transferred into His Kingdom**

Having been transferred into His kingdom, we await the future reality seen in the next verses.

> Philippians 3:20 and 21:
> For our conversation [citizenship] is in heaven; from whence also we look for the Saviour, the Lord Jesus Christ.
> Who shall change our vile body, that it may be fashioned like unto his glorious body, according to the working whereby he is able even to subdue all things unto himself.

Our bodies were fashioned from the dust of the earth and will be changed into a glorious body, like his, at his coming from heaven. On that day, the Church will fully share in this total transport into God's realm. Until that day, we are to look with patience and expectation for the return of our savior.

---

[24] *New American Bible.*

The Wave or Elevation Offering

The first fruits waved or elevated to God represented a transfer from the domain of man into God's domain. When Christ arose he did so with a spiritual body. Therefore, we, like him, will be utterly transferred into God's dominion. At Christ's return, we will be literally elevated to heaven with new bodies:

> I Thessalonians 4:16 and 17:
> For the Lord himself shall descend from heaven with a shout, with the voice of the archangel, and with the trump of God: and the dead in Christ shall rise first:
> Then we which are alive and remain shall be caught up together with them in the clouds, to meet the Lord in the air: and so shall we ever be with the Lord.

As we have seen in Leviticus 23:11 and the Gospels, the waving of the first fruits offering gives us a precise pattern of Christ's resurrection.

> I Corinthians 15:20-23:
> But now is Christ risen from the dead, and become the firstfruits [offering] of them that slept.
> For since by man came death, by man came also the resurrection of the dead.
> For as in Adam all die, even so in Christ shall all be made alive.
> But every man in his own order: Christ the firstfruits [offering]; afterward they that are Christ's at his coming.

Christ, raised from the dead, is the first fruits of the others who would be resurrected from the dead. I Corinthians 15:23 says everyone is resurrected in the proper order: "Christ the firstfruits" and then those who belong to Christ at his coming. First fruits indicate there is a harvest to follow.

JESUS CHRIST OUR COMPLETE OFFERING

God's great harvest will include the raising of those who are Christ's at his return. What a day that will be!

Name of Sacrifice	Hebrew Name	Functions	Distinctive Characteristic	Parallel to Christ
Wave Offering --- Heave Offering Elevation Offering	*tenuphah* --- *terumah*	To transfer to God's ownership and then given to the priests	To transfer to God's ownership, into His domain	"Christ the First Fruits" I Cor. 15:23 "For He delivered us from the domain of darkness, and transferred us to the Kingdom of His beloved Son." Colossians 1:13 (*New American Standard*)

Chapter 16

The Day of Atonement: The Grand Portrayal of Christ

Leviticus 16 is the pinnacle of the Old Testament revelation insofar as the shadows, patterns, and types of Christ are concerned. In this chapter on the Day of Atonement, we discover a momentous apex of the tutorial lessons of the coming redeemer in the Old Testament.

Only on the Day of Atonement did the high priest enter the holy of holies to sprinkle it with the blood of two different sin offerings. Once yearly, the high priest cast lots between two sin offerings. One became a scapegoat and the other a standard purification sacrifice. Only on this momentous holy day, did the priest, sacrifice and tabernacle interact and were utilized to an extent seen on no other day of the year. Only on this day was the holy of holies accessible and in full use. On this high and holy day, the various patterns and types of Christ come into sharp focus and into full motion.[1]

Since the sin offerings take a prominent place on the Day of Atonement, it is essential to recall the central function of the sin offering. As described in Chapter 8, its primary purpose

---

[1] To review, see the section in Chapter 5: "The Day of Atonement: A Pattern of the True Things to Come."

JESUS CHRIST OUR COMPLETE OFFERING

was purification. In fact, we saw that the Hebrew word for sin offering, *chattath*, could be translated as "purification offering." The sprinkling of the blood of the sin offering represented cleansing and purification.

Many burnt offerings were sacrificed as well on this most holy day. We saw in the chapter on the burnt offering that it could literally be translated from the Hebrew as "ascending offering." This is noteworthy since the Day of Atonement has remarkably clear parallels to the ascension of our Lord Jesus Christ.

Understanding the matters that were dealt with previously in this book is essential to fully appreciating the magnitude of the events of this day. With a firm grasp of the significance of these sacrifices of the Old Covenant, let's now examine the Day of Atonement in its entirety.

> Leviticus 16:1 and 2:
> And the LORD spake unto Moses after the death of the two sons of Aaron, when they offered before the LORD, and died;
> And the LORD said unto Moses, Speak unto Aaron thy brother, that he come not at all times into the holy *place* within the vail before the mercy seat, which is upon the ark; that he die not: for I will appear in the cloud upon the mercy seat.

The Lord's instruction to Moses was to speak to the high priest, Aaron, that he "come not at all times" into the holy of holies "that he die not." To grasp this statement that "he die not," we must understand what occurred in Leviticus prior to chapter 16.

The Day of Atonement: The Grand Portrayal of Christ

In chapters 8 and 9, the priesthood was instituted, after which Aaron and his sons were ordained as priests. Chapter 9 closes out in a rather dramatic fashion.

> Leviticus 9:22-24:
> And Aaron lifted up his hand toward the people, and blessed them, and came down from offering of the sin offering, and the burnt offering, and peace offerings.
> And Moses and Aaron went into the tabernacle of the congregation, and came out, and blessed the people: and the glory of the LORD appeared unto all the people.
> And there came a fire out from before the LORD, and consumed upon the altar the burnt offering and the fat: *which* when all the people saw, they shouted, and fell on their faces.

When Moses and Aaron came out of the tabernacle and blessed the people, they saw the glory of the Lord. Then a miraculous fire started and burned up the offering on the altar.[2] The people then cried out and fell on their faces. Chapter 9 ends on a note of triumph and awe.

At this time in history, tribes and nations had their multiple gods. Most had their sacrificial rites, priests, and holy places. Their priests would have offered blessings and prayers. But only the God of Israel—the True God—manifested such miraculous wonders to His people: His glory appeared to all and fire ignited and burned up the sacrifices. Their covenant God was a true and powerful God, as opposed to a dead, silent idol of all the other nations. Israel's God was not some inert statue collecting dust in a stone temple, like the Philistine god, Dagon, in

---

[2] This fire was never allowed to die out (Leviticus 6:5 and 6). That fire, which Israel saw God ignite that day, was to be kept burning from this point on so it could consume all future offerings.

JESUS CHRIST OUR COMPLETE OFFERING

Ashdod. Israel's God demonstrated His power showing that He was truly among them.

The next chapter opens with an event so horrifying it must have stunned the entire nation. There is an incredibly jarring contrast between the exaltation of chapter 9 and the anguish of chapter 10.

> Leviticus 10:1-3:
> And Nadab and Abihu, the sons of Aaron, took either of them his censer, and put fire therein, and put incense thereon, and offered strange fire before the LORD, which he commanded them not.
> And there went out fire from the LORD, and devoured them, and they died before the LORD.
> Then Moses said unto Aaron, This *is it* that the LORD spake, saying, I will be sanctified in them that come nigh me, and before all the people I will be glorified. And Aaron held his peace.

Fire came out from the Lord and killed Nadab and Abihu. Nadab and Abihu had been anointed as priests along with their father, Aaron, and brothers, Eleazar and Ithamar.[3] God had provided miraculous fire on the altar, but they entered the tabernacle with fire from outside the tabernacle area. Their approach was illegitimate because they brought in "strange fire" rather than the fire God had previously ignited on the altar.

The opening verses of Leviticus 16 directly address the concern of death by an illegitimate approach. These verses refer back to Leviticus 10, where the sons of Aaron defiled the sanctuary with strange fire and died.

---

[3] To read about the anointing of the priests see Exodus 28 and Leviticus 8.

The Day of Atonement: The Grand Portrayal of Christ

When the Scripture states of Aaron in Leviticus 16:2, that he "come not at all times" into the holy of holies, "that he die not," it is not a pedantic concern with man-made protocol. Since the episode in Leviticus 10, it may have appeared that the profession of high priest had become rather high-risk, literally a matter of life and death. One can imagine the cautious and somber demeanor of Aaron carrying God's commands concerning the Day of Atonement.

This cautious or hesitant frame of mind in approaching God may seem disconcerting or even chilling to those of us with such freedom and boldness to enter into God's presence. But before the sacrifice of Jesus Christ, the way was not yet open. But now we are exhorted to approach God incessantly with boldness: "Therefore, brothers, since we have confidence to enter the Most Holy Place by the blood of Jesus."[4] The work of Christ has wrought quite a radical change.

> Leviticus 16:3 and 4:
> Thus shall Aaron come into the holy place: with a young bullock for a sin offering [*chattath*], and a ram for a burnt offering [*olah*].
> He shall put on the holy linen coat, and he shall have the linen breeches upon his flesh, and shall be girded with a linen girdle, and with the linen mitre shall he be attired: these are holy garments; therefore shall he wash his flesh in water, and so put them on.

Normally, the high priest was attired in bright-colored garments "for glory and beauty"(Exodus 28:2, 5). However, only on this particular day was he dressed entirely in unadorned linen. In the Scriptures, linen can represent

---

[4] Hebrews 10:19, NIV. Hebrews 4:16: "Let us therefore come boldly unto the throne of grace, that we may obtain mercy, and find grace to help in time of need." Also see David Bergey, *Jesus Christ Our Approach Offering*, Chapter 6, "Our Right of Boldness in Approach."

JESUS CHRIST OUR COMPLETE OFFERING

purity or righteousness.[5] When the high priest bathed, this also represented purification and cleansing.[6]

> Verses 5 and 6:
> And he shall take of the congregation of the children of Israel two kids of the goats for a sin offering [*chattath*], and one ram for a burnt offering [*olah*].
> And Aaron shall offer his bullock of the sin offering [*chattath*], which is for himself, and make an atonement[7] for himself, and for his house.

These verses relate the sacrifices to be offered. There is one ram for a burnt (ascending) offering and then three different prominent sin (purification) offerings were to be presented: a bull and two male goats. These sin offerings were the overarching focus on the Day of Atonement. The first of these sin offerings, the bull, was offered for the high priest and for his household.

> Verses 7-10:
> And he shall take the two goats, and present them before the LORD at the door of the tabernacle of the congregation.
> And Aaron shall cast lots upon the two goats; one lot for the LORD, and the other lot for the scapegoat.
> And Aaron shall bring the goat upon which the LORD'S lot fell, and offer him *for a* sin offering [*chattath*].
> But the goat, on which the lot fell to be the scapegoat, shall be presented alive before the LORD, to make an

---

[5] Revelation 15:6: "pure and white linen;" Revelation 19:8: "fine linen is the righteousness of the saints."
[6] See *Jesus Christ Our Approach Offering*, 126-129.
[7] The word, atonement, in Leviticus 16 is translated from the Hebrew word, *kaphar*. We defined this word in Chapter 11 of our study in Genesis 32:20.

The Day of Atonement: The Grand Portrayal of Christ

atonement with him, and to let him go for a scapegoat into the wilderness.

According to verse 5, the scapegoat is also a sin offering, howbeit a rather unusual one because it was never actually killed by the priest. The scapegoat sacrifice was never presented any other time of the year. Yet this scapegoat bearing the sins of the people was an integral part of this most holy day, presenting him alive and "to make an atonement with him."

Three Sin (Purification) Offerings on the Day of Atonement:

Bull (for high priest and his household)
Goat (for scapegoat)
Goat (for purification)

Verses 11-14:
And Aaron shall bring the bullock of the sin offering [*chattath*], which is for himself, and shall make an atonement for himself, and for his house, and shall kill the bullock of the sin offering which is for himself: And he shall take a censer full of burning coals of fire from off the altar before the LORD, and his hands full of sweet incense beaten small, and bring it within the vail:
And he shall put the incense upon the fire before the LORD, that the cloud of the incense may cover the mercy seat that is upon the testimony, that he die not:
And he shall take of the blood of the bullock, and sprinkle it with his finger upon the mercy seat

JESUS CHRIST OUR COMPLETE OFFERING

eastward; and before the mercy seat shall he sprinkle of the blood with his finger seven times.

The sin (purification) offering of the bull, which Aaron presented, was for himself and his household. As he entered the holy of holies, he was to place incense into the censer of burning coals that he got from the altar. Then he was to take some of the bull's blood and sprinkle it upon and before the mercyseat, seven times.[8] The bull served as a purification offering to cleanse the holy place.

Aaron was to sprinkle the blood with his finger "upon the mercy seat eastward; and before the mercy seat." The approach of the high priest into the holy places of the tabernacle was from the east so this blood fell upon the pathway the high priest had walked, purifying it.[9] Even the very place that the feet of the priest tread was defiled and unclean, in need of cleansing by sprinkling of the blood of the *chattath* offering. Again, this was in pointed contrast to our pathway to the throne of grace. Cleansed by the blood of our savior's sacrifice, we have boldness and freedom to enter in God's presence at any time.

Hebrews 9:25 spoke of this sin offering of the bull on the Day of Atonement: "the high priest entereth into the holy place every year with blood of others." The Greek word for

---

[8] "Mercyseat" translated with the Hebrew word, *kapporeth*, was a pure gold lid with a cherubim at each end that rested on top of the ark. This was the "place of atonement" where God was to meet with Moses and later with the high priests on the Day of Atonement. (Exodus 25:22). Walter J. Cummins, *Scripture Consulting Select Studies*, 342-345.

[9] Both the tabernacle and the temple faced east so the approach of the high priest would have been from the east. Numbers 3:38: "But those that encamp before the tabernacle toward the east, even before the tabernacle of the congregation eastward..."

The Day of Atonement: The Grand Portrayal of Christ

"others" may be rendered "strange" or "foreign."[10] The blood of a bull or goat was not equivalent to the blood of a human being, thus it was not an equivalent substitute sacrifice.

Hebrews 9:12 says of Christ, "Neither by the blood of goats and calves, but by his own blood he entered in once into the holy place, having obtained eternal redemption for us." By "his own" blood, he entered into the tabernacle of the heavenlies having obtained our eternal redemption. Also, in Hebrews 13:12 it states that he sanctified us "with his own blood."

Christ's blood was an equivalent sacrifice for humanity while the sacrifice of animals was not. Since sin came by a human being, Adam, it had to be absolved by a human being. Christ's precious blood had the power to obtain our redemption and sanctification.

The events of this Day of Atonement continue with the high priest sacrificing the next sin offering.

> Verses 15 and 16:
> Then shall he kill the goat of the sin offering [*chattath*], that is for the people, and bring his blood within the vail, and do with that blood as he did with the blood of the bullock, and sprinkle it upon the mercy seat, and before the mercy seat:
> And he shall make an atonement for the holy place, because of the uncleanness of the children of Israel, and because of their transgressions in all their sins: and so shall he do for the tabernacle of the

---

[10] "Others" is Greek word, *allotrios*. Hebrews 11:9: "By faith he sojourned in the land of promise, as in a strange [*allotrios*] country…" 11:34: "…turned to flight the armies of the aliens [*allotrios*]."

congregation that remaineth among them in the midst of their uncleanness.

Here, he repeats the same ceremony performed with the blood of the bull, but now with a goat on behalf of the whole congregation. As before, he sprinkles the goat blood on and around the mercy seat. The blood of this goat would accomplish an atonement for the holy place because of the nation of Israel's uncleanness.

Hebrews 9:7 also refers to these activities of the high priest: "But into the second [section] went the high priest alone once every year, not without blood, which he offered for himself, and for the errors of the people."

> Leviticus 16:17:
> And there shall be no man in the tabernacle of the congregation when he goeth in to make an atonement in the holy place, until he come out, and have made an atonement for himself, and for his household, and for all the congregation of Israel.

Verse 17 declares that no other person was to enter the tabernacle until the work of purification and reconciliation was completed. No one of the congregation or of Aaron's household could enter. It was not a team effort as Nadab and Abihu had undertaken. From start to finish, the high priest alone accomplished this important work of atonement on this holy day.

In parallel to the New Covenant, the entire work of our salvation and redemption was accomplished by Jesus Christ alone from beginning to end. By his one sacrifice for sins forever, he alone completed the whole work of our reconciliation to God.

The Day of Atonement: The Grand Portrayal of Christ

On occasion, some have suggested that established institutions or churches can secure for the believer salvation or reconciliation to God. Prominent status, solemn rituals or impressive facilities cannot add one iota to what Christ alone has done. Our salvation fully rests on his work and nothing else.

> Verses 18 and 19:
> And he shall go out unto the altar that *is* before the LORD, and make an atonement for it; and shall take of the blood of the bullock, and of the blood of the goat, and put it upon the horns of the altar round about.
> And he shall sprinkle of the blood upon it with his finger seven times, and cleanse it, and hallow it from the uncleanness of the children of Israel.

Next, the high priest exited the tabernacle and placed and sprinkled the blood of the bull and of the goat on the altar. Just as with the mercy seat, the altar received a seven-fold sprinkling of blood to purify it and sanctify it from uncleanness of the Israelites. The blood of the bull and the goat served to ceremonially cleanse the altar.

To review, the high priest sacrificed a bull and goat as sin (purification) offerings. He then took the blood of these offerings and entered into the tabernacle and sprinkled the blood. The blood of the sin offerings served to cleanse and purify the holy places.

The following verse in Hebrews explains how these activities on the Day of Atonement under the Law were a precise model of Christ's work.

JESUS CHRIST OUR COMPLETE OFFERING

>Hebrews 9:11 and 12:
>But Christ being come an high priest of good things to come, by a greater and more perfect tabernacle, not made with hands, that is to say, not of this building [creation];
>Neither by the blood of goats and calves, but by his own blood he entered in once into the holy place, having obtained eternal redemption *for* us.

Jesus Christ became a high priest, not of the Mosaic sanctuary, but in the "greater and more perfect tabernacle" in the heavens. At his ascension, he entered into the holy place in the heavens by his own blood. Aaron and the subsequent high priests of Israel needed sin (purification) offerings of bulls and goats to enter into the holy of holies on the Day of Atonement each year. Jesus Christ entered once into the heavenly tabernacle by the sin offering of himself.

>Hebrews 9:22 and 23:
>And almost all things are by the law purged with blood; and without shedding of blood is no remission. It was therefore necessary that patterns of things in the heavens should be purified with these; but the heavenly things themselves with better sacrifices[11] than these.

What are the "patterns of things in the heavens?" In the opening pages of chapter 5 of our study, we noted that the earthly, Mosaic tabernacle was modeled after the heavenly tabernacle. When it says the "pattern of things in the heavens," it is a reference to the Mosaic tabernacle. On the Day of Atonement, the earthly tabernacle was purified with

---

[11] Christ's sacrifice is stated in the plural here. The figure, heterosis (of number), is where the plural is put for the singular: "this is so put when great excellence or magnitude is denoted." E.W. Bullinger, *Figures of Speech Used in the Bible*, 529-531.

The Day of Atonement: The Grand Portrayal of Christ

the blood of sacrifices. But the heavenly holy places were purified with a far superior sacrifice.

> Verses 24 and 25:
> For Christ is not entered into the holy places made with hands, which are the figures [copies] of the true; but into heaven itself, now to appear in the presence of God for us:
> Nor yet that he should offer himself often, as the high priest entereth into the holy place every year with blood of others;

The Mosaic tabernacle, built by the hands of the Israelites, was a copy of the true tabernacle in heaven. Every year on the Day of Atonement, the high priest entered into it with blood from the sin offerings to purify and cleanse.

In contrast, Christ entered into heaven itself by his own blood, purifying the heavenly places. Look at this high priest we have! He has not entered into an earthly sanctuary built by men, but he has ascended into heaven itself to appear before the face of God to intercede on our behalf.

Day of Atonement	
High Priest:	Entered into earthly tabernacle
Tabernacle:	Cleansed by blood of sacrifices
Sacrifice:	Sin Offerings

JESUS CHRIST OUR COMPLETE OFFERING

> **Christ at His Ascension**
>
> **High Priest:** Enters into heavenly tabernacle
>
> **Tabernacle:** Cleansed by Christ's blood
>
> **Sacrifice:** Christ, The final offering for sin

On the Day of Atonement, the tabernacle, high priest and offerings formed a wondrous pattern to illustrate Christ and his accomplishments. On this great solemn feast of the Old Testament calendar, the sacrificial law reaches its supreme expression. Here, the high priest attains to his highest mission. At this time, the tabernacle receives it fullest use. These models of the coming one are put in motion, interacting with each other to depict Christ's sacrifice as well as his ascension.

Scapegoat

After the high priest had cleansed the holy places, the live goat was brought forth.

> Leviticus 16:20-22:
> And when he hath made an end of reconciling [atoning for] the holy *place*, and the tabernacle of the congregation, and the altar, he shall bring the live goat:
> And Aaron shall lay both his hands upon the head of the live goat, and confess over him all the iniquities of the children of Israel, and all their transgressions in all their sins, putting them upon the head of the goat,

The Day of Atonement: The Grand Portrayal of Christ

and shall send him away by the hand of a fit man into the wilderness:
And the goat shall bear upon him all their iniquities unto a land not inhabited: and he shall let go the goat in the wilderness.

He laid both hands on the head of the animal and confessed, "**all** the iniquities of the children of Israel, and **all** their transgressions in **all** their sins." This confession would have to include not just sins done in ignorance, as Leviticus 4 stipulated, but all sins. The scapegoat gives us a rather striking portrayal of the coming Messiah who would bare all our iniquities and all our transgressions and all our sins.[12]

> **Scapegoat**
> -Cast lots
> -Lay hands on head
> -Confess all sins
> -Send away into the wilderness
> -Bear all the sins

Hebrews 10:2 and 3:
For then would they not have ceased to be offered? because that the worshippers once purged should have had no more conscience of sins.
But in those *sacrifices* there is a **remembrance** again made of sins every year.

---

[12] Colossians 2:13: "And you, being dead in your sins and the uncircumcision of your flesh, hath he quickened together with him, having forgiven you **all** trespasses." Also see Chapter 4 in this book: "The Law: A Shadow of Christ."

JESUS CHRIST OUR COMPLETE OFFERING

Every year, the confession of sin over the scapegoat on the Day of Atonement brought into remembrance all of their sins. However, after Christ's singular sacrifice, God promised: "And their sins and iniquities will I remember no more" (Hebrews 10:17). With Christ there is not yearly listing of iniquities and offenses. After his once-and-for-all sin offering, there is no recollection of sin by our heavenly Father.

> **Sacrifices of Bulls and Goats:**
> "…**remembrance again made** of sins every year."
>
> **Christ's sacrifice:**
> "…their sins and iniquities will I **remember no more**."

If the worshippers on the Day of Atonement had been cleansed once and for all, they would no longer have carried the guilt and remembrance of sins. Those sin (purification) offerings served to reinforce the sense of sin. But **how much more** shall the blood of Christ cleanse our consciences! In the eyes of God, we have a consciousness cleansed of guilt and condemnation. He remembers our sins and iniquities no more. That is a considerable contrast to the yearly sacrifice of the scapegoat that actually had the opposite effect.

Hebrews 10:4 tells us that, "it is not possible that the blood of bulls and of goats should take away sins." Those sacrifices on the Day of Atonement had no intrinsic power to take away sins.[13] But those sin (purification) offerings,

---

[13] "Take away" in Hebrews 10:4 is the Greek word, *aphaireō*, meaning "to remove, to take away from.: In verse 11, "take away" is *periaireō*, meaning to

The Day of Atonement: The Grand Portrayal of Christ

anticipated Christ and depicted he who would put away sin by the sacrifice of himself. As God beheld the detailed patterns of the coming Messiah in the rituals of the Day of Atonement, He granted some measure of cleansing and sanctification.

The scapegoat offering was a unique and graphic picture of the good things that were to come. The sins were put upon the goat and he bore them away. Here, we have quite an explicit tutorial of he on whom God would lay "the iniquity of us all." Yet our Lord Jesus Christ carried more than all our sins. As Isaiah 53 states, this righteous servant of the Lord carried our sickness and sorrow as well. The completeness of his sacrifice enables us to live as complete and empowered sons and daughters of the Highest.

Ascending Sacrifices on the Day of Atonement

There was another notable offering to be presented on this very significant holy day.

> Leviticus 16:23-25:
> And Aaron shall come into the tabernacle of the congregation, and shall put off the linen garments, which he put on when he went into the holy *place*, and shall leave them there:
> And he shall wash his flesh with water in the holy place, and put on his garments, and come forth, and offer his burnt offering [*olah*], and the burnt offering [*olah*] of the people, and make an atonement for himself, and for the people.

"take away what is round about, to take away wholly." The sacrifices of the Old Testament, such as the scapegoat, may have taken away sins, but they were powerless to rout it out or to nullify sin as did Christ's sacrifice.

JESUS CHRIST OUR COMPLETE OFFERING

> And the fat of the sin offering [*chattath*] shall he burn upon the altar.

Another prominent sacrifice on the Day of Atonement was burnt offering, or as translated literally from the Hebrew: ascending offering. The high priest then went into the holy place and took off the linen clothes. After he bathed, he put on his garments and then sacrificed his burnt (ascending) offering on the altar.

Since verse 24 mentions "**his** burnt offering," it may be a reference to Leviticus 16:3 where he brought a bull for a sin offering and a ram for burnt (ascending) offering. After he offered "his burnt offering," it said he was also to present "the burnt offering of the people." While Leviticus 16 mentions burnt (ascending) offerings only in verses 3, 5 and 24, the following passage in Numbers mentions other specific burnt (ascending) offerings to be sacrificed on the Day of Atonement.

> Numbers 29:7-11:
> And ye shall have on the tenth day of this seventh month an holy convocation [Day of Atonement]; and ye shall afflict your souls: ye shall not do any work therein:
> But ye shall offer a burnt offering [*olah*] unto the LORD for a sweet savour; one young bullock, one ram, and seven lambs of the first year; they shall be unto you without blemish:
> And their meat [meal] offering shall be of flour mingled with oil, three tenth deals to a bullock, and two tenth deals to one ram,
> A several tenth deal for one lamb, throughout the seven lambs:
> One kid of the goats for a sin offering; beside the sin offering of atonement [scapegoat], and the continual

The Day of Atonement: The Grand Portrayal of Christ

burnt offering, and the meat [meal] offering of it, and their drink offerings.

The burnt (ascending) offerings presented on this day were very abundant: one young bull, one ram and seven lambs with the accompanying meal offerings. In addition to these sacrifices, Numbers 29:11 reminds the reader that the daily sacrifices called the "continual burnt offering" on this most busy day of the year are not to be neglected. As noted previously, the daily burnt offering consisted of one lamb, a meal offering and a drink offering done in the morning and then repeated in the evening (Numbers 28:3-7).

Almost a dozen animals were presented as burnt or ascending sacrifices on this holy day.[14] While the sin (purification) offerings were certainly of prominent importance, these burnt (ascending) offerings were more numerous. It is fitting that quite an emphasis should be placed on the ascending offerings. When the high priest entered into the holy places with blood of purification sacrifices, it looked forward to the day when the true sacrifice would ascend into the holy places of heaven to appear in the presence of God for us.

> Hebrews 4:14-16:
> Seeing then that we have a great high priest, that is passed into the heavens, Jesus the Son of God, let us hold fast our profession.
> For we have not an high priest which cannot be touched with the feeling of our infirmities; but was in all points tempted like as we are, yet without sin.

---

[14] Rabbinical scholars differ whether the ram mentioned Numbers 29:8 was identical to the one mentioned in Leviticus 16:3 and 8. If they were two different rams, then 12 *olah* sacrifices were offered that day.

JESUS CHRIST OUR COMPLETE OFFERING

> Let us therefore come boldly unto the throne of grace, that we may obtain mercy, and find grace to help in time of need.

After Jesus Christ's sacrificial work, he ascended into the heavens. With this great high priest, we have complete access to God. We are to approach the throne of grace fearlessly and freely. Is this not a striking contrast to the Aaronic priest who was told to "come not at all times" into the holy of holies "that he die not?"[15]

Leviticus 16 closes, reviewing the significance of the Day of Atonement.

> Leviticus 16:29-34:
> And this shall be a statute for ever unto you: that in the seventh month, on the tenth day of the month, ye shall afflict your souls, and do no work at all, whether it be one of your own country, or a stranger that sojourneth among you:
> For on that day shall the priest make an atonement for you, to cleanse you, that ye may be clean from all your sins before the LORD.
> *It shall* be a sabbath of rest unto you, and ye shall afflict your souls, by a statute for ever.
> And the priest, whom he shall anoint, and whom he shall consecrate to minister in the priest's office in his father's stead, shall make the atonement, and shall put on the linen clothes, even the holy garments:
> And he shall make an atonement for the [most] holy sanctuary, and he shall make an atonement for the tabernacle of the congregation, and for the altar, and he shall make an atonement for the priests, and for all the people of the congregation.

---

[15] Leviticus 16:2.

The Day of Atonement: The Grand Portrayal of Christ

> And this shall be an everlasting statute unto you, to make an atonement for the children of Israel for all their sins once a year. And he did as the LORD commanded Moses.

This Day of Atonement was to continue yearly on the tenth day of the seventh month.[16] Verse 30 sums up in one verse the purpose of the Day of Atonement and the essence of the sin offering: "For on that day shall the priest make an atonement for you, to cleanse you, that ye may be clean from all your sins before the LORD." The sin offering functioned to cleanse God's people from their sins.

Models in Motion

A popular hobby is model railroading. These miniature scale models include a locomotive with rolling stock which hauls cargo around a track. Often, miniature train stations, railroad yards, loading platforms, other buildings and landscapes are included. Railroad models have moving parts. The train moves around the tracks, often through tunnels and miniature towns. In the more intricate models, the loading of the cargo may be portrayed. These models can be impressive according to the skill and resources of the hobbyist. One of world's largest models is exhibited in Hamburg, Germany, extending over three floors.[17] These models in motion give an expansive view of the big picture.

The interactive models of the high priest, tabernacle, and sacrifices on the Day of Atonement may seem as a totally unfamiliar concept to the modern reader. Yet we have

---

[16] Seventh month is called Ethanim or Tishri. The Jewish holiday, Yom Kipper, occurs on the 10th of Tishri by their current calendar reckoning.
[17] "Miniatur Wunderland" is a major tourist attraction.

JESUS CHRIST OUR COMPLETE OFFERING

contemporary examples of active models operating together, giving a panoramic display of a much larger scene.

On the Day of Atonement, the high priest selected three sin offerings and then he entered into the tabernacle with the blood to purify the holy places. As the blood was sprinkled, the holy places were cleansed and atoned for. The high priest then brought the scapegoat, laid his hands on it, confessing the sins of people. Then, this goat was lead out from the land of the living into the wilderness bearing all the sins. The events on the Day of Atonement were a precise visual display speaking prophetically about the coming Christ.

This momentous feast day under the Law depicted Christ and his work. He laid down his life as the ultimate once-and-for-all sin offering. After his resurrection, he entered the heavenly tabernacle at his ascension, cleansing it by his blood.

The tabernacle, high priest and sacrifices of ancient Israel all served as models or patterns of the coming Christ. Most sacrifices under the Law were to be offered before the tabernacle by the priest. On the Day of Atonement all three of these models interacted to the fullest extent—models in motion.

Indeed, the Day of Atonement was a model in action depicting Christ's towering achievements. To look at this interactive model in Leviticus 16 and take it all in, we can get a sense of perspective and see the big picture.

While we may find it challenging to become familiar with the overview of the events of this day, this series of sacrifices and procedures was engrained in Israelite culture and practice. When the true Messiah would arrive, the Day of

The Day of Atonement: The Grand Portrayal of Christ

Atonement would present an interactive model of Christ's accomplishments for those that had eyes to see and ears to hear.

Part Three

The Complete Offering

Chapter 17

Christ's Complete Sacrifice on Display:
Viewing the Old Testament Offerings as a Whole

While it has taken some time and effort, we have considered many offerings of the Old Testament and how they corresponded to the coming savior. Each offering had unique attributes and distinct functions that depicted Christ's once-and-for-all sacrifice. Our Lord's sacrifice was so massive in its scope and magnitude that no one sacrifice could give a full pattern of the good things to come. Rather, the distinct characteristics of each sacrifice illustrated one or more of the aspects of Christ's work. Viewing the offerings as a group allows us to glimpse an entire spectrum of Christ's accomplishments. The scope of the ultimate sacrifice can be appreciated when the offerings are looked at as a whole.

Let's briefly review the distinguishing aspects of these Old Testament offerings and how they give a vivid portrayal of him who was to come. The sin and trespass offerings were both for sin but had very different roles.

The function of the Old Testament **trespass offering** was to restore, recompense, and return; to make amends. The trespass offering was the only sacrifice under the Law of

JESUS CHRIST OUR COMPLETE OFFERING

Moses that involved a restitution payment for the wrong done, plus an extra twenty percent.

The trespass offering looked forward to the restitution payment the Lord Jesus Christ would make by the sacrifice of himself. The loss that Adam perpetrated on God, Christ restored in full. The redeemer's sacrifice recompensed Adam's original trespass. By the sacrifice of Christ, what God was defrauded of in Adam has been fully repaid. The savior paid the price to return what Adam forfeited plus "much more." Christ's sacrifice made whole the broken relationship between God and man.

As a result of Christ fulfilling the aspects of the trespass offering, there is no verdict of condemnation that can be laid against us because Christ paid it all and more. He made full restitution for us giving us a "much more" salvation.

We saw that the focus of the **sin offering** in the Law of Moses was on the blood of the sacrifice. Hebrews 9:22 informs us of the significance of the blood of the sacrifice: "…almost all things are by the law purged [cleansed, purified] with blood…" The function of the sin offering and the blood was to purge or cleanse. We noted that the cleansing faculty of this offering functioned to forgive sins, sanctify, and atone.

The sin offering looked forward to the cleansing and purification wrought by the blood of Christ which forgives sins, sanctifies, and atones. Christ fulfilled the sin offering for our cleansing, wiping away all sin and imparting to us the righteousness of God. As a result, we are set apart for eternal life and reconciled to God. Nothing can separate us from Him.

Christ's Complete Sacrifice on Display

We also read about two profoundly unusual sin offerings, the scapegoat and the red heifer offering. Both illustrated the coming savior in remarkable ways. The **scapegoat** was not even killed by the priest, but rather was sent out into the wilderness to face destruction while bearing the sins of the people. In like manner, Christ bore our sins. He was lead away: "…cut off from the land of the living."[1]

The **red heifer sacrifice** was noteworthy because of its mention in Hebrews 9:13. This rare sacrifice was the only priestly offering commanded to be sacrificed outside the camp or outside of the city gates. Our lord was crucified outside the gates of Jerusalem, which we will cover in Appendix One. Likewise the red heifer offering in the first century was carried out on the Mount of Olives.

The **peace offering** was the only altar sacrifice where a portion was given back to the offerer to eat. The priests ate of many of the sacrifices offered before the altar, but only with the peace offering were people of Israel allowed to eat thereof.[2]

We considered what it meant in ancient times to eat a sacrifice. The significance of eating of a sacrifice was a full sharing and union with that sacrifice and the God or gods it was offered to. Therefore it became clear that the peace offering graphically illustrated the full sharing or identification the believer would have with the great sacrifice to come.

The **meal offering** had the unique attribute of not being an animal sacrifice. Unlike the other offerings, no innocent

---

[1] Isaiah 53:8.
[2] The Passover offering was eaten by the people of Israel but it was not sacrificed on the altar.

JESUS CHRIST OUR COMPLETE OFFERING

animal died as a substitute for the offerer. There was no sprinkling of blood representing cleansing.

We read that in the case of the priestly offerings, the meal offering was usually paired with a **drink offering** of wine. These meal and drink offerings were a precursor to the bread and wine of "holy communion" set forth in the New Testament. While the bread and cup of the New Testament look back in remembrance to the sacrifice of Christ, so the meal and drink offering looked forward to the future ultimate sacrifice. Just as the bread of communion represent the body of Christ given in sacrifice, so the meal offering foreshadowed the great sacrifice to come.

We also noted an important truth that the meal offering was to be presented as a memorial, in remembrance. Likewise, the bread and wine of communion is also to be received in remembrance. While we are to recall what Christ has accomplished when we eat the bread and drink of the cup; additionally we also invoke God's remembrance on our behalf. We may look to God to remember and act miraculously to bring about our deliverance.

The distinctive characteristic of the **burnt** (ascending) **offering** was that the entire sacrifice was completely consumed on the altar. This looked forward to the savior who would, in complete devotion, give himself totally to secure a complete salvation for us. Another unique feature of the burnt offering was its meaning in the Hebrew: the ascending offering. When we understand that the sacrifice ascended, in the form of smoke, we see a wonderful parallel to Christ. He also was the sacrifice that ascended.

The peace, meal and burnt offerings were not sacrifices for sin, but rather were "sweet savor" offerings that functioned to intercede on behalf of the offerer. This intercessory

Christ's Complete Sacrifice on Display

function looked forward to the sacrificial work of the righteous servant of Isaiah 53:12 who "made intercession for the transgressors."

We also considered the **wave or elevation offering** that uniquely signified a transfer into God's realm. To raise or wave an offering to God signified a legal transfer of ownership. This offering looked forward to God's people being transferred into His Kingdom.

All these offerings had profound parallels to Christ's complete sacrifice. Each of them displays at least one distinctive function of the person of Christ or the work of Christ. Each glistens with at least one aspect of the multifaceted diamond of our savior's work. Taken as a whole, these sacrifices reveal facets of our redemption and salvation with a brilliant radiance.

While we have seen notable ways these Levitical sacrifices foreshadowed Christ, other people have had difficulty understanding these truths.

> II Corinthians 3:13-16:
> And not as Moses, which put a vail over his face, that the children of Israel could not stedfastly look to the end [Christ] of that which is abolished [the law]:[3]
> But their minds were blinded: for until this day remaineth the same vail untaken away **in the reading of the old testament**; which vail is done away in Christ.
> But even unto this day, **when Moses is read**, the vail is upon their heart.
> Nevertheless when it shall turn to the Lord, the vail shall be taken away.

---

[3] Romans 10:4: "For Christ is the end [*telos*] of the law for righteousness to every one that believeth."

JESUS CHRIST OUR COMPLETE OFFERING

It says in the reading of the Law of Moses they were blinded, with their hearts veiled. What were they blind to in the Law? Many sections of the Law of Moses were about sacrifices that looked forward to and had striking parallels to Christ's great sacrifice. When these people of Israel read about the Levitical sacrifices, they were blinded to how these offerings portrayed the coming one.

In reading the Old Testament, some of the people of Israel were blinded. In contrast, we had quite a different experience. Although it took us some time and effort, we saw how Christ was depicted in these sacrifices. We had to examine various Hebrew words, ancient customs and, most importantly, read what the Scriptures said to learn the functions and significance of the various sacrifices.

In contrast to us, these people of Israel of the first century would have had an innate comprehension of these Levitical sacrifices; their instructions and their practices. They would have been intimately acquainted with the Day of Atonement. They would not only have read the book of Leviticus in the Hebrew language, but they would have lived it in their culture and worship under the Old Covenant.

They would have known that the trespass offering involved a restitution payment, yet many of them did not connect it to Christ and his great payment. They knew that sprinkling the blood of the sin offering represented a cleansing, yet many of them were blind to the parallel to Christ. They understood how the eating of the peace offering indicated a full sharing. But many of them were in the dark about how then God's people shared fully with the Messiah. They knew exactly what it meant to eat of a sacrifice. They were familiar with the significance of the laying of the hands of the high

Christ's Complete Sacrifice on Display

priest on the scapegoat and how that transferred the sins of the nation onto that goat. But many of them did not see how this sacrifice corresponded to Jesus of Nazareth dying on Golgotha.

The people of Israel who could read the Hebrew language would never have stumbled over the term "meat offering" that we read in the Authorized King James Version. They would never have been puzzled why it says "meat offering" when these offerings never contain any meat. The Hebrew text of the Old Testament should have been unambiguously plain to them, yet true meaning of the meal offering was hidden to those whose minds were blinded.

They knew the Hebrew word for "burnt offering" literally meant "ascending," yet they did not grasp that Christ was the ultimate fulfillment of the sacrifice that ascended.

As we look to Christ and his sacrificial work, we behold the paramount truths depicted by the Old Testament sacrifices. What grace God has poured out on us that our eyes should see what our savior has wrought!

JESUS CHRIST OUR COMPLETE OFFERING

Name of Sacrifice	Hebrew Name	Functions	Distinctive Characteristic	Parallel to Christ
Trespass Offering -- Restitution Offering	asham	Restitution: Forgave: - unintentional sins - property violations - unfaithfulness to God	monetary payment plus 20%	Isaiah 53:10 Romans 8:3 Romans 5
Sin Offering -- Purification Offering	chattath	-Forgiveness -Cleansing -Sanctifying -Atonement	Blood applied	Hebrews 9:12-14; 10:22; 13:12 I Peter 1:2 II Cor. 5:21 I John 1:7-2:2
Peace Offering --- Fellowship Offering	shelem	Sweet savour: Sharing fully with the sacrifice -thanksgiving -vow -freewill	Sacrifice eaten by the offerer	Our Identification, with Christ I Cor. 10:18 Eph. 2:14
Meal/Bread Offering	minchah	Sweet savour: Asking for God's remembrance	Not an animal sacrifice, often paired with drink offering	The body of Christ given in sacrifice: precursor to the bread in communion
Burnt Offering -- Ascending Offering	olah	- Sweet savour: -Intercession -Atonement -Dedication	a complete sacrifice, entirely burned up on the altar	Sacrifice that ascended, complete Sacrifice -Complete obedience
Wave Offering ---- Heave Offering ---- Elevation Offering	tenuphah --- terumah	To transfer to God's ownership and then given to the priests	To transfer to God's ownership; into His domain	Christ the First Fruits I Cor. 15:23 Colossians 1:13

Chapter 18

His Complete Offering

We will now look at another characteristic of Christ's complete sacrifice that was foreshadowed by the Mosaic sacrifices.

> I Peter 1:18 and 19:
> Forasmuch as ye know that ye were not redeemed with corruptible things, as silver and gold, from your vain conversation received by tradition from your fathers;
> But with the precious blood of Christ, as of a lamb without blemish and without spot:

As a lamb without blemish or spot, Jesus Christ fully paid for our complete redemption. As we will see, the sacrifices of Leviticus were also to be without blemish and without spot.

Leviticus 1:3 required the following of a burnt (ascending) offering: "If his offering be a burnt sacrifice of the herd, let him offer a male without blemish [*tamim*]..." The words

JESUS CHRIST OUR COMPLETE OFFERING

"without blemish" are translated from the Hebrew word, *tamim*, meaning complete or whole.[1]

> **Hebrew: *tamim* = complete or whole**

> Leviticus 3:1: "...a sacrifice of peace offering...he shall offer it without blemish [*tamim*] before the LORD."

In the case of the peace offering, the animal sacrificed also was to be whole or complete.

> Leviticus 4:3: "...a young bullock without blemish [*tamim*] unto the LORD for a sin offering."

The sin offering was also to be "without blemish."

> Leviticus 5:18: "And he shall bring a ram without blemish [*tamim*] out of the flock, with thy estimation, for a trespass offering, unto the priest."

The Law of Moses also decreed that the ram presented as a trespass offering was to be whole or complete.

This stipulation of completeness is common to almost all of the animal sacrifices. The burnt, peace, sin, and trespass offerings were all required to be "without blemish," meaning complete or whole. While these animal sacrifices were not equivalent substitutes to pay the full price for mankind's redemption, they served to depict the completeness of our Lord's ultimate sacrifice.

---

[1] *The New Brown Driver Briggs*, 1071; *Gesenius' Hebrew and Chaldee Lexicon*, 867.

His Complete Offering

Leviticus 22 defined what it meant for the sacrifices to be whole or complete.

> Leviticus 22:18-23:
> ... which they will offer unto the LORD for a burnt offering;
> Ye shall offer at your own will a male without blemish [*tamim*], of the beeves [cattle], of the sheep, or of the goats.
> But whatsoever hath a blemish, that shall ye not offer: for it shall not be acceptable for you.
> And whosoever offereth a sacrifice of peace offerings unto the LORD to accomplish his vow, or a freewill offering in beeves or sheep, it shall be perfect [*tamim*] to be accepted; there shall be no blemish therein.
> Blind, or broken, or maimed, or having a wen [running sore], or scurvy, or scabbed, ye shall not offer these unto the LORD, nor make an offering by fire of them upon the altar unto the LORD.
> Either a bullock or a lamb that hath any thing superfluous [deformed] or lacking in his parts, that mayest thou offer for a freewill offering but for a vow it shall not be accepted.

With the lone exception of a freewill offering in verse 23, any defective offering was barred from the altar. Any animal deformed or "lacking in its parts," diseased or broken was not acceptable. The sacrifice was to be presented to God in a state of perfection.

Let's take a moment to look at these offerings from the vantage point of the Creator. As noted earlier, in Genesis chapter 1 and 2, God made the first man and woman with body, soul and spirit. They were complete as three-fold beings. God made and formed animals as well with soul life. At the time of Adam's creation, these animals with body and soul life were never given spirit. These beasts of the earth were whole or complete exactly the way God made them.

However, Adam and Eve sinned and lost the spirit God had created in them. From the fall of Genesis 3, humanity lacked the spirit; they were only soul and body. Death passed upon all men as Romans 5 states, even upon those who "had not sinned after the similitude of Adam's transgression." The death that passed upon all humanity was the lack of the spirit life. Men and women had soul life or breath life, but no spirit life. Therefore, they faced life incomplete; lacking one of their three vital parts: the spirit that God had originally placed within them.

In a very real sense, humanity was defective, lacking an integral part with which it had been originally created. Like a prohibited blemished sacrifice, after the fall of Adam and Eve, their descendents would be "superfluous or lacking in its parts" without the spirit of God. By the offense of Adam, humanity had no holy spirit to access their loving Creator.

From God's viewpoint, that sacrificial animal came before Him as a complete, whole sacrifice who would give its life for one who was incomplete: a person of body and soul. That animal was indeed whole, just as God had originally made it. God would transfer the acceptableness, the completeness of that animal to the Israelite offering the sacrifice. Then the unworthiness, the incompleteness of the offerer was transferred to the offering that died on his behalf.

We were defective and incomplete—dead in trespasses and sin. But by the crucifixion, Jesus Christ's completeness was transferred to us, while all our lack, our disease and sin were

His Complete Offering

transferred to him. Jesus Christ was our complete offering, our perfect and complete sacrifice. What a portrait of our Lord's sacrifice is displayed by these Old Testament sacrifices!

The Scriptures speak of a created being who was originally "*tamim*," perfect, complete and without blemish.

> Ezekiel 28:12:
> Son of man, take up a lamentation upon the king of Tyrus, and say unto him, Thus saith the Lord GOD; Thou sealest up the sum, full of wisdom, and perfect [*kalil*] in beauty.

The Hebrew word, *kalil*, is translated as "perfect" in the sense of perfect or complete beauty.[2]

> Verses 13-15:
> Thou hast been in Eden the garden of God; every precious stone was thy covering, the sardius, topaz, and the diamond, the beryl, the onyx, and the jasper, the sapphire, the emerald, and the carbuncle, and gold: the workmanship of thy tabrets and of thy pipes was prepared in thee in the day that thou wast created.
> Thou art the anointed cherub that covereth; and I have set thee so: thou wast upon the holy mountain of God; thou hast walked up and down in the midst of the stones of fire.
> Thou wast perfect [*tamim*] in thy ways from the day that thou wast created, till iniquity was found in thee.

---

[2] *Kalil* is a Hebrew word for full or complete. Both *kol* and *kalil* are related "to the root *kll*, which produces the Hebrew verb form qal "to finish, make complete. *Theological Lexicon of the Old Testament,* 614 and *The New Brown Driver Briggs Hebrew and English Lexicon,* 480. *Kalil* is also used in referring to complete or "whole burnt offerings." (Psalm 51:19).

JESUS CHRIST OUR COMPLETE OFFERING

This description goes well beyond the glory of an earthly monarch to depict Lucifer.[3] At the moment of his creation, Lucifer was entirely complete [*tamim*] and perfect [*kalil*] in beauty—nothing lacking, in total splendor in heaven with God. This glorious state continued until Lucifer sinned and "iniquity was found" in him. These verses describe the fall of this heavenly being:

> Verse 16 and 17:
> ...thou hast sinned: therefore I will cast thee as profane out of the mountain of God: and I will destroy thee, O covering cherub, from the midst of the stones of fire.
> Thine heart was lifted up because of thy beauty, thou hast corrupted thy wisdom by reason of thy brightness...

Lucifer was cast out from God's glorious presence because his heart became proud on account of his beauty. The life of our Lord Jesus Christ took a radically different course. He faced a situation far removed from that of Lucifer:

> Isaiah 53:2 and 3:
> ...a root out of a dry ground: he hath no form nor comeliness; and when we shall see him, there is no beauty that we should desire him.
> He is despised and rejected of men...

Here, we behold the righteous servant in the context of his crucifixion, with no beauty, despised and rejected of men. The original honor and splendor of Lucifer in heaven forms an extreme contrast to our Lord's suffering. Christ is

---

[3] In Isaiah 14, Lucifer is also compared to an earthly king as in Ezekiel 28.

His Complete Offering

described as "a root out of dry ground," forming a drastic distinction to the Lucifer basking in heavenly effulgence.

> Hebrews 2:9 and 10:
> But we see Jesus, who was made a little lower than the angels for the suffering of death, crowned with glory and honour; that he by the grace of God should taste death for every man.
> For it became him, for whom are all things, and by whom are all things, in bringing many sons unto glory, to make the captain of their salvation perfect through sufferings.

Having tasted death for all humanity, he was raised from the dead and "crowned with glory and honor." He was made "perfect through sufferings." Again, this is quite a contrast to Lucifer who was created in perfection strolling in the midst of heavenly beauty. While Lucifer's heart was lifted up because of his beauty and dignity, Christ lowered himself to suffer death, utterly bereft of beauty and dignity.

> Hebrews 5:7-9:
> Who in the days of his flesh, when he had offered up prayers and supplications with strong crying and tears unto him that was able to save him from death, and was heard in that he feared;
> Though he were a Son, yet learned he obedience by the things which he suffered;
> And being made perfect he became the author [source] of eternal salvation unto all them that obey him

Verse 7 refers to our Lord's prayers in the Garden of Gethsemane where he demonstrated his unparalleled devotion and obedience to do God's will.

JESUS CHRIST OUR COMPLETE OFFERING

Also the Scripture states that Christ "learned obedience by the things which he suffered." By his act of unmatched obedience and subsequent suffering, he learned and understood the awesome profit of doing God's will: the salvation for all humanity. Not until after the crucifixion did Jesus see the full results of his total obedience: the mystery of Jews and Gentiles becoming joint heirs.[4]

He was made perfectly complete and became the source of eternal salvation. Again, this is the polar opposite from Lucifer who once basked on the holy mountain of God in the midst of heavenly glory reveling in celestial riches. Lucifer was created as perfect and complete in heaven, but his heart was lifted up because of his beauty and his splendor.

In stark contrast, Jesus Christ, by his suffering on earth and his total obedience to God, accomplished a perfect and complete work for us. He gave his all, fulfilling God's will in every respect by sacrificing himself. Because of his humiliation and suffering, now we are sons of God, brought to glory!

---

[4] Ephesians 3:6: "That the Gentiles should be fellowheirs, and of the same body, and partakers of his promise in Christ by the gospel:"

Chapter 19

Complete in Him: Our Identification with Christ

Christians generally understand that Christ died for them on the cross at Golgotha. They may also recognize that the savior took their place as a substitute on the tree. Others have grown in their understanding to see that the Son of God bore their sin. However, few have grown to appreciate the full sharing and identification we have with Christ.

Some have grasped that Christ's great sacrifice involved our sins being transferred to him. However, it seems that few have understood the extent of our full sharing with Christ as expressed in the following verse:

> II Corinthians 5:21:
> For He hath made him *to be* sin [offering] for us, who knew no sin; that we might be made the righteousness of God in him.

In this verse, we see a double transfer of our sin **to** Christ, and God's righteousness in Christ **to** us. In this sense, we are identified with Christ, sharing fully with him.

> Romans 6:4-8:
> Therefore we are buried **with** him by baptism into death: that like as Christ was raised up from the dead

JESUS CHRIST OUR COMPLETE OFFERING

> by the glory of the Father, even so we also should walk in newness of life.
> For if we have been planted [identified[1]] together in the likeness of his death, we shall be also in the likeness of his resurrection:
> Knowing this, that our old man is crucified **with** him, that the body of sin might be destroyed, that henceforth we should not serve sin.
> For he that is dead is freed from sin
> Now if we be dead **with** Christ, we believe that we shall also live **with** him.

This passage tells us a lot about our identification with Christ. The word "with" in this context speaks to what we fully shared with our savior. "With" has been put in bold print because it is an undersized word with an oversized significance when referring to our identification with Christ.

The "old man" and the "body of sin" are both graphic expressions depicting our sin nature. Since we are identified with Christ in his death, our sin nature died with him. Look at the vivid words in these verses describing the state of our old sin nature: **crucified, buried, destroyed, dead.**

Identified with Christ
The status of your sin nature:
  -crucified
  -dead
  -buried
  -destroyed

---

[1] From the Working Translation in *A Journey through the Acts and Epistle* by Walter J. Cummins.

Complete in Him: Our Identification with Christ

We not only fully shared with his death, but now we also fully shared in his resurrection life. Verse 5 says we are identified with his resurrection as well as with his death. Verse 8 states, since "...we be dead **with** Christ, we believe that we shall also live **with** him."

This statement, "...we shall also live **with** him," if taken out of the context of identification with Christ, might be understood as referring to living in heaven with Christ in the future. However, the subject of Romans 6 is walking in newness of life, not future glory. Romans 6:11 declares that we are to walk in this present time considering ourselves "...to be dead indeed unto sin, but alive unto God through Jesus Christ our Lord." Verse 13 says we should yield ourselves "...unto God, as those that are alive from the dead..." God's will is that we walk in this world realizing our identification with Christ.

The book of Ephesians tells us more about our identification.

> Ephesians 2:5-9:
> But God, who is rich in mercy, for his great love wherewith he loved us,
> Even when we were dead in sins, hath quickened [made alive] us together **with** Christ, (by grace ye are saved;)
> And hath raised us up together, and made us sit together in heavenly places in Christ Jesus:
> That in the ages to come he might shew the exceeding riches of his grace in his kindness toward us through Christ Jesus.
> For by grace are ye saved through faith; and that not of yourselves: it is the gift [offering] of God:
> Not of works, lest any man should boast.

JESUS CHRIST OUR COMPLETE OFFERING

Verse 9 proclaims God's ultimate gift offering: the finished work of Christ and our subsequent salvation.

According to verse 5, we are made alive with Christ. We have already seen in Romans 6 how we were identified not only with Christ's death, but his resurrection as well. Ephesians 2:6 gives additional truth: "And hath raised us up together, and made us sit together in heavenly places in Christ Jesus." We have not only been made alive in Christ, but we are raised and seated together in the heavenlies.

Our identification with Christ extends into the heavenly places! The completeness of our salvation is almost beyond earthly comprehension. Our legal standing before God includes not only righteousness, but being made alive, raised, and seated with Christ.

Your status as a son of God
Identified with Christ:

- made the righteousness of God in him
- newness of life
- in the likeness of his resurrection
- made alive
- raised
- seated in the heavenly places

We have utter oneness and union with him. Herein is the great sacrificial transfer: our old sin nature was transferred to him and died with him. Then his righteousness and his resurrection life was transferred to us.

Complete in Him: Our Identification with Christ

Sacrificial Identification in the Old Testament

Is our identification with Christ a sparkling new revelation that was first revealed in the Church Epistles? Is it one of God's hidden mysteries?

Our identification with Christ's sacrifice is surely revealed by revelation in the Church Epistles. And our full sharing with the savior is without doubt a mystery to many born again Christians today. However, as we have noted in previous chapters, God has made an effort to communicate this concept of sacrificial identification repeatedly throughout the Scriptures.[2]

Let's review how the sacrifices of the Old Testament demonstrated this two-way exchange. Not only was the sin and guilt transferred onto the sacrifice, but the innocence of that offering was transferred back to the Israelite. There was a full sharing or identification between the sacrifice and the one presenting it.

We read in Leviticus how sacrifices depicted the full sharing between offerer and offering in two ways: by laying hands on the sacrifice and eating the sacrifice. On the Day of Atonement, the high priest laid his hands on the head of the goat and confessed the sins of the people, "putting them upon the head of the goat...and the goat shall bear upon him all their iniquities..." (Leviticus 16:21) The sin of the nation of Israel was laid upon the scapegoat by the high priest, and then, in turn, all the innocence of the offering was transferred to the Israelites.

---

[2] See David Bergey, *Our Identification with Christ's Sacrifice* (Redlands, California, 2000) 13.

JESUS CHRIST OUR COMPLETE OFFERING

From God's point of view, there was a two-way exchange between the offerer and the animal sacrificed. The offering shared fully in sin and the consequences—death. And, in turn, the one presenting the sacrifice shared fully in the innocence of the offering. This laying of the hands on the animal to be sacrificed signified, in essence, a double transfer.

Laying Hands on Sacrifices:	
Scapegoat	Leviticus 16:21
Burnt Offering	1:4
Peace Offering	3:2, 8, 13
Sin Offering	4:4, 24, 29, 33

Laying hands on a sacrifice was not part of some cryptic Levitical code. God declares very plainly that the sins of the people were put upon the head of the scapegoat. Since this transfer between the sacrifices and the offerer was so clearly presented and explained, God must have a reasonable level of expectation that we recognize this truth. Also, this gesture is repeated so often with the sacrifices, that one cannot suppose that this is some secret God kept to Himself. God made quite an effort to convey this truth.

We saw that eating a sacrifice also indicated a full sharing or identification. The following verse tells us the precise significance of eating the sacrifice:

> Leviticus 10:17:
> Wherefore have ye [Aaron and his sons] not **eaten the sin offering** in the holy place, seeing it is most holy, and God hath given it you **to bear the iniquity** of the

congregation, to make atonement for them before the LORD?

Aaron and his sons were to bear the iniquity of the congregation by eating the sin offering. The priest shared fully in what that sin offering represented, thus bearing the sin of God's people. By consuming the sacrifice, the priest was identified with the sin offering and the sins of the congregation were transferred to him.

As we read, many of the Old Testament sacrifices were to be eaten:

Sacrifices to be eaten:
The Passover Offering:	Exodus 12:8
The Peace Offering:	Leviticus 19:6
The Meal Offering:	Leviticus 6:16
The Sin Offering:	Leviticus 6:26
The Trespass Offering:	Leviticus 7:1-6

This truth that eating a sacrifice signifies a full sharing with the sacrifice is also mentioned in the following verse in the New Testament.

> I Corinthians 10:18:
> Behold Israel after the flesh: are not they which eat of the sacrifices partakers [*koinōnos*] of the altar?

This verse leads us to take a good look at how those who eat of the sacrifices share fully with the altar and what the sacrifices represented.

JESUS CHRIST OUR COMPLETE OFFERING

While there are mysteries in the Scriptures, this concept of identification was not one of them. God repeatedly commanded that these sacrifices were to be eaten indicating a full sharing, a union with the sacrifice. Just in case we may have missed it in the Old Testament, He brings it up again in I Corinthians 10:18. Clearly, God did not intend for this topic to be an obscure mystery that only biblical scholars could studiously contemplate. God desires for His people to understand this subject of identification in His Word.

God instituted these sacrificial practices to express the central theme of identification. He wanted people to recognize the full sharing Israel had with the sacrifices because they looked forward to our identification with Christ.

Identification illustrated in the Old Testament Sacrifices:

1. Laying hand(s) on the head of the sacrifice:
    Leviticus 16:21
2. Eating the sacrifice: Leviticus 10:17

In the Scriptures, God has made a consistent effort to reveal and clarify this great truth of identification or full sharing with the sacrifices.

At Jesus Christ's last supper before the crucifixion, he established the practice of eating of the bread and drinking of the cup in remembrance of his death. He said that the wine represented his blood and the bread represented his body. As we drink the wine and eat the bread, the full sharing with his sacrifice is demonstrated.

Complete in Him: Our Identification with Christ

The bread and the cup are not some unintelligible sacred mystery. Rather, it is a demonstration of a truth God has been illustrating plainly throughout the Scriptures. The Old Testament sacrifices looked forward to how the redeemer of all humanity would save God's people. In communion, we look backward to the finished work of Christ. Both the sacrifices of the Old Testament and the communion of the New Testament serve as object lessons of the substitution and identification we have in Christ.

> ## Lessons of Identification and Substitution in the Scriptures:
> ### In Old Testament: Sacrifices
> ### In New Testament: Communion

The offerings of the Old Testament could be called "little pictures" of Christ's sacrificial work. Viewed as a whole, the offerings of the Old Covenant give the "big picture," portraying Christ's substitution for us and identification with us.

In looking at the sacrifices of the Law of Moses, we saw many variations and details. At times, the complexity may have been difficult. However, the more we looked at the sacrifices of the Law, the more we saw how with one clarion voice they spoke of our identification with the great sacrifice who was to come. The layers of elaborate detail in the Old Testament sacrificial system may have been challenging. But a simple message rang out: what we shared with him! With one voice they proclaimed one united message: the Christ who was made "to be sin [offering] for us, who knew no sin; that we might be made the righteousness of God in him" (II Corinthians 5:21). All the sacrifices looked forward to the Son of God who loved us, and gave himself for us (Galatians 2:20). In one rolling crescendo, they all broadcasted the double transfer that would take place with the complete sacrifice who was to come.

These Levitical sacrifices are not merely obscure rites and practices of some ancient tribes. No, these are tutorials of redemption. They foreshadowed the coming Christ and taught God's people of the salvation the Messiah would bring. Furthermore, as students of God's Word, we see the continuity of the Scriptures, the unity of God's Word, from Genesis to Revelation. Whether in Leviticus or in Galatians, they all speak with one end: to awaken our minds to what Christ has accomplished.

Walking in Newness of Life: Living our Identification with Christ

Romans 6:4 states what should be the practical result of our identification with Christ: "...like as Christ was raised up from the dead by the glory of the Father, even so we also should walk in newness of life." Our walk in this world should take on a newness because of our full sharing with the savior.

How do we apply these fabulous truths to our day-to-day life? How do we walk in newness of life? The Church Epistles have much to say about living our identification with Christ. Here, we will cover only a portion of what they reveal.

Romans 6:11 addresses how to practically apply our identification with Christ: "Likewise reckon [*logizomai*] ye also yourselves to be dead indeed unto sin, but alive unto God through Jesus Christ our Lord." The linchpin verb of

Complete in Him: Our Identification with Christ

this verse is "reckon" from the Greek word, *logizomai*. Elsewhere this word, *logizomai*, is translated as "account," "count," or "think" in the sense of to consider.

As sons of God, we are told to take into account and consider ourselves to be dead to sin and alive to God. Living in this world, we have learned to consider many things. Most of us have taken some account of our sins and weaknesses as well as our difficulties and setbacks. Perhaps you have taken an exam to determine your academic strengths and weaknesses. You may have read self-help books or taken courses to assess and then improve your performance. Romans 6:11 tells us how to assess ourselves: "…dead indeed unto sin, but alive unto God…" We are to take account of the truth that our sin died when Christ died and now we are to walk in his resurrection life.

The epistle to the Colossians addresses how we should take into account the new reality of our identification with Christ.

> Colossians 3:1-4:
> If [since] ye then be risen with Christ, seek those things which are above, where Christ sitteth on the right hand of God.
> Set your affection on things above, not on things on the earth.
> For ye are dead, and your life is hid with Christ in God.
> When Christ, *who is* our life, shall appear, then shall ye also appear with him in glory.

The word, "if" in verse one should be rendered "since." There is no "if," "maybe," or "perhaps" about it—Ephesians 2 states explicitly that you are made alive, raised and seated with Christ. Our full identification with Christ is an unequivocal reality.

JESUS CHRIST OUR COMPLETE OFFERING

In light of being "risen with Christ," we are to seek and set our affections on things above. Christ has done so much for us and now we are asked to put forth some effort to seek out those realities that God has accomplished. Since we are dead with Christ, we should set our minds on things above. Again, we are to take account and be cognizant of the fact that we are dead and risen with him.

Verse 4, looking forward to future realities, promises that when Christ appears, you too will appear with him in glory. Our union with Christ extends into eternity! To realize this extent of our identification frees us from the fear of death and future punishment. Knowing we shall be appearing with Christ in glory should certainly have a positive impact on our attitude in the here and now!

> Colossians 3:5-9:
> Mortify [put to death] therefore your members which are upon the earth; fornication, uncleanness, inordinate affection, evil concupiscence, and covetousness, which is idolatry:
> For which things' sake the wrath of God cometh on the children of disobedience:
> In the which ye also walked some time, when ye lived in them.
> But now ye also put off all these; anger, wrath, malice, blasphemy, filthy communication out of your mouth.
> Lie not one to another, seeing that ye have put off the old man [nature] with his deeds;

We are to "put to death" and "put off" the practices of the old nature. Blasphemy, filthy communication out of your mouth and lying are all in the category of speech. We are to get rid of this type of communication since it is a part of the old nature.

Complete in Him: Our Identification with Christ

Ephesians 4:25 says we are to put "…away lying, speak every man truth with his neighbour: for we are members one of another." A substantial part of putting away lying and speaking the truth would include declaring our identity as sons of God.

Jesus Christ fearlessly declared who he was as the Son of God. He did not accept the disbelief, slander, and lies concerning his identity. He was unwavering in his mission to fulfill what the Scriptures said about him in the written Word of God. Likewise, we should declare what the Word of God in the New Testament says about us. We should also be unwavering in our commitment to affirm what the Scriptures state concerning our identification with Christ.

According to Colossians 3:5, we are to put to death the negative practices of our sin nature. To wallow in sin-consciousness when you are dead to sin would be the acceptance of a lie. To dwell on and declare negatives about yourself could be in the category of "filthy communication." Declaring your lack of ability to walk with God could be slander against what God made you to be in Christ. It is no badge of honor to confess the negatives of this age. Sin consciousness, negatives about oneself, and a sense of lack of ability are all part of the systemic lies of this world.

While we should not be in denial of our sins or human frailties, neither should we be in denial of what God has made us in Christ. We should align our speech with the reality of our identification with Christ. Let's consider some examples of how we might do that.

II Corinthians 5:21 states: "He hath made him to be sin [offering] for us, who knew no sin; that we might be made the righteousness of God in him." In light of this, we can

JESUS CHRIST OUR COMPLETE OFFERING

declare: "I will not confess sin-consciousness for I have been made righteous. I stand in the presence of God without any sense of sin, guilt or shortcomings."

As Galatians 2:20 declares, "...I was crucified with Christ, nevertheless I live..." In light of this statement, we could confess: "I will not dwell on negatives about myself because I was crucified with Christ, nevertheless I live, yet not I but Christ lives in me."

Since Romans 6:11 says we are to consider ourselves "...to be dead indeed unto sin, but alive unto God through Jesus Christ our Lord," we would be well within our rights to say: "I will not declare any lack of ability to walk with God or live for God. I am dead to sin and alive to God by Christ Jesus my Lord."

Let's return to Colossians chapter 3.

> Colossians 3:10-14:
> And have put on the new man, which is renewed in knowledge after the image of him that created him:
> Where there is neither Greek nor Jew, circumcision nor uncircumcision, Barbarian, Scythian, bond nor free: but Christ is all, and in all.
> Put on therefore, as the elect of God, holy and beloved, bowels of mercies, kindness, humbleness of mind, meekness, longsuffering;
> Forbearing one another, and forgiving one another, if any man have a quarrel against any: even as Christ forgave you, so also do ye.
> And above all these things put on charity, which is the bond of perfectness.

As human beings, we may take into account our ethnic heritage and family background. As sons of God, we should

Complete in Him: Our Identification with Christ

give more importance to what Christ accomplished than to our ethnicity and our social standing. Actually, God's Word declares rather categorically that these ethnic and social distinctions don't even exist in the new man! People can have fondness for their heritage—or they may deride it at times. Either way, these factors of this earth are no longer a distinction in the new man. We are members of the body of Christ, a part of the heavenly kingdom.

We are to put on the new man "…which is renewed in knowledge…" As we have seen, there is so much God does not want us to be ignorant of. According to Romans 12:2, we are told to "…be not conformed to this world: but be ye transformed by the renewing of your mind."

The new man has been created within us. Now we are to put it on in our thinking and actions. We are to acknowledge the actuality of who we are in Christ and walk accordingly.

This passage of Colossians 3 goes beyond a listing of "dos and don'ts" or virtues and vices. It speaks to our identity in union with Christ. These are not presented as moral obligations to attain righteousness, but rather these are choices that we can make because we are righteous. These are ways to think and act that stem from what we have already received in Christ.

You may have been told at some point in your life that you need to "deal with reality." As Christian believers, we need to deal with the reality of what our Lord Jesus Christ has accomplished. We need to take into account that we were crucified with Christ.

A change in our self-image can be dramatic and quick when we realize our identification into all that was and is Christ.

JESUS CHRIST OUR COMPLETE OFFERING

When we start developing the realization of our full identification with our Lord, a new day will dawn in our lives. Life will take on a certain crispness and vigor. The fashions of this present time will become dimmer as the light shines on the path before us.

Chapter 20

Complete Deliverance in the Lamb of God

This study of the Levitical offerings and their correspondence to Christ's great sacrifice has helped us to behold the breadth and magnitude of what our Lord accomplished. Since Jesus Christ achieved a full and complete work of our redemption and salvation, we have complete deliverance.

In chapter 3 of this study, we saw that Isaiah 53 revealed that the promised redeemer would bear the sickness and sorrow of God's people, as well as their sin. Luke 4 features another prophecy from Isaiah that Jesus Christ fulfilled concerning the deliverance of God's people.

> Luke 4:16-21:
> And he came to Nazareth, where he had been brought up: and, as his custom was, he went into the synagogue on the sabbath day, and stood up for to read.
> And there was delivered unto him the book of the prophet Esaias [Isaiah]. And when he had opened the book, he found the place where it was written,
> **The Spirit of the Lord is upon me, because he hath anointed me to preach the gospel to the poor; he hath sent me to heal the brokenhearted, to preach**

JESUS CHRIST OUR COMPLETE OFFERING

> **deliverance to the captives, and recovering of sight to the blind, to set at liberty them that are bruised, To preach the acceptable year of the Lord.**
> And he closed the book, and he gave it again to the minister, and sat down. And the eyes of all them that were in the synagogue were fastened on him.
> And he began to say unto them, This day is this scripture fulfilled in your ears.

Luke 4:18 and 19 (in bold print) is a quote from Isaiah 61:1 and 2. Jesus Christ fulfilled this prophecy of Isaiah 61 which sheds much light on his healing ministry.

"The Spirit of the Lord is upon me, because he hath anointed me to preach the gospel to the poor..." In this opening sentence we have two essential elements in play to receive mental or physical healing from God: the spirit of God and the Word of God set forth in the gospel.

The spirit of God was in operation in the ministry of Jesus Christ. It was not only latent or potential; it was in action. Secondly, Jesus Christ preached the gospel. A more accurate translation of the word "preach" is "to announce a joyful proclamation."[1] The word "gospel" literally means "good news." So, with the spirit of God in operation, Jesus joyfully proclaimed the good news. Luke 4:18 is certainly good news! Whether mental healing or physical healing, Jesus Christ brought this deliverance into manifestation by the spirit and by the Word of God.

"...he hath sent me to heal the brokenhearted..."
In this phrase, we have the absolute will of God—to heal the broken hearts of God's people. Life has shattered many. Yet Christ has been dispatched by God to bind up the heart, that

---

[1] Walter J. Cummins, *A Journey through the Acts and Epistles*, 39.

Complete Deliverance in the Lamb of God

innermost part of our being. This provides us a real, authentic mental healing that cannot be found anywhere else. All the therapies contrived by man cannot bring the peace and deliverance that Christ can bring.

"...to preach deliverance to the captives..."

The captivity of humanity began with Adam and Eve. Enslavement to sin and death came upon all mankind when these first humans rejected God's Word in Genesis 3. By Christ's redemptive work, God has so lovingly provided a way for us to be released from the bondage of sin. Christ has set us free from the power of darkness of this world. God wants us to be delivered from every trauma, every psychosis, and every phobia that has ever oppressed us. Whether a minor heartache or life-shattering experience, Christ is our deliverer.

> John 8:31, 32 and 36:
> ...If ye continue in my word, then are ye my disciples indeed;
> And ye shall know the truth, and the truth shall make you free.
> If the Son therefore shall make you free, ye shall be free indeed.

God, through Christ, is able to deliver us from any mental prison that enslaves us. This is true freedom.

"...and recovering of sight to the blind..."

The Gospels record instances of Christ healing the physically blind.[2] In the following verse, he spoke of the difficult issue of healing those who are mentally blinded to the truth of God's Word.

---

[2] Luke 7:21, Mark 10:46-52 and John 9.

JESUS CHRIST OUR COMPLETE OFFERING

> Matthew 13:15 and 16:
> ...their eyes they have closed; lest at any time they should see with *their* eyes, and hear with *their* ears, and should understand with *their* heart, and should be converted, and I should heal them.
> But blessed *are* your eyes, for they see: and your ears, for they hear.

Conversion and healing requires the eyes of the spiritual understanding being opened. The healing power of Christ extends to mental as well as physical blindness.

"...to set at liberty them that are bruised."
"Bruised" is translated as "downtrodden, bruised, crushed and broken by calamity" by the *Amplified Bible*. Whether broken in heart or body, Christ is our liberator. God sent Jesus Christ to set His people free. Where we are injured or broken, Christ is able to bring about our release. Jesus Christ heals God's people's crushed and broken hearts.

These declarations clearly indicate that Christ's work involves deliverance from emotional and mental as well as physical oppression. Our Lord Jesus Christ offers us release from our mental prisons. Where we have been broken by adversity, hardship or mental anguish, he brings liberty and peace.

How does Christ heal the brokenhearted? By the operation of the spirit and the joyful proclamation of the good news. Part of his mission was, and is, to bring mental and physical healing to God's people.

Our current society is desperate for mental healing. They seek relief with antidepressants and other medications. Some seek a solution in psychotherapy. The need for mental

Complete Deliverance in the Lamb of God

healing is just as great, if not greater, than when Jesus first spoke these words. And these words are just as real, true, and applicable today as when first spoken. The ministry of Jesus Christ, first proclaimed in Nazareth, continues to this day. He is still able to "save to the uttermost" (Hebrews 7:25).

The Lord Jesus Christ is our complete sacrifice—bearing **both** our sickness and our sorrows. Jesus Christ achieved a complete salvation. In addition to spiritual salvation, he gives us both physical and mental healing.

It is well known that some mental problems are caused by physical deficiencies or chemical imbalances. Some physical sicknesses are caused by mental pain or stress. Had Christ merely carried our mental and not our physical problems, our mental healing would be incomplete. By the same token, if Christ only bore our physical sicknesses without the mental anguish and weakness, our physical healing would remain unfinished. Christ bore it all, saving us to the uttermost!

The New Testament repeats the revelation in Isaiah: both mental and physical healing have been accomplished by the Lord Jesus Christ who bore our sins, sorrows and sickness. He is a complete savior! Not only were our transgressions laid on him, but also our sorrows and disease. We have not only forgiveness of sins but peace and healing as well. Our physical and mental healing is complete by the sacrifice of Jesus Christ.

Christ bearing our sin and sickness is an objective reality whether anyone believes it or not. Just because forgiveness and healing are available does not mean all will access it. The prevailing presence of sin in the world does not mean

JESUS CHRIST OUR COMPLETE OFFERING

Christ did not bear our sin. By the same token, the presence of sickness does not mean Christ did not bear our diseases.

In spite of the fears and frailties of this life, we have physical and mental healing. How simple and clear this is—yet how seemingly difficult it has been for Christians to come to an understanding of what our savior has accomplished on our behalf. When we read the truth of God about Christ bearing our sin, sickness and sorrow explained so clearly, we may wonder why we do not see this deliverance manifested more in our daily lives.

The Word of the Cross is the Power of God

I Corinthians gives us valuable insight on how to manifest God's deliverance.

> I Corinthians 1:17 and 18:
> For Christ sent me not to baptize, but to preach the gospel: not with wisdom of words, lest the cross of Christ should be made of none effect.
> For the preaching [*logos*=word] of the cross is to them that perish foolishness; but unto us which are saved it is the power of God.

There is power in believing the specifics of what Christ accomplished from the Word of God. To see God's power more at work in our lives is indeed the point of this examination of Old Testament sacrifices. To view the details of Christ's sacrifice in a new light can help us to accept what Christ has given us. Manifesting deliverance in our lives begins with filling our thinking with the reality of precisely what he has accomplished for us.

Verse 17 says: "…lest the cross of Christ should be made of none effect." Therefore, it must be possible for the cross of

Complete Deliverance in the Lamb of God

Christ to be "made of none effect." Jesus said in Matthew 15:6 that the Word of God was nullified by the traditions of men.

As earnest Christians, we may find it difficult to fathom that such a monumental accomplishment as Christ bearing the sins of humanity could be made void or nullified. However, we must face the hard fact that preaching the gospel mixed with man's wisdom and man's traditions will cause the accomplishments of Christ to become of none effect in the lives of people. This truth in I Corinthians 1:17 and Matthew 15:6 goes a long way to explain the lack of results in the Church today. The reality of Christ bearing our sin, sickness and sorrows can be invalidated in the lives of people when the wisdom and traditions of men are mixed with the Word of God.

Verse 18 says that "the preaching [*logos* or word] of the cross is to them that perish foolishness..." The "word of the cross" is nonsense or silliness to those who do not believe. Many look at the crucifixion with the eyes of the senses. All they see in the death of Christ is a tortured, but gallant martyr who inspired his followers to start a major religion. But we see so much more. We see a suffering savior who carried our sins and our sicknesses. We behold a resurrected Lord giving us the power of God to live what he has accomplished.

We have taken an in-depth look at the sacrifice of our Lord in this study, allowing His Word to dwell in us. In examining the specifics of the Old Testament sacrifices, we can grow in understanding the monumental effects of his great sacrifice. Then, Christ's work can become less abstract and less academic. Christ's accomplishments can then be seen with greater clarity and certainty.

JESUS CHRIST OUR COMPLETE OFFERING

Again, verse 18 states concerning the word of the cross, "…unto us which are saved it is the power of God." When the word of the cross is proclaimed without man's wisdom or without man's tradition—it is the power of God!

As we behold exactly what happened that afternoon at Golgotha and the events that followed, we can begin to manifest that power of God in our lives. We must take care not to become preoccupied with the wisdom and the traditions of men. There is no power in the sterile traditions and wisdom of this world. May we become immersed in the full reality of what Christ accomplished that day on Golgotha. May we become less absorbed with the words and traditions of men and more absorbed with the Word of God. When we read the words of God with our spiritual eyes open, we'll manifest what Christ achieved by his death, resurrection, and ascension into the heavenly tabernacle.

The Lamb of God: The Sacrifice for the Ages

When John the Baptist first saw Jesus, he proclaimed: "Behold the Lamb of God, which taketh away the sin of the world…" (John 1:29). According to the Greek texts and the marginal note in the Authorized King James Version, the verse could read: "Behold the Lamb of God, which beareth away the sin of the world…"

> **"Behold the Lamb of God, which beareth away the sin of the world…"**

Complete Deliverance in the Lamb of God

In the Mosaic Law, the most prominent and most frequent sacrifice was the lamb. The number of lambs commanded to be sacrificed by the priests in public offerings was well over 900 a year.[3] This did not include the lambs brought at the Israelite's own discretion for a burnt, peace, or sin offering. Nor did this number include the lambs sacrificed at Passover.[4]

The prominence of the sacrificial lamb in the Old Testament may explain why the Lamb is a dominant symbol of Christ in the New Testament as well. Christ is called the "Lamb" 30 times in the New Testament, mostly in Revelation. In the book of Revelation, the title the "Lamb," is used a resounding 26 times, referring to the Lord Jesus Christ.

Throughout the Scriptures, the lamb is used to illustrate the Messiah and his sacrifice on our behalf. We saw how the daily sacrifice of two lambs foreshadowed Christ in Numbers 28. One of the first mentions of a lamb in the Bible is in Genesis 22:7 when Isaac asks Abraham, "Behold, the fire and the wood: but where is the lamb for a burnt offering?" This passage has been covered in detail in chapter 14 on the burnt offering.

Genesis 22 is one of the great accounts of Scripture illustrating the coming Christ. Herein, one of the first occurrences of "lamb" in the Bible provides a vivid foreshadowing of Christ's substitution. Then, in the closing book of the Bible, the term lamb is used 26 times referring to Christ. From the beginning to the end of the Scriptures,

---

[3] Lambs sacrificed yearly in the public offerings included: daily offerings at 2 lambs a day: 730; feast days: 21; Sabbath days: 100; new moon: 80.
[4] Although, in the case of the Passover, a lamb was not specified by the Law. The Passover sacrifice could be "…of the flock [sheep or goats] and the herd [cattle]…" Deuteronomy 16:2.

JESUS CHRIST OUR COMPLETE OFFERING

Christ is pictured as a lamb, as the great substitute for humanity. Talk about the big picture!

The first time Christ is portrayed as a lamb in Revelation, the meaning is explained:

> Revelation 5:2-6:
> And I saw a strong angel proclaiming with a loud voice, Who is worthy to open the book, and to loose the seals thereof?
> And no man [no one] in heaven, nor in earth, neither under the earth, was able to open the book, neither to look thereon.
> And I wept much, because no man [no one] was found worthy to open and to read the book, neither to look thereon.
> And one of the elders saith unto me, Weep not: behold, the Lion of the tribe of Juda, the Root of David, hath prevailed to open the book, and to loose the seven seals thereof.
> And I beheld, and, lo, in the midst of the throne [in heaven] and of the four beasts, and in the midst of the elders, stood **a Lamb as it had been slain**, having seven horns and seven eyes, which are the seven Spirits of God sent forth into all the earth.

Revelation 5:6 clearly says, "...a Lamb as it had been slain..." Christ is symbolized as a slain lamb—a sacrifice. He laid down his life at Golgotha. Christ alone was worthy because he has sacrificed himself as the Lamb of God. He was the redeemer; he paid the price for God to repurchase humankind.

In the future, a great question is proclaimed in heaven: who is worthy or qualified to open the book? "Opening the book" is an ancient biblical expression referring to redemption of

Complete Deliverance in the Lamb of God

land. If one was able to pay for the redemption of the land, the seven seals were opened as a sign that the mortgage had been released.[5]

When the question was proclaimed: who is worthy? — all the heavenly principalities and powers stood mute. No one met the requirements to recover or redeem the lost state of humanity. All creation shrank back in inability, unable to reclaim what Adam had forfeited. While all the angels of heaven stood mute, Jesus Christ alone stood qualified and worthy. No one in heaven qualified; no one on earth was worthy; no one "under the earth" — who had died — was able to open the book.

If Jesus Christ is the only one worthy to stand before the entire host of heaven and earth and open the final ages, why can't we esteem him worthy today to bring to pass everything he has already accomplished for us? This includes our mental deliverance, our physical healing, our forgiveness and cleansing of all sin. God completely took away all of our sin, our inadequacy and sickness and laid them on Christ. If, in the future, all of the heavenly realm can declare him qualified and capable by his substitution, so can we today. We should declare in our own hearts that Jesus Christ is fully able to forgive, deliver, supply and heal. As the redeemed ones, we can indeed manifest health in both mind and body, walking in the love and the power he has achieved for us. If the whole realm of heaven will esteem him as worthy, may we also esteem him capable to work in our lives today — worthy to heal, worthy to forgive, worthy to supply. Just as he will prevail to open the book as the mighty redeemer, in this very hour he can prevail with all he has accomplished in our lives.

---

[5] See Bishop K. C. Pallai, *Orientalisms of the Bible, Volume 1,* 115. Also see: Walter J. Cummins and Daniel J. Bader, *Volume 2, A Journey through the Acts and Epistles,* 208.

JESUS CHRIST OUR COMPLETE OFFERING

In this future hour recorded in Revelation 5, our savior will be the only one worthy to open the book. Jesus stands before the heavenly realm as the only one qualified, having the right of redemption because of his sacrificial payment. Now, from this verse forward, the title most often used of the Lord Jesus Christ throughout Revelation is "the Lamb."

The final two chapters of Scripture introduce the new and final age:

> Revelation 21:1-4:
> And I saw a new heaven and a new earth: for the first [former] heaven and the first [former] earth were passed away; and there was no more sea.
> And I John saw the holy city, new Jerusalem, coming down from God out of heaven, prepared as a bride adorned for her husband.
> And I heard a great voice out of heaven saying, Behold, the tabernacle of God *is* with men, and he will dwell with them, and they shall be his people, and God himself shall be with them, *and be* their God.
> And God shall wipe away all tears from their eyes; and there shall be no more death, neither sorrow, nor crying, neither shall there be any more pain: for the former things are passed away.

All the consequences of the fall of Lucifer and the sin of Adam will be wiped away. The devastation caused by these cataclysmic events will be terminated. Death itself will be abolished. The misery of the previous ages will pass away. This wonderful new epoch is spoken of in II Peter:

Complete Deliverance in the Lamb of God

> II Peter 3:11-13:
> Seeing then that all these things shall be dissolved, what manner of persons ought ye to be in all holy conversation and godliness,
> Looking for and hasting unto [eagerly expecting] the coming of the day of God, wherein the heavens being on fire shall be dissolved, and the elements shall melt with fervent heat?
> Nevertheless we, according to his promise, look for new heavens and a new earth, wherein dwelleth righteousness.

This new heaven and earth, where we will live forever with God, is the great promise of our Father to His people.

> Isaiah 65:17:
> For, behold, I create new heavens and a new earth: and the former shall not be remembered, nor come into mind.

Even in the Old Testament, the prophets foretold of a day coming when there would be a new heaven and a new earth. Paradise will be restored. Resurrected humanity will live forever in God's presence. The former things will have passed away; the heartache of the previous age of humanity's existence will be put out of mind. Death and anguish will be no more.

In this final age, we will bask in the light of God and His Son. In this new heaven and new earth, what title will Jesus Christ hold?

> Revelation 21:23:
> And the city had no need of the sun, neither of the moon, to shine in it: for the glory of God did lighten it, and the Lamb is the light thereof.

JESUS CHRIST OUR COMPLETE OFFERING

As seen in this verse, the title for our Lord continues to be "the Lamb" even in Revelation 21 and 22. Seven times in these closing two chapters of Scripture, Christ is called the Lamb.[6] This title will be used throughout eternity. Our sins are forgotten. Yet how the redeemer purchased us to God is never forgotten! The Lamb of God who laid down his life will never escape the memory of God's people.

Like a lamb, Christ faced an undeserved death with no objection. Isaiah 53:7 says, "...he opened not his mouth: he is brought as a lamb to the slaughter, and as a sheep before her shearers is dumb, so he openeth not his mouth." He could have called over twelve legions of angels to his rescue (Matthew 26:53). But he remained silent. As the lamb, he faced his unjust death without complaint — the innocent laid down his life for the guilty. He raised no legal objections. He allowed his own rights to be violated so the lost estate of humanity could be redeemed. We call him Savior and Lord and rightly so, and throughout eternity, one additional great title belongs to our Lord: **the Lamb.**

Again, if the sacrifice of Jesus Christ is to be kept in mind throughout eternity, we should keep it in mind today. Let's share the efficacy of Christ's redemptive power with others. Since his accomplishments continue to tower in the future ages, we should keep them in the forefront of our thinking now. When there is lack in our lives, when there is sickness or sin, may we regard and esteem his sacrificial work of far greater importance than our failings and frailties. When the so-called wisdom and logic of this present age of man is gone from memory, our Lord will still be called the Lamb — his great sacrifice will be recognized universally and eternally.

---

[6] Revelation 21:9, 14, 22, 23, 27; 22:1, 3.

Complete Deliverance in the Lamb of God

God sets forth the big picture which extends into eternity. Jesus Christ is the Lamb, our substitute. Whether in the opening book or the closing book of Scripture, God illustrates the Christ as the slain lamb. The Scripture, from beginning to end, trumpets out with one voice—this man, our redeemer has taken our place! The more we grow in our understanding of the Old Testament sacrifices, the louder they speak. With one voice they declare: **He paid it all.**

Appendix One

The Probable Location of the Crucifixion

In chapter 8 on the sin offering, we considered the remarkable parallel between Christ and the red heifer offering: both were sacrificed **without the gate**. Please recall that the sin offerings were killed at the altar before the tabernacle and then were **burned** outside the camp. However, only the red heifer was to be **sacrificed** outside the camp.[1] Now we will look at the exact location of the sacrifice of the red heifer and the probable location of the crucifixion.

In *Archaeology of the Bible: Book by Book*, it states that the "...Mishnah and Talmud say that the "red heifer was taken out of the Temple courts and slain on the Mount of Olives."[2]

The Mishnah also states, referring to the Temple of Herod in the first century:

> All the [temple] walls were high, except the wall in the east, so that the priest who burned the [red] heifer, standing on the top of the Mount of Olives should be able to look directly into the entrance of the

---

[1] Numbers 19:3 says of the red heifer: "that he may bring her forth **without the camp**, and one shall slay her before his face."
[2] *Archaeology of the Bible: Book by Book*, Gaalyah Cornfeld, Harper and Row: New York, 1976) 55.

Probable Location of the Crucifixion

sanctuary at the time when he sprinkled the blood [of the red heifer].[3]

These ancient rabbinic sources said that the priest exited through an eastern gate of the temple to the Mount of Olives to burn the red heifer offering.[4] From this evidence, the location of the sacrifice and burning of the red heifer, in the first century, was on the Mount of Olives that was east of the city and temple.

Location of the red heifer offering:
The Mount of Olives
East of the city and the temple

Hebrews 13:10-12:
We have an altar, whereof they have no right to eat which serve the tabernacle.
For the bodies of those beasts, whose blood is brought into the sanctuary by the high priest for sin [offerings], are burned **without the camp**.
Wherefore Jesus also, that he might sanctify the people with his own blood, suffered **without the gate**.

Verse 11 speaks of the bodies of the sin offerings that were brought to a location outside of the camp and burned.[5] At

---

[3] Massecheth Middoth Perek II:4. The translation of sections of the Mishnah are in Appendix I, Alfred Edersheim, *Sketches of Jewish Social Life* (Peabody, Mass.: Hendrickson, 1994) 269.
[4] Massecheth Middoth Perek I:3 says: "the eastern gate…by it the high priest who burned the red heifer and all who assisted, went out upon the Mount of Olives.
[5] Leviticus 4:12: Even the whole bullock shall he carry forth without the camp unto a clean place, where the ashes are poured out, and burn him on the wood with fire: where the ashes are poured out shall he be burnt.

JESUS CHRIST OUR COMPLETE OFFERING

this same location the red heifer was also sacrificed and burned.[6] As mentioned, the rabbinic sources say that in the first century, this location was on the Mount of Olives

What is noteworthy is that verse 12 connects the crucifixion of Christ to this location: "Wherefore Jesus also, that he might sanctify the people with his own blood, suffered without the gate."

In tying together Hebrews 13:11 and 12, there is an implication that Jesus was crucified, not just without the gate, but in the same location the red heifer was offered and burned along with the other sin offerings. While Hebrews 13 is not explicit about the location of the crucifixion, a verse in the Gospels is.

Golgotha: A Place of Polling

Let's look at what the Gospel records tell us about the place where Jesus was crucified.

> Luke 23:33:
> And when they were come to the place, which is called Calvary, there they crucified him...

This word "Calvary" is from the Latin Vulgate where *calvaria* is the Latin word for head or skull. While "Calvary" is a common word to describe the location of Christ's death, looking at the Hebrew word is more helpful in defining the location.

---

[6] Ernest Martin, *Secrets of Golgotha*, 24. Rabbinic sources say location of red heifer sacrifice and where sin offerings were burned was identical.

Probable Location of the Crucifixion

John 19:17:
And he bearing his cross went forth into a place called the place of a skull, which is called in the Hebrew Golgotha:

The Hebrew equivalent of "Golgotha" is the word *gulgoleth* used 12 times in the Old Testament.

> Exodus 16:16 ...according to the number of your persons [*gulgoleth*]; take ye every man for them which are in his tents. (margin: Hebrew by the poll, or, head)
>
> Exodus 38:26 A bekah for every man [*gulgoleth*], that is, half a shekel, after the shekel of the sanctuary... (margin: Heb. a poll)
>
> Numbers 1:2: Take ye the sum of all the congregation of the children of Israel, after their families...every male by their polls [*gulgoleth*];
>
> Numbers 1:18 ...from twenty years old and upward, by their polls [*gulgoleth*].
>
> Numbers 1:20: ...according to the number of the names, by their polls [*gulgoleth*], every male from twenty years old and upward...
>
> Numbers 1:22: ...according to the number of the names, by their polls [*gulgoleth*], every male from twenty years old and upward.
>
> Numbers 3:47: Thou shalt even take five shekels apiece by the poll [*gulgoleth*].

JESUS CHRIST OUR COMPLETE OFFERING

> Judges 9:53: And a certain woman cast a piece of a millstone upon Abimelech's head, and all to brake his skull [*gulgoleth*].
>
> II Kings 9:35: And they went to bury her: but they found no more of her than the skull [*gulgoleth*], and the feet, and the palms of her hands.
>
> I Chronicles 10:10: And they put his armour in the house of their gods, and fastened his head [*gulgoleth*] in the temple of Dagon.
>
> I Chronicles 23:3: Now the Levites were numbered from the age of thirty years and upward: and their number by their polls [*gulgoleth*].
>
> I Chronicles 23:24: …they were counted by number of names by their polls [*gulgoleth*].

Of the 12 times this word *gulgoleth* is used, three times it refers to an actual skull or head, nine times it refers to a poll or numbering in a census. So Golgotha, "a place of a skull," may be translated as "the place of polling or numbering or registry" referring to a location where the census was taken. So, we see that the crucifixion likely took place at a place of registry or polling.

> **Golgotha:**
> **the place of polling or numbering**

Knowing that Golgotha was most likely a place of polling, is there any place in the Scripture that mentions **the location** of polling or numbering?

Probable Location of the Crucifixion

> Ezekiel 43:18 and 21:
> These are the ordinances of the altar in the day when they shall make it...
> Thou shalt take the bullock also of the sin offering, and he shall burn it in the appointed place [*miphkad*] of the house [temple], **without** the sanctuary.

The "appointed place" is translated from the Hebrew word *miphkad,* meaning the place of registry or polling.[7] The *miphkad,* or place of polling, was also the same location of where the sin offerings were burned. Here in Ezekiel, we have an explicit statement that says the place of polling and the location of the incinerating of the sin offerings are identical. Jesus was sacrificed at Golgotha: the polling or numbering place. Also, remember that ancient rabbinical sources locate the place the sin offerings were burned on the Mount of Olives. With this in mind, we see that Ezekiel 43:21 is a key verse that ties together the site of polling with the location of the incineration of the sacrifices.[8] If the prophecy of Ezekiel can be applied to the first century temple, then Christ was crucified at the location where the sin offerings were burned on the Mount of Olives.

The word *miphkad* also is used in Nehemiah:

> Nehemiah 3:31:
> After him repaired Malchiah the goldsmith's son unto the place of the Nethinims, and of the merchants, over against the gate Miphkad, and to the going up of the corner.

---

[7] These references have a closely related word: II Samuel 24:9: "And Joab gave up the sum of the number [*miphqad*] of the people unto the king..." I Chronicles 21:5: "And Joab gave the sum of the number [*miphqad*] of the people unto David..."

[8] Martin calls this the *miphkad* altar, the "third altar," where the sin offerings were incinerated and, in the first century, where people were counted for the temple tax prior to the feasts.

JESUS CHRIST OUR COMPLETE OFFERING

This "gate Miphkad," or numbering gate, was on the east side of Jerusalem and faced the Mount of Olives and would have led to the area where the people went to be registered or polled. While this gate may not be mentioned in the 1st and 2nd century sources, it indicates the site of the polling was east toward the Mount of Olives.

"The Place of the City"

John tells us more about the location where Jesus was crucified.

> John 19:20:
> This title then read many of the Jews: for **the place** where Jesus was crucified was nigh to the city: and it was written in Hebrew, and Greek, and Latin.

John 19:20 may also be translated, "This title then read many of the Jews, for the place of the city was near where Jesus was crucified." The place of the city was evidently a location where many could read the title placed on the cross by Pilate. What was "the place of the city" mentioned in this record?

> Acts 21:28:
> Crying out, Men of Israel, help: This is the man, that teacheth all men every where against the people, and the law, and **this place**: and further brought Greeks also into the temple, and hath polluted **this holy place**.

In Acts 21:28, the Temple at Jerusalem was referred to as the place or the holy place.

Probable Location of the Crucifixion

John 11:47 and 48:
Then gathered the chief priests and the Pharisees a council, and said, What do we? for this man doeth many miracles.
If we let him thus alone, all men will believe on him: and the Romans shall come and take away both **our place** and nation.

The council at Jerusalem expressed concern that the Romans might take away their place and nation. We have seen the Temple referred to as "the place," and it may well have been that they were concerned that the Romans might take away that Temple.

John 19:20 says Jesus was crucified near "the place of the city," that is, the temple. Yet bear in mind that he also had to be without the gates of the city.

> **Crucified near the temple**
> **Yet without the gates of the city**

Also, the place where he was crucified was called Golgotha, which was "the place of numbering" and which was on the Mount of Olives near where the sacrifices were burned.

The ancient Jewish sources say that through the eastern temple gate "the high priest who burned the red heifer and all who assisted, went out upon the Mount of Olives."[9] The east temple gate led directly to the Mount of Olives where the red heifer was slain and burned. The Mount of Olives would have qualified as near the temple.

---

[9] Massecheth Middoth, Perek I:3.

JESUS CHRIST OUR COMPLETE OFFERING

At any rate, this location rules out the Garden tomb, also called "Gordon's Calvary," as a location of the crucifixion. This beautiful site is situated north of Jerusalem, rather than east.[10]

The older traditional site, commonly shown in many Bible atlases as "Golgotha," west of Jerusalem, was picked by Helena the mother of Emperor Constantine in the fourth century after she had a vision. This location is **far west** of the temple area, located beyond the "second wall," on the west side of Jerusalem. Since the temple was on the **southeast** side of the city, this site also could **not** be "near to The Place of the city."

Let's return to the verse in Ezekiel 43:21:

> Thou shalt take the bullock also of the sin offering, and he shall burn it in the appointed place [*miphkad*] **of the house** [temple], **without** the sanctuary.

Note that the *miphkad* altar was "of the house" or temple, yet outside the temple area: "without the sanctuary."

> Ezekiel 44:1:
> Then he brought me back the way of the gate of the **outward sanctuary** which looketh toward the east; and it was shut.

This verse refers to an east gate that was shut and "the outward sanctuary." This *miphkad* altar, while outside the city, was "of the house" that is, "of the temple." Thus, a

---

[10] The only reason General Gordon in the 1800's located the crucifixion at this lovely site north of the city was because the cliffs at this site looked like a skull. Martin says these cliffs are recent—in the last 250 years or so. Even today these cliffs hardly look like a skull, due to erosion.

Probable Location of the Crucifixion

crucifixion on the Mount of Olives would have been "nigh unto" this "outward" temple area.

Arrest and Punishment at the Scene of the Crime

According to Roman law, a criminal was to be executed at the site of the crime and/or at the site of capture.[11] Jesus' "crime" was put on the cross: "this is the king of the Jews" (Luke 23:38). Where was he publicly proclaimed as king?

> Luke 19:37 and 38:
> And when he was come nigh, even now at the **descent of the mount of Olives**, the whole multitude of the disciples began to rejoice and praise God with a loud voice for all the mighty works that they had seen;
> Saying, Blessed be the King that cometh in the name of the Lord: peace in heaven, and glory in the highest.

He was proclaimed as king "at the descent of the mount of Olives." Here, his triumphal entry into Jerusalem began.

Where was Jesus arrested?

> Luke 22:39 and 40; 46-48:
> And he came out, and went, as he was wont, **to the mount of Olives**; and his disciples also followed him. And when he was at the place, he said unto them, Pray that ye enter not into temptation...
> And said unto them, Why sleep ye? rise and pray, lest ye enter into temptation.

---

[11] Ernest Martin, *Secrets of Golgotha*, 72-78.

JESUS CHRIST OUR COMPLETE OFFERING

> And while he yet spake, behold a multitude, and he that was called Judas, one of the twelve, went before them, and drew near unto Jesus to kiss him.
> But Jesus said unto him, Judas, betrayest thou the Son of man with a kiss?

Jesus was arrested on the Mount of Olives; the site of his "crime" was "at the descent of the mount of Olives." So in accordance with Roman law, that is where he would have been crucified.

As we have considered, the ancient rabbinical records concur that the red heifer offering was sacrificed outside the city on the Mount of Olives. While all the sin offerings were to be burned outside the camp or outside the city (in the first century) only the red heifer was sacrificed at this location. Therefore, Hebrews 13 suggests a direct parallel to Christ's sacrifice.

Also we saw that in all likelihood, the correct translation of the "the place of the skull" should be "the place of numbering, registration, or polling." Ezekiel 43:21 makes mention of a site called *miphkad* meaning numbering or polling. On this site an altar was to be built where the sin offerings were to be burned. Additionally, the crucifixion was near the temple: "The Place of the city," according to John 19:20.

If the crucifixion was carried out according to Roman law and practice, then the Mount of Olives would have been where it occurred. Putting together this information from biblical and historical records, the most probable location of the crucifixion of our Lord Jesus Christ would have been on the Mount of Olives just east of the temple near the location where the red heifer was offered.

Probable Location of the Crucifixion

Significance of the Mount of Olives

We first saw the significance of the Mount of Olives in Genesis 22 where Abraham took Isaac to be sacrificed. As we noted in chapter 14, in the area of Jerusalem the highest mountain is the Mount of Olives. Normally the highest peak in an area would be selected as an altar. Also since Abraham saw the mountain "afar off" (Genesis 22:4) it would have been the highest peak. Therefore, Abraham's sacrifice most likely took place on the Mount of Olives.

How else is the Mount of Olives significant? The following verse states that the crucifixion and resurrection would have been in the same general area.

> John 19:41:
> Now in the place where he was crucified there was a garden; and in the garden a new sepulcher, wherein was never man yet laid.

Besides the probable site of the crucifixion and the subsequent burial and resurrection of Christ, the Mount of Olives has immense importance in the end times.

> Zechariah 14:1-4:
> Behold, the day of the LORD cometh, and thy spoil shall be divided in the midst of thee.
> For I will gather all nations against Jerusalem to battle; and the city shall be taken, and the houses rifled, and the women ravished; and half of the city shall go forth into captivity, and the residue of the people shall not be cut off from the city.
> Then shall the LORD go forth, and fight against those nations, as when he fought in the day of battle.

JESUS CHRIST OUR COMPLETE OFFERING

> And his feet shall stand in that day **upon the mount of Olives**, which is before Jerusalem on the east, and **the mount of Olives** shall cleave in the midst thereof toward the east and toward the west, and there shall be a very great valley; and half of the mountain shall remove toward the north, and half of it toward the south.

In the period known as the "Day of the Lord," a great battle will ensue over the city of Jerusalem. At that time, the Lord will return to earth and his feet will stand on the Mount of Olives" before Jerusalem on the east." Then the Mount of Olives shall "cleave in the midst," forming a great valley.

So the area of the Mount of Olives is the scene of quite a lot of activity in the Bible. Allowing the crucifixion occurred here, then, his burial in a nearby tomb and resurrection would have also happened in this area. And finally, this cataclysmic event occurs on the Mount of Olives in the Day of the Lord.

Sources for this Appendix:

Ernest L. Martin, *Secrets of Golgotha, The Lost History of Jesus' Crucifixion Second Edition* (Associates of Scriptural Knowledge: Portland, Oregon, 1996).

Walter J. Cummins, *The Place – Golgotha*. The Way International Sunday Service audiocassette #1323.

Gaalyah Cornfeld, *Archaeology of the Bible: Book by Book*. Harper and Row: New York, 1976) 55.

Appendix Two

Defining *telos* and related Greek words used in *Jesus Christ Our Complete Offering*

This appendix defines *telos* and its related or cognate Greek words. These words are footnoted in this book because they connect and encompass the completeness of Christ's sacrifice and the completeness we have in him.

telos:
- **a full and complete end**, not merely a cessation but a total fulfillment and completion.
- End or goal toward which a movement is being directed, outcome (AG 811).
- The fulfillment or completion of any thing (EWB 248).
- What "end" is intended the reader must determine by context (T 620).

> Luke 22:37: an end [*telos*] in the sense of fulfillment (T 620).
> Hebrews 9:26: consummation or fulfillment [*telos*] of the ages.
> II Corinthians 3:13; Romans 10:4.

teleioō:
- **to complete, to finish**, , to make perfect as to be full; to be brought to a full end, consummated, accomplished in full, fully mature (WT 443).
- Complete, bring to an end, finish, accomplish (AG 809)

JESUS CHRIST OUR COMPLETE OFFERING

- To carry through completely, to accomplish, finish, bring to an end; to perfect or consummate; (T 618)
- Perfect or accomplish (PV 63).

John 19:28: to accomplish, bring to a close or fulfillment by an event (T 619); final fulfillment (AG 809).
John 4:34, 5:36; 17:4; 19:28; Hebrews 2:10, 5:9; 7:19, 28; 9:9; 10:1,14.

teleō:
- **to accomplish**
- Generally involving a notion of time, to perform the last act which completes a process, to accomplish, fulfill (T 619)
- Carry out, accomplish (AG 811).

John 19:28 and 30; Luke 12:50; 18:31; 22:37
Teleō in John 19:30 "contains both the chronological sense of "ended" and also the theological sense of "achieved… everything that God commissioned Jesus to do has been completed." (K 8. 59).

Panteles : (from *pan* [all] and *telos*)
- **completely**, fully, wholly (AG 608)
    Hebrews 7:25: "save them to the uttermost [*panteles*]." NIV: "save them completely;" totality of the saving work of Jesus Christ (K 8. 67).

Teleios:
- **perfect,** brought to its end, finished, (T 618)
    Hebrews 9:11: "more perfect tabernacle"
    "more excellent tabernacle" (T 618 and WT 42).

Key to sources

T: Joseph Henry Thayer, *Greek-English Lexicon of the New Testament* (Milford, MI: Baker House, 1977).

WT: Walter J. Cummins, *A Journey through the Acts and Epistles* (Franklin, Ohio: Scripture Consulting, 2006).

K: Gerhard Kittel, *Theological Dictionary of the New Testament* (Grand Rapids: MI: Eerdmans, 1967).

EWB: E. W. Bullinger, *Critical Lexicon* (London: Bagster, 1974).

AG: William Arndt and Wilbur Gingrich, *A Greek-English Lexicon of the New Testament and Other Early Christian Literature,* Second Edition: translated and adapted from Walter Bauer's fourth edition (Chicago: University of Chicago Press, 1979).

PV: The Concordance of the Peshitta Version of the Aramaic New Testament, (New Knoxville OH: American Christian Press 1985.)

Appendix Three

The Hebrew word *Choli*

The 22 occurrences of the Hebrew word, *choli*, in the Hebrew Old Testament are all used in the context of sickness and disease.

Deuteronomy 7:15:
And the LORD will take away from thee all sickness [*choli*], and will put none of the evil diseases of Egypt, which thou knowest, upon thee; but will lay them upon all them that hate thee.

Deuteronomy 28:59:
Then the LORD will make thy plagues wonderful, and the plagues of thy seed, even great plagues, and of long continuance, and sore sicknesses [*choli*], and of long continuance.

Deuteronomy 28:61:
Also every sickness [*choli*], and every plague, which is not written in the book of this law, them will the LORD bring upon thee, until thou be destroyed.

I Kings 17:17:
And it came to pass after these things, that the son of the woman, the mistress of the house, fell sick; and his sickness [*choli*] was so sore, that there was no breath left in him.

The Hebrew word, *Choli*

II Kings 1:2:
And Ahaziah fell down through a lattice in his upper chamber that was in Samaria, and was sick: and he sent messengers, and said unto them, Go, enquire of Baalzebub the god of Ekron whether I shall recover of this disease [*choli*].

II Kings 8:8:
And the king said unto Hazael, Take a present in thine hand, and go, meet the man of God, and enquire of the LORD by him, saying, Shall I recover of this disease [*choli*]?

II Kings 8:9:
So Hazael went to meet him, and took a present with him, even of every good thing of Damascus, forty camels' burden, and came and stood before him, and said, Thy son Benhadad king of Syria hath sent me to thee, saying, Shall I recover of this disease [*choli*]?

II Kings 13:14:
Now Elisha was fallen sick of his sickness [*choli*] whereof he died. And Joash the king of Israel came down unto him, and wept over his face, and said, O my father, my father, the chariot of Israel, and the horsemen thereof.

II Chronicles 16:12:
And Asa in the thirty and ninth year of his reign was diseased in his feet, until his disease [*choli*] was exceeding great: yet in his disease [*choli*] he sought not to the LORD, but to the physicians.

II Chronicles 21:15:
And thou shalt have great sickness [*choli*] by disease of thy bowels, until thy bowels fall out by reason of the sickness day by day.

JESUS CHRIST OUR COMPLETE OFFERING

II Chronicles 21:18:
And after all this the LORD smote him in his bowels with an incurable disease [*choli*].

II Chronicles 21:19:
And it came to pass, that in process of time, after the end of two years, his bowels fell out by reason of his sickness [*choli*]: so he died of sore diseases. And his people made no burning for him, like the burning of his fathers.

Psalms 41:3:
The LORD will strengthen him upon the bed of languishing: thou wilt make all his bed in his sickness [*choli*].

Ecclesiastes 5:17: All his days also he eateth in darkness, and he hath much sorrow and wrath with his sickness [*choli*].

Ecclesiastes 6:2:
A man to whom God hath given riches, wealth, and honour, so that he wanteth nothing for his soul of all that he desireth, yet God giveth him not power to eat thereof, but a stranger eateth it: this is vanity, and it is an evil disease [*choli*].

Isaiah 1:5:
Why should ye be stricken any more? ye will revolt more and more: the whole head is sick [*choli*], and the whole heart faint.

Isaiah 38:9:
The writing of Hezekiah king of Judah, when he had been sick, and was recovered of his sickness [*choli*]:

Isaiah 53:3:
He is despised and rejected of men; a man of sorrows, and acquainted with grief [*choli*=sickness]: and we hid as it were

The Hebrew word, *Choli*

our faces from him; he was despised, and we esteemed him not.

Isaiah 53:4:
Surely he hath borne our griefs [*choli*=sickness], and carried our sorrows: yet we did esteem him stricken, smitten of God, and afflicted.

Jeremiah 6:7:
As a fountain casteth out her waters, so she casteth out her wickedness: violence and spoil is heard in her; before me continually is grief [*choli*=sickness] and wounds.

Jeremiah 10:19:
Woe is me for my hurt! my wound is grievous: but I said, Truly this is a grief [*choli*=sickness], and I must bear it.

Hosea 5:13:
When Ephraim saw his sickness [*choli*], and Judah saw his wound, then went Ephraim to the Assyrian, and sent to king Jareb: yet could he not heal you, nor cure you of your wound.

Appendix Four

The First Sin Offering in the Bible

Genesis 4 relates events surrounding the first offering specifically mentioned in the Bible.

> Genesis 4:1-5:
> And Adam knew Eve his wife; and she conceived, and bare Cain, and said, I have gotten a man from the LORD.
> And she again bare his brother Abel. And Abel was a keeper of sheep, but Cain was a tiller of the ground.
> And in process of time it came to pass, that Cain brought of the fruit of the ground an offering unto the LORD.
> And Abel, he also brought of the firstlings of his flock and of the fat thereof. And the LORD had respect unto Abel and to his offering:
> But unto Cain and to his offering he had not respect. And Cain was very wroth, and his countenance fell.

These two brothers both brought an offering to the Lord. Abel's offering was regarded favorably, while God had no regard for Cain's. God's non-acceptance of Cain's offering caused him to be very upset.

> Verses 6-8:
> And the LORD said unto Cain, Why art thou wroth? and why is thy countenance fallen?
> If thou doest well, shalt thou not be accepted? and if thou doest not well, sin [*chattath*] lieth at the door.

The First Sin Offering

And unto thee shall be his desire, and thou shalt rule over him
And Cain talked with Abel his brother: and it came to pass, when they were in the field, that Cain rose up against Abel his brother, and slew him.

God reached out to Cain and addressed this acute problem saying, "If thou doest well, shalt thou not be accepted?" We can see from the passage that Cain was not doing well. So God presented Cain with another way to get help: "if thou doest not well, sin [*chattath*] lieth at the door."

As noted in chapter 6, "sin" and "sin offering" are translated from one Hebrew word, *chattath*. The usage in the context determines how the word should be translated.

> *Chattath* **may be translated as:**
> -sin
> -sin offering

Translators often render the word "lieth" in verse 7 as "crouches" which may suggest that sin is personified as an animal "crouching at the door."[1] While sin is rarely, if ever, personified as a crouching animal in the Scriptures, the word, *chattath*, is translated as "sin offering" 116 times.[2] While there is sin in this context, the subject of offerings is also at the forefront.

---

[1] *Amplified*, *New American Standard*, and *New International Version*. But "lieth" in Genesis 4:7 is elsewhere rendered: Genesis 29:2: "...flocks of sheep lying by it..." and Psalm 23:2: "He maketh me to lie down in green pastures..."
[2] The Hebrew word, *chattath*, is translated as "sin offering" 116 times and as "sin" 169 times in the *Authorized King James Version*.

JESUS CHRIST OUR COMPLETE OFFERING

The New Brown Driver Briggs lexicon classifies the Genesis 4:7 occurrence of *chattath* as a sin offering, saying that the crouching beast is a sin offering.[3] Both E. W. Bullinger in *Figures of Speech Used in the Bible* and Julia Hans in *Go Figure! An Introduction to Figures of Speech in the Bible* cites this as an example of the figure metonymy where "sin is put for the offering for sin." Dr. Hans states: "It was a sin offering lying at the door, not sin."[4]

> Genesis 4:7: *Young's Literal Translation*
> Is there not, if thou dost well, acceptance? and if thou dost not well, at the opening a sin-offering is crouching, and unto thee its desire, and thou rulest over it.

With extraordinary love, God reaches out His hand to Cain to help bring him back. God initiates a solution and instructs him to offer a sin offering. His brother Abel had offered "the firstlings of his flock and of the fat thereof," which God approved of. Cain had only offered "the fruit of the ground" which was not sufficient for an offering. God wanted a sacrifice of shed blood, which foretold of the ultimate sacrifice of the Christ. Cain evidently rejected God's provision for sin and later murdered his brother.

As we can see from this record, sacrifices were established very early in the book of Genesis. Since Jesus Christ referred to Abel as a prophet, this record of Genesis suggests that Abel established these sacrifices by revelation from God.[5] Also, God instructed Cain concerning a sin offering. This

---

[3] Francis Brown, *The New Brown Driver Briggs Hebrew and English Lexicon*, 308.
[4] Julia B. Hans, *Go Figure! An Introduction to Figures of Speech in the Bible*, 152. E.W. Bullinger, *Figures of Speech Used in the Bible*, 584.
[5] Luke 11:50 and 51: "That the blood of all the prophets, which was shed from the foundation of the world, may be required of this generation; From the blood of Abel unto the blood of Zacharias…"

The First Sin Offering

passage in Genesis shows that near the beginning of man's history, God desired offerings. Many centuries later, God instituted sacrifices in detail, by revelation to Moses in the Law. All these sacrifices looked forward to the Christ who was to come.

Scripture Index

Genesis

Genesis 1:28	111
Genesis 1:29	111
Genesis 1:31	20
Genesis 2:17	21, 110
Genesis 3	20, 49, 110, 127, 378, 401
Genesis 4:1-5	433
Genesis 4:3 and 4	285, 325
Genesis 4:3-5	231
Genesis 4:6-8	434
Genesis 4:7	435, 441
Genesis 8:1	275
Genesis 8:20 and 21	181, 286
Genesis 8:4	182
Genesis 14:18 and 19	248
Genesis 22:1-4	296
Genesis 22:5-14	298
Genesis 22:7	407
Genesis 22:13	66
Genesis 22:15-18	300
Genesis 27:41	233
Genesis 32:3-7	233
Genesis 32:9-12	234
Genesis 32:13-15, 16-18	235
Genesis 32:16-21	241
Genesis 32:19-21	236
Genesis 32:20	239
Genesis 33:1 and 2	236
Genesis 33:5-11	237

Exodus

Exodus 3:7 and 8	53
Exodus 6:5	275
Exodus 12:2, 3 and 6	82
Exodus 12:8	216, 389
Exodus 12:15	335
Exodus 20:25	321
Exodus 28:2, 5	347
Exodus 29:38-42	246
Exodus 32:1-6	255
Exodus 35:21 and 22	322

Leviticus

Leviticus 1-7	83, 85, 92, 99, 102, 103, 210, 227
Leviticus 1:1	90, 91
Leviticus 1:1 and 2	90
Leviticus 1:2 and 3	97
Leviticus 1:3	280, 375
Leviticus 1:3-5	280
Leviticus 1:4	69, 238
Leviticus 1:6-9	281
Leviticus 1:9	99, 172, 176, 180, 291
Leviticus 1:10-13	283
Leviticus 1:13	177, 180
Leviticus 1:14-17	283
Leviticus 1:15	177
Leviticus 1:17	177, 180
Leviticus 2:1	97, 226, 274
Leviticus 2:2	177, 180
Leviticus 2:4	228, 271

Scripture Index

Leviticus 2:4-7 228
Leviticus 2:8-10 229
Leviticus 2:9 .... 177, 180, 274
Leviticus 2:11 .... 177, 229, 336
Leviticus 2:12 .... 230, 326
Leviticus 2:12 and 13 230
Leviticus 2:13 .... 198, 212
Leviticus 2:14-16 230
Leviticus 2:16 .... 177, 274
Leviticus 3:1-5 190
Leviticus 3:1 .... 190, 218, 376
Leviticus 3:5 .... 177, 180
Leviticus 3:7-11 191
Leviticus 3:11 178
Leviticus 3:12-15 192
Leviticus 3:16 .... 178, 193, 195
Leviticus 4:1-7 138
Leviticus 4:3 .... 95, 376
Leviticus 4:8-10 139
Leviticus 4:11, 12, 13-20 140
Leviticus 4:12 .... 159, 178, 179
Leviticus 4:22-26 142
Leviticus 4:27-31 143
Leviticus 5:6 .... 92, 93, 94
Leviticus 5:14-16 .... 104, 108
Leviticus 5:15 112
Leviticus 5:16 .... 123, 124
Leviticus 5:17-19 106
Leviticus 5:18 376
Leviticus 6:1-7 .... 107, 108
Leviticus 6:2 113
Leviticus 7:11-19 199
Leviticus 7:28-34 319
Leviticus 7:29-34 195
Leviticus 7:30 322
Leviticus 7:37-38 91
Leviticus 8:13-15 148
Leviticus 8:15 ... 147, 152, 153, 261
Leviticus 9:22-24 345
Leviticus 10:1-3 346
Leviticus 10:17 216, 217, 221, 388, 390
Leviticus 10:17 and 18 216
Leviticus 12:6-8 150
Leviticus 16:1 and 2 344
Leviticus 16:3 and 4 347
Leviticus 16:5 and 6 348
Leviticus 16:7-10 .... 67, 348
Leviticus 16:11-14 349
Leviticus 16:12-14 175
Leviticus 16:15 .... 77, 351
Leviticus 16:17 352
Leviticus 16:18 and 19 ..... 147, 353
Leviticus 16:20-22 356
Leviticus 16:21 .... 12, 68, 387, 388, 390
Leviticus 16:21 and 22 .... 12, 68
Leviticus 16:22 ... 70, 166, 217, 221
Leviticus 16:23-25 359
Leviticus 16:29-34 362
Leviticus 16:30 152
Leviticus 19:5 and 6 196
Leviticus 22:18-23 377
Leviticus 23:15-17 334
Leviticus 23:37 247
Leviticus 23:4-8 328

JESUS CHRIST OUR COMPLETE OFFERING

Leviticus 23:9-14 329

Numbers
Numbers 5:6-8 .... 122, 124
Numbers 8:15 and 16 324
Numbers 8 :7 and 8 149
Numbers 8:9-14 323
Numbers 16: 44-48 174
Numbers 18:12 194
Numbers 18:15-17 106
Numbers 18:8,11-14 326
Numbers 19:11-13 157
Numbers 19:1-3 154
Numbers 19:3 .... 159, 414
Numbers 19:4-6 155
Numbers 19:5 179
Numbers 19:7-9 156
Numbers 25:1-3 213
Numbers 28:17, 23 and 24 331
Numbers 28:3-6 289
Numbers 28:3-7 361
Numbers 28:4-8 249
Numbers 28:9 and 10 290
Numbers 28 and 29 .... 99, 249, 250, 290
Numbers 29:7-11 360
Numbers 31:29 326

Deuteronomy
Deuteronomy 23:25 321
Deuteronomy 27:7 .... 197, 201
Deuteronomy 33:10 282

Joshua
Joshua 7:1 113
Joshua 22:20 114

Judges
Judges 11:30 and 31,32-36 305
Judges 11:37-40 306

Samuel
I Samuel 1:11,19 276
I Samuel 5:1-4 117
I Samuel 5:5 and 6 118
I Samuel 5:9 119
I Samuel 6:2, 3-6 120
I Samuel 6:3, 4, and 8 122
I Samuel 6:7 and 8 121
I Samuel 7:9 .... 282, 292
I Samuel 11:15 201
II Samuel 24:25 292

Chronicles
I Chronicles 23:31 65
II Chronicles 2:4 65
II Chronicles 3:1 296
II Chronicles 29:1-8 202
II Chronicles 29:30 and 31 204
II Chronicles 29:35 and 36 204
II Chronicles 30:1-3 205
II Chronicles 30:18-20,21-23 206
II Chronicles 30:24-27 208

Nehemiah
Nehemiah 3:31 419

Ezra
Ezra 8:28 200

Psalms
Psalm 106:28 .... 212, 213
Psalm 23:3 122
Psalm 51:19 282
Psalm 68:18 287

Scripture Index

Psalm 81:16 194
Psalm 107:22 201
Psalm 141:2 .... 173, 291

Isaiah
Isaiah 1:11-14 65
Isaiah 28:11 and 12 182
Isaiah 46:1-5 266
Isaiah 52:10 48
Isaiah 52:13 and 14 49
Isaiah 52:14 .... 167, 310
Isaiah 52:15-53 1 50
Isaiah 53 . ... 28, 47, 48, 50, 51, 52, 53, 54, 55, 58, 59, 60, 61, 66, 70, 95, 103, 104, 124, 130, 136, 166, 167, 168, 183, 217, 266, 267, 270, 272, 310, 359, 369, 374, 399, 412
Isaiah 53:2 and 3 380
Isaiah 53:3 432
Isaiah 53:4 .. 70, 166, 189, 271, 433
Isaiah 53:4 and 5 .... 189, 271
Isaiah 53:5 .... 55, 271
Isaiah 53:5 and 6 55
Isaiah 53:6 310
Isaiah 53:7-9 56
Isaiah 53:10 ....57, 94, 102, 103, 112, 124
Isaiah 53:11 and 12 58
Isaiah 53:12 ..48, 70, 167, 310, 371
Isaiah 61:1, 2 401
Isaiah 65:17 410

Jeremiah
Jeremiah 33:11 202

Ezekiel
Ezekiel 28:12 379
Ezekiel 28:13-15 379
Ezekiel 28:16 and 17 380
Ezekiel 43:18 and 21 419
Ezekiel 43:19-22 146
Ezekiel 43:21 422
Ezekiel 44:1 422

Hosea
Hosea 6:7 .... 112, 115

Amos
Amos 4:5 336

Zechariah
Zechariah 14:1-4 425

Matthew
Matthew 8 :16 and 17 54
Matthew 13:15 and 16 402
Matthew 15:6 405
Matthew 26:36-39 308
Matthew 26:40-45 309
Matthew 26:53 412
Matthew 27:57-60 57

Mark
Mark 15:22-28 48
Mark 16:1 and 2 332

Luke
Luke 2:21-24 151
Luke 4:5 and 6 110
Luke 4:16-21 399
Luke 18:31-34 26
Luke 19:37 and 38 423
Luke 22:17-20 250
Luke 22:37 ...... 28, 47, 60, 310, 427
Luke 22:39 and 40 423
Luke 23:33 416

JESUS CHRIST OUR COMPLETE OFFERING

Luke 24:25-27 27
Luke 24:44 and 45 62
Luke 24 51 287

John
John 1:29 406
John 4:31-34 24
John 5:36 24
John 5:37-39 25
John 6:47-52 253
John 6:53-57 220
John 8:31, 32 and 36 401
John 11:47 and 48 421
John 17:1-4 29
John 19:16-30 29
John 19:17 417
John 19:20 ....420, 421
John 19:41 425
John 20:16 and 17 333

Acts
Acts 5:15 65
Acts 10:1-4 276
Acts 10:30 and 31 277
Acts 21:28 420

Romans
Romans 5:6-9 242
Romans 5:10 and 11 242
Romans 5:12 ....21, 110
Romans 5:19 313
Romans 5:21 313
Romans 5:6-21 125
Romans 6:1-5 268
Romans 6:4 ....270, 383, 392
Romans 6:4-8 383

Romans 6:5 ....219, 269
Romans 6:6 ....129, 269
Romans 6:8,11-13 314
Romans 6:9 334
Romans 6:10 ....39, 314
Romans 6:11 .....315, 316, 385, 392, 396
Romans 6:16 and 17 316
Romans 7:14 111
Romans 8:1 ....127, 129
Romans 8:26-28 187
Romans 8:31 and 32 ....23, 131
Romans 8:33 and 34 128
Romans 8:33-39 131
Romans 8:34 186
Romans 12:1 ....314, 316
Romans 12:2 317
Romans 15:16 337

I Corinthians
I Corinthians 1:18 14
I Corinthians 1:17 and 18 404
II Corinthians 3:13-16 371
I Corinthians 5:7 ....82, 333, 335
I Corinthians 6:19, 20 .... 339I
I Corinthians 10:1 and 2 252
I Corinthians 10:3 and 4 253
I Corinthians 10:5-15 254
I Corinthians 10:16 ....224, 256
I Corinthians 10:16-18 224
I Corinthians 10:17 257
I Corinthians 10:18 ...211, 214, 225, 257, 389
I Corinthians 10:25-31 215

Scripture Index

I Corinthians 11:23-26 258
I Corinthians 11:27-29 262
I Corinthians 11:29 and 30 264
I Corinthians 13:3 308
I Corinthians 14:14-18 209
I Corinthians 14:21 and 22 183
I Corinthians 15:20 and 23 328

II Corinthians
II Corinthians 5:14 .... 165, 169
II Corinthians 5:14-21 165
II Corinthians 5:21 ... 167, 168, 170, 185, 260, 383, 391, 396
II Corinthians 9:15 245

Galatians
Galatians 1:4 340
Galatians 2:20 .. 169, 220, 269, 315, 392, 396
Galatians 3:8 300
Galatians 3:16 303
Galatians 3:23-25 86

Ephesians
Ephesians 1:14 339
Ephesians 1:6 and 7 241
Ephesians 2:4-9 243
Ephesians 2:5-9 385
Ephesians 2:7 80
Ephesians 2:8-10 45
Ephesians 2:12 and 13 22
Ephesians 2:13 .... 222, 223, 261
Ephesians 2 13-16 .... 222, 223
Ephesians 4:8 287
Ephesians 4:25 395
Ephesians 5:2 ..... 40, 101, 171, 172, 184, 188

Philippians
Philippians 3:10 .... 219, 220
Philippians 3:20 and 21 340

Colossians
Colossians 1:13 339
Colossians 1:20 261
Colossians 2:16 and 17 .... 64, 250
Colossians 2:17 66
Colossians 3:1-4 393
Colossians 3:5-9 394
Colossians 3:10-14 396

Thessalonians
I Thessalonians 4:16 and 17 341

Timothy
II Timothy 2:15 84

Hebrews
Hebrews 2:9 .... 33, 381
Hebrews 2:10 34
Hebrews 2:11 and 12, 13-15 35
Hebrews 2:16 and 17 37
Hebrews 4:14-16 .... 39, 361
Hebrews 4:16 45
Hebrews 5:7-9 381
Hebrews 5:8 and 9 37
Hebrews 7:19 41
Hebrews 7:22-28 .... 38, 293
Hebrews 7:25 ..... 44, 186, 188, 318, 403, 428
Hebrews 8:1 and 2 73
Hebrews 8:3, 4 and 5 74
Hebrews 8:5 75
Hebrews 9:1-6 76
Hebrews 9:7 352

JESUS CHRIST OUR COMPLETE OFFERING

Hebrews 9:8 77
Hebrews 9:9 .... 41, 78
Hebrews 9:10-12 79
Hebrews 9:11 and 12 354
Hebrews 9:12 .... 170, 351
Hebrews 9:13 .... 157, 160, 369
Hebrews 9:13 and 14 157
Hebrews 9:21 and 22 145
Hebrews 9:21-25 79
Hebrews 9:22 .... 153, 354, 368
Hebrews 9:22 and 23 354
Hebrews 9:23 75
Hebrews 9:24 and 25 355
Hebrews 9:25 350
Hebrews 9:26 ...... 80, 169, 313, 427
Hebrews 9:26 and 28 169
Hebrews 9:28 .... 63, 66, 101, 294
Hebrews 10:1 .... 41, 43, 69
Hebrews 10:2 .... 64, 357
Hebrews 10:3 64
Hebrews 10:4 .... 311, 358
Hebrews 10:4-7 311
Hebrews 10:6 96
Hebrews 10:8 .... 96, 284, 311
Hebrews 10:10 35
Hebrews 10:10-14 42
Hebrews 10:14 43
Hebrews 10:17 .... 158, 358
Hebrews 10:19 .... 45, 261
Hebrews 10:22 262

Hebrews 11:4 232
Hebrews 11:17-19 301
Hebrews 11:19 .... 301, 302, 315
Hebrews 13:10-12 415
Hebrews 13:10-13 158
Hebrews 13;11 .... 96, 416
Hebrews 13:12 .... 35, 159, 160, 351
Hebrews 13;15 and 16 209

I John
I John 1:3-7 161
I John 1:8-10 162
I John 2:1 and 2 163
I John 3:19-22 164

Peter
I Peter 1:2 148
I Peter 1:18 and 19 .... 32, 375
I Peter 2:24 .... 52, 265, 267, 270
II Peter 1"21 90
II Peter 3:11-13 411

James
James 1:18 336
James 2:21 288

Revelation
Revelation 5:2-6 408
Revelation 5:3, 4, 8 173
Revelation 20:10 37
Revelation 21:1-4 410
Revelation 21:23 412
Revelation 21 and 22 .... 19, 412

Subject Index

Abraham, 37, 66, 67, 234, 248, 287, 288, 295, 296, 297, 298-304, 314, 315, 316, 407, 425

Achan, 113, 114, 326

Ahaz., 203

allotrios, 351

Ammon, 305, 306

anabainō, 287

anapherō, 287, 288

antithesis (figure of speech), 49

antitupos, 79

aphaireō, 358

Ararat, 182

ascension, 40, 50, 78, 79, 287, 288, 333, 344, 354, 356, 364, 406

asham, 11, 57, 58, 85, 92, 93, 94, 102-109, 112, 115, 116, 120-126, 128, 130, 133, 135, 167, 185, 374

ashes, 140, 156, 157, 158, 159, 160, 161, 178, 284, 415

atonement, 67, 69, 77, 93, 105, 106, 108, 123, 125, 141-144, 147, 148, 149, 151, 152, 153, 159, 163, 164, 174, 175, 217, 236, 238-242, 260, 280, 281, 291, 323, 348, 349, 350-353, 359, 360, 362, 363, 389

azkarah, 274, 275

Baal, 212, 213

baptism, 253, 254, 268, 269, 383

between the two evenings, 82, 246, 249, 289

Bishop K. C. Pallai, 134, 238, 307, 409

blood of Christ, 22, 23, 32, 155, 157, 158, 222, 223, 224, 257, 259, 260, 261, 262, 358, 368, 375

boldness, 45, 88, 261, 347, 350

bread offering, 229, 336, 338

by his stripes we are healed, 272

cabal, 267

Cain, 194, 228, 231, 232, 325, 434, 435, 436

ceremonial cleansing, 147, 158

chalal, 271

challah, 228, 271

chata, 150

chattath, 85, 93, 95, 103, 138, 139, 141, 142, 144, 146-152, 154, 156, 158, 160, 161, 162, 170, 185, 344, 347, 348-351, 359, 374, 435, 436

childbirth, 150, 151

choli, 51, 52, 430, 431, 432, 433

Church Epistles, 171, 387, 392

cleanse the altar, 147, 353

cleansing of the leper, 227

communion, 197, 213, 221, 223, 224, 252-259, 264, 277, 279, 370, 374, 391

complete in him, 9, 44, 285

condemnation, 126, 127, 128, 129, 130, 131, 132, 164, 358, 368

condescension (figure of speech), 184, 275

consummation of the ages, 170, 313

continual burnt offering, 99, 288, 289, 318

JESUS CHRIST OUR COMPLETE OFFERING

Cornelius, 276, 277

cup of the Lord, 262

Dagon, 117, 118, 346, 418

daily burnt offering, 294, 361

Day of Atonement, 67, 69, 76, 77, 79, 80, 81, 98, 139, 152, 153, 154, 166, 168, 175, 178, 181, 293, 343, 344, 347-364, 372, 387

dead with Christ, 269, 314, 384, 385, 394

discerning the Lord's body, 262, 263, 264, 265, 268, 272

dōron, 232, 244

double demonstration of the full sharing, 218

double transfer, 68, 383, 388, 392

drink of the cup, 260, 370

drink offering, 92, 204, 247, 248, 249, 250, 251, 279, 288, 290, 330, 361, 370, 374

drink the cup, 214, 257, 259, 261, 277, 278

earthly sanctuary, 74, 75, 355

earthly tabernacle, 75, 79, 80, 81, 355

eating of the sacrifice, 86, 210, 211

Eleazar, 154, 155, 326, 346

elevation offering, 322, 371

ephapax, 38, 39, 42

equivalent sacrifice, 37, 46, 244, 351

Esau, 233, 234, 235, 236, 237, 238, 240, 242, 243

examples, 65, 75, 84, 96, 123, 133, 183, 221, 227, 254, 257, 291, 292, 295, 363, 395

Ezra, 155, 200

fat, 139, 140, 141, 142, 144, 178, 179, 190, 191, 192, 193, 194, 195, 196, 199, 204, 205, 223, 231, 281, 283, 320, 325, 345, 359, 434, 436

Feast of Unleavened Bread, 207, 227, 328, 329, 330, 332, 333, 335

feasts, 65, 98, 207, 247, 250, 290, 328, 419

fermentation, 230

first fruits, 194, 227, 228, 231, 246, 325, 326, 327, 328, 330, 331, 332, 333, 334, 335, 337, 341, 342

first fruits from the dead, 333

firstborn, 105, 317, 323, 324

forgiveness, 64, 71, 100, 105, 106, 108, 109, 115, 116, 133, 138, 141, 143, 144, 151, 152, 153, 161, 162, 164, 237, 240, 241, 260, 261, 302, 357, 403, 404, 409

fragrance, 87, 99, 172, 176, 182, 183, 184, 185, 191, 193, 195, 286

frankincense, 177, 226, 227, 228, 231, 246, 274

freewill offering, 200, 377

gate of the temple, 159, 415

Gethsemane, 308, 309, 310, 312, 313, 381

gift offering, 226, 232, 235, 238, 239, 240, 241, 242, 244, 246, 279, 386

Gilgal, 201

ginōskō, 164, 165

Subject Index

golden censer, 76, 173, 174

grace, 33, 34, 39, 44, 45, 46, 80, 126, 127, 134, 143, 179, 187, 206, 215, 224, 233, 235, 237, 238-241, 244, 262, 268, 313, 347, 361, 373, 381, 385

grain, 85, 227, 230, 231, 246, 272, 279, 331

gulgoleth, 417, 418

hagiazo, 337

hamartias, 96, 130, 141

healing, 19, 52, 54, 55, 59, 120, 190, 206, 208, 266, 270, 271, 272, 273, 278, 400, 401, 402, 403, 404, 409

heave offering, 196, 199, 319, 320, 322, 326, 327, 336

heavenly tabernacle, 74, 75, 78, 81, 354, 356, 364, 406

Helena the mother of Emperor Constantine, 422

heterosis (figure of speech), 354

Hezekiah, 202, 203, 204, 205, 206, 208, 432

hilasmos, 163

holokautōma, 284

holy of holies, 76, 77, 139, 153, 175, 343, 344, 347, 350, 354, 362

horns of the altar, 138, 139, 141, 142, 143, 144, 147, 148, 353

hupodeigma, 74, 79

identification, 13, 14, 48, 68, 69, 87, 43, 168,169, 191, 213, 215, 216, 218, 219, 225, 226, 254, 253, 256, 257, 259, 267-269, 316, 369, 383-395, 398

idolatry, 113, 255, 257, 258, 394

incense, 65, 87, 99, 138, 139, 140, 172-180, 184, 185, 191, 194, 195, 203, 205, 226, 227, 229, 282, 284, 286, 287, 291, 346, 349, 350

iintercession, 38, 40, 44, 58, 100, 128, 131, 132, 176, 178, 179, 181, 184, 186, 187, 188, 206, 292, 293, 294, 318, 371

Isaac, 67, 233, 234, 287, 288, 296, 298-303, 314, 315, 407, 425

issue of blood, 147, 151

Jacob, 94, 150, 192, 198, 229, 230, 233-242, 244, 267, 285, 321, 331

jealousy offering, 227

Jehovahjireh, 299

Jephthah, 7, 304, 305, 306, 307, 314

Joseph of Arimathea, 57

Josephus, 82, 198, 230, 249, 329

kalil, 282, 379, 380

kaphar, 239, 240, 348

koinōnia, 209, 212, 214, 219, 224, 256, 257

koinōnos, 211, 212, 214, 389

Korah, 174

Lamb of God, 10, 72, 87, 399, 406, 407, 408, 412

lay his hand upon the head, 138, 139, 142, 144, 190, 191, 192, 218

leaven, 177, 227, 229, 335, 336, 338

Levites, 91, 146, 174, 202, 203, 204, 206, 207, 208, 211, 323, 324, 326, 418

logos, 14, 404, 405

Lucifer, 380, 381, 382, 411

JESUS CHRIST OUR COMPLETE OFFERING

maal, 112, 113, 114

makob, 51, 53

manna, 76, 253, 254, 256, 258

Mary, 30, 152, 332, 333

meal offering, 83, 84, 85, 86, 87, 92, 97, 99, 101, 116, 171, 172, 176, 177, 179, 198, 211, 226-228, 229, 231, 244, 246-249, 251, 272, 273, 274, 275, 277, 288, 319, 335, 336, 361, 369, 370, 373

mediator, 294

Melchisedec/Melchizedek, 241, 248, 326

memorial portion, 179, 227, 229, 274, 275, 277

mercy seat, 77, 139, 175, 176, 344, 349, 350, 351, 352, 353

mercyseat, 76, 163, 350

metonymy (figure of speech), 95, 129, 223, 436

minchah, 85, 226, 227, 228, 231, 232, 233, 235-240, 244, 246, 247, 249, 251, 272, 274, 275, 279, 374

miphkad/Miphkad, 146, 419, 420, 422, 423, 424

Mishnah, 155, 414

mnēmosunon, 275, 276

model, 74, 82, 101, 248, 303, 353, 363, 364

Moriah, 296, 297, 299, 303

Mount of Olives, 19, 160, 297, 309, 369, 414, 415, 416, 419, 420, 421, 423, 424, 425, 426

much more, 14, 18, 23, 65, 71, 112, 125, 126, 127, 128, 134, 135, 136, 157, 242, 263, 358, 368, 405

The Mystery, 214, 301, 338

Nadab and Abihu, 249, 346, 352

nasa, 70, 217, 266, 267

newness of lfe, 7, 392

nichoach, 180, 181, 182

Noah, 181, 275, 286

nuach, 182, 183

nuph, 320, 321, 322, 323, 324, 330

obedience, 37, 126, 134, 149, 252, 299, 300, 303, 308, 310, 313, 316, 317, 318, 374, 381, 382

olah, 85, 280, 281, 283, 284, 285, 286, 287, 292, 296, 298, 304, 310, 318, 347, 348, 359, 360, 361, 374

oneness, 169, 220, 221, 222, 224, 261, 315, 386

outside the camp, 140, 155, 156, 159, 160, 161, 178, 193, 369, 414, 424

panteles, 428

parable (figure of speech), 78, 243, 301, 302

paradise, 19, 21, 411

Passover, 4, 82, 83, 84, 85, 87, 160, 205, 206, 207, 208, 211, 216, 230, 282, 329, 330, 332, 333, 335, 369, 389, 407

peace offering, 83, 84, 86, 99, 101, 140, 143, 144, 171, 172, 176-180, 189-193, 195, 196, 197-204, 209, 210, 211, 216, 218, 219, 222, 223, 224, 281, 286, 289, 295, 319, 320, 336, 369, 372, 376

Pentecost, 44, 183, 186, 210, 227, 330, 334, 335, 336, 338

perfect tabernacle, 79, 354, 428

Philistines, 116, 117, 118, 119, 120, 121, 292

pierced, 228, 271, 310

pigeons, 151, 152, 283

Subject Index

Pilate, 30, 57, 329, 420

plēmmeleia, 130

polling place, 418, 419, 420, 424

prayer, 15, 29, 100, 173, 174, 175, 176-179, 184, 187, 206, 208, 234, 277, 292

propitiation, 143, 163

purification offering, 94, 149, 150, 151, 152, 153, 154, 156, 157, 158, 167, 344, 350

qatar, 176, 177, 178, 179, 180, 191, 192, 193, 196, 226, 229, 231, 281, 282, 283, 284, 286, 291

qorban., 91

ram, 66, 67, 104, 105, 106, 108, 123, 298, 299, 303, 347, 348, 360, 361, 376

ratsah, 238

reconciliation, 19, 37, 143, 148, 151, 154, 165, 224, 238, 239, 240, 242, 243, 244, 260, 262, 352, 353

red heifer, 137, 146, 154, 155, 158, 159, 160, 161, 178, 369, 414, 415, 416, 421, 424, 425

Red Sea, 252

redeem, 10, 22, 23, 32, 71, 86, 105, 131, 170, 336, 409

redemption, 11, 19, 32, 33, 37, 43, 46, 47, 50, 54, 60, 63, 70, 71, 79, 87, 102, 106, 131, 132, 135, 241, 244, 297, 299, 301, 302, 311, 312, 319, 340, 351, 352, 354, 371, 375, 376, 392, 399, 409, 410

renewing, 134, 317, 397

reparation, 94, 115, 122, 133, 149

Reptitio (figure of speech), 290

restitution, 58, 105, 106, 108, 109, 112, 116, 121, 123, 124, 132, 133, 134, 145, 149, 172, 179, 189, 368, 372

resurrection, 27, 40, 50, 219, 220, 222, 269, 270, 315, 319, 328, 332, 333, 334, 341, 364, 384, 385, 386, 393, 406, 425, 426

righteousness, 122, 126, 127, 128, 166, 168, 185, 260, 261, 266, 268, 270, 313, 315, 316, 317, 348, 368, 371, 383, 386, 391, 396, 397, 411

Sabbath, 64, 65, 98, 249, 250, 290, 329-335, 407

sacrificalese, 221

sacrifice of praise, 202, 209, 210

sacrifices of thanksgiving, 199, 201, 202, 204, 209

sacrificial language, 220, 269

sacrificial meal, 197, 211

sacrificial terminology, 219, 221, 239, 315

salt, 198, 212, 213, 216, 230

salt of the covenant, 198, 212, 230

salted offerings, 198, 230

sanctification, 35, 42, 43, 46, 148, 149, 262, 351, 359

sanctified, 35, 42, 43, 148, 150, 153, 158, 205, 208, 240, 312, 337, 338, 346, 351

saraph, 178, 179, 282, 286

Saul, 201

scapegoat, 12, 67, 68, 69, 70, 77, 98, 137, 152, 154, 161, 166, 167, 168, 191, 221, 268, 343, 348, 349, 357, 358, 359, 360, 364, 369, 373, 387, 388

shadow of good things, 41, 63, 64, 65, 80, 125, 250

shadow outline, 63, 66

shalam, 123, 124

shelem, 85, 197, 225, 374

shub, 120, 121, 122, 123, 124

silhouette, 63, 66, 69

sin nature, 129, 130, 169, 270, 316, 384, 386, 395

Solomon's temple, 297

speaking in tongues, 183, 210

sprinkling of the blood, 77, 138, 147, 175, 190, 191, 192, 249, 281, 350, 353, 414

substitution, 56, 66, 67, 71, 84, 85, 87, 166, 169, 391, 408, 409

sweet savor offerings, 101, 102, 171, 176, 179, 184

sweetsmelling savour, 40, 101, 171, 184

tabernacle of the heavenlies, 351

tamid, 289

tamim, 375, 376, 377, 379, 380

teleioō, 24, 29, 31, 34, 38, 41, 43, 427

teleō, 26, 28, 31, 428

telos, 8, 28, 44, 169, 371, 427, 428

tenuphah, 85, 320, 321, 322, 323, 324, 335, 342, 374

terumah, 320, 322, 342, 374

throne of grace, 39, 45, 262, 347, 350, 361, 362

tithes, 326, 327

transfer of sin, 60, 71, 143, 217

transference of sin, 70, 217

true tabernacle, 73, 75, 78, 80, 88, 355

tupos, 74, 254, 255, 257

tutor, 86

tutorial, 10, 86, 161, 219, 222, 280, 343, 359

type, 15, 26, 31, 60, 67, 72, 74, 79, 82, 126, 154, 232, 256, 258, 280, 290, 303, 312, 343, 338, 395

vow offering, 200

water of purifying, 149, 156

water of separation, 156, 157

wave loaves, 227, 335

wave offering, 12, 92, 195, 196, 228, 319, 320, 321, 322, 323, 324, 327, 333, 334, 335, 336

whole burnt offering, 284, 310, 314

wine, 48, 194, 247, 248, 249, 251, 259, 276, 278, 289, 312, 327, 330, 370, 390

without blemish, 32, 95, 97, 104, 106, 108, 138, 142, 143, 147, 190, 191, 218, 280, 281, 283, 330, 360, 375, 376, 377, 379

word of the cross, 14, 15, 405, 406

zebach, 92

www.ingramcontent.com/pod-product-compliance
Lightning Source LLC
Chambersburg PA
CBHW071644160426
43195CB00012B/1353